Full Praise for *Communication Highwire*

"Finally, a culture-based book on communication styles! . . . a refreshing and engaging framework for understanding communication styles. Tons of examples and activities should be especially useful to educators and trainers alike."

—Judith N. Martin, Professor, Intercultural Communication,
School of Human Communication, Arizona State University

"This is an ultimate approach for discussing global diversity using communication styles as the numerator for human capital."

—Curtis Mathews, Jr., Vice President, Corporate People Diversity, CIGNA

"In a lively and lucid style, *Communication Highwire* introduces the reader to the powerful impact of culture on communication styles. Grounded in theory, and richly elaborated through experience, this book provides a much-needed overview for business professionals, educators, trainers and anyone else who is culturally curious!"

—Janet Bennett, Executive Director,
Intercultural Communication Institute

"If you want to move up to the next rung on the ladder in the arena of communication, you need to read and experience *Communication Highwire*. Its concepts are supported by tools and activities that will enable you to be a more effective manager, leader and collaborator."

—Maggie Fischer, Manager, Worldwide Procurement & Logistics
Business Process Development, Texas Instruments Inc.

"For those of us engaged in global development, the issues and problems accurately described in *Communication Highwire* are a major part of our daily challenge. I am so glad to finally find a book which goes beyond the well meaning, often used phrase of *valuing diversity*, and offers simple explanations and practical ideas on improving communication to *leverage diversity*—a much more valuable concept in effectively working together."

—Ken Brown, Assembly Technology Development for
Communication & Wireless Products at Intel Corporation

"Communication Highwire: Leveraging the Power of Diverse Communication Styles is a valuable and much needed contribution to the intercultural literature. The authors do a splendid job of making a vast literature and an array of complex communication concepts accessible through the masterful use of metaphor and storytelling. A wide variety of learning activities allows the reader to work with these ideas and the 'four-step method' (reflection, analysis, discussion, decision making) supports the reader in applying them."

—R. Michael Paige, University of Minnesota

Communication Highwire

Leveraging the Power of Diverse Communication Styles

Dianne Hofner Saphiere,
Barbara Kappler Mikk, and
Basma Ibrahim DeVries

INTERCULTURAL PRESS
A NICHOLAS BREALEY PUBLISHING COMPANY

Yarmouth, ME • Boston • London

First published by Intercultural Press, a Nicholas Brealey Publishing Company, in 2005

Intercultural Press, Inc.
A Nicholas Brealey Publishing Company
PO Box 700
Yarmouth, ME 04096
Information: 1-888-BREALEY
Orders: 207-846-5168
Fax: 207-846-5181
www.interculturalpress.com

Nicholas Brealey Publishing
3-5 Spafield Street, Clerkenwell
London, EC1R 4QB, UK
Tel: +44-(0)-207-239-0360
Fax: +44-(0)-207-239-0370
www.nbrealey-books.com

Printed in the United States of America

09 08 07 06 05   1 2 3 4 5

ISBN: 1-931930-15-5

Library of Congress Cataloging-in-Publication Data
Saphiere, Dianne Hofner.
    Communication highwire : leveraging the power of diverse communication
  styles / Dianne Hofner Saphiere, Barbara Kappler Mikk, and Basma Ibrahim DeVries.
      p. cm.
  Includes bibliographical references and index.
    ISBN 1-931930-15-5 (pbk. : alk. paper)   1. International business enterprises—
Social aspects.   2. Communication in management—Social aspects.   3. Intercultural
communication.   I. Mikk, Barbara Kappler.   II. DeVries, Basma Ibrahim.   III. Title.

  HD2755.5.S27 2005
  658.4'5—dc22   2005007807

This book is dedicated to our wonderfully supportive families,
with whom we are blessed to enjoy plenty of great communication
style experiences every day, and to the incredibly collaborative process
that we were privileged to experience while writing this book—
a process that allowed each of us to contribute fully and in our
unique styles. We hope it has resulted in content and methods that
you will find useful and that you will continue developing.

Contents

Acknowledgments

This book has been a collaborative effort in every sense of the word. We want to thank our immediate family members, Jon, Tonu, Greg, Danny, Annika, and Oliver. We are incredibly appreciative of the time, resources, culture-specific insights, stories, expertise, critique, and love and support shared by so many of our family members, colleagues, friends, clients, students, and employers.

Among those to whom we are especially indebted are Ulan Asanov, Gilles Asselin, Janet Bennett, Thorunn Bjarnadottir, Eleonore Breukel, Carrie Cameron, Lori Charron, Jean Choe, Andrew Cohen, Antonella Corsi-Bunker, Jon DeVries, Tatyana Fertelmeister, Amy Hoeft, Anna Janke, Yuko Kipnis, Bruce LaBrack, Ann Marie Lei, Esther Louie, Judith Martin, Ruth Mastron, Liudmila Mikhailova, Tonu Mikk, Kristin Mishra, Tomi Nagai, Nancy O'Brien, Michael Paige, Peggy Pusch, Marilyn Reineck, Shannon Murphy Robinson, Heather Robinson, Lucy Shahar, Vitaliy Shyyan, Donna Stringer, Kay Thomas, Stella Ting-Toomey, Olga Trofymenko, Greg Webb, Barbara West, members of Intercultural Insights—an online resource group—and participants in our communication style workshops at congresses of SIETAR–USA: Virginia, Minneapolis, Portland, and Austin, and at NASAGA 2003 in Montreal.

We are grateful to our publisher, who from the beginning shared our vision for this book, especially Toby Frank, who as president of Intercultural Press encouraged us to develop this theme, and Trish O'Hare, president of Nicholas Brealey–North America, for her continued support. Judy Carl-Hendrick, our editor, contributed the invaluable gift of seeing the core and helping us to develop it while removing distractions. Our sincere appreciation to our illustrator, Marko Fields, for creatively transforming our ideas into inspiring artwork.

We would also like to acknowledge each other and the commitment we made to write this book together—literally! It is a joy for the three of us that we cannot figure out which one of us wrote what phrase or who initiated a specific idea or chapter. We are delighted we have journeyed the road less traveled.

Given the collaborative nature of our writing, and that we have truly co-created the ideas we present to you, it was extremely challenging to determine how to put our names in the required linear order for authorship. The order listed reflects our commitment to work together on future projects and a continual rotation of our names. We encourage you to consider viewing our names in one continuous circle, with each name forming an arch, both supporting and being supported by the others.

Introduction

Mike and Tanaka

Nearly twenty years ago Dianne was asked by a U.S. American corporate president, Mike, to "help him out" with a Japanese subsidiary president, Tanaka-san,* whom he was on the verge of firing. Mike asked Dianne to help him discover whether he was missing something. He just couldn't communicate with Tanaka-san, and Mike worried that Tanaka had no viable strategy for creating a return on investment.

Dianne interviewed Mike and Tanaka-san individually and found that Tanaka-san felt his strategy was the only hope of creating a return on investment. He felt he'd presented his strategy to Mike repeatedly but that Mike just "didn't get it."

Dianne worked with them extensively both individually in their native languages and together. After about four months, during a face-to-face meeting Mike growled at Tanaka-san in exasperation, "This is just not working out. You say you understand but then you don't take action! I have no idea where you're coming from or where you're going!" Tanaka-san stood up, walked over to Mike, pointed his finger in Mike's face, and shouted, "You don't listen! I have told you and told you, clearly, directly, over and over, and you don't hear! You have your own priorities and what I tell you just doesn't fit your thinking!"

San is a gender-neutral honorific that is commonly used after a Japanese person's last name. Its equivalent in English might be "Mr." or "Mrs.," and it is commonly used in business in Japan. We use *san* in this story as it reflects how the individuals are truly called in this real example. We return to this Mike and Tanaka story at various points throughout this book because it "speaks" so well to the topic of communication style, and we refer to Mr. Tanaka both as Tanaka-san and Tanaka.

Dianne shrank under the table hoping to disappear. All her efforts seemed fruitless. Surely Tanaka-san, an executive she perceived as highly competent, was about to be fired. To her surprise, Mike leaned back in his chair, smiled, and said calmly, "Tanaka-san, I think that for the first time in the five years we've worked together, I finally know where you stand. Thank you." It was a breakthrough. Things didn't get rosy after that, but Mike and Tanaka-san worked together more productively for several more years.

This story shows how powerful communication style can be—whether it serves as an impediment to productivity and enjoyment or as a conduit to seeing and benefiting from differences. In this case, differences in communication style led Mike to evaluate Tanaka-san as an ineffectual and incompetent executive. But Mike was only evaluating Tanaka-san's ability to communicate with him in a way that Mike found credible.

Mike and Tanaka-san's communication styles were so disjointed that despite Herculean efforts and active facilitation they remained unable to understand one another. It was only a moment of "nothing-more-to-lose" exasperation on both sides that caused Mike and Tanaka to see beyond the communication patterns each person was hooked into using. We authors have each had many similar encounters in which communication style disconnects wreaked havoc on the people involved and the jobs they were doing. We were convinced that there had to be less painful and more successful ways to enhance communication between people with differing styles, so we decided to do some focused work together on the topic.

As we researched and discussed communication style, we were surprised how little has been published on this topic. We wrote this book because we feel it is a very important topic that has lacked and yet deserves focused attention and development. It is our hope that trainers, organization development consultants, facilitators, team leaders, educators, community activists, and anyone interested in productivity and relationships will find this book helpful. (For details on how communication style has been approached throughout the years by various disciplines and how this heritage has influenced this book, see the Appendix.)

As we began our work together, the first perception that the three of us shared was that the labels commonly used to identify communication styles, such as *direct* and *indirect,* while easy to talk about and to understand, are culturally relative and thus are open to misinterpretation. In the Mike and Tanaka story, Mike felt that Tanaka-san was overly indirect and inscrutable. Tanaka-san personally felt that for months he had been very direct in his communication approach. He felt like he had been jumping up and down to make his point but that Mike was refusing to hear it. It was as if the two of them were lost in a house of mirrors, banging against walls, neither able to be sure of what he or his colleague was seeing. If Tanaka-san, for example, had been told to be direct, his response would likely have been "I am!" While the style labels currently used in the intercultural communication field are convenient and provide initial insight into differences, communication style is much more complex than what these labels reveal.

It also struck us that communication style is not some static thing that we "are." Communication style is a pattern of behavior; it is something we "do." In this story, Tanaka-san was not "indirect" while Mike was "direct." Both men communicated directly *and* indirectly. Mike never told Tanaka directly that he doubted the viability of Tanaka's strategy; he repeatedly reminded him to emphasize return on investment. Tanaka-san, for his part, never made the point explicitly that he felt his approach would in fact produce the required return on investment more effectively than the approach Mike was suggesting. Tanaka-san repeatedly and directly explained his strategy and why it would work well. However, Tanaka and Mike defined *direct* and *indirect* in very different ways and on very different scales. Existing communication style labels did not help them to understand and navigate the complexity of their interaction. We sought a model that allowed for such dynamism and robustness.

To work together more effectively, Tanaka-san needed to learn what sort of *actual behavior* he could exhibit to get Mike to hear him. He needed to understand that the respect he wanted to show Mike might indeed be communicated using these behaviors. He needed to be able to interpret *direct* from Mike's experience. This breakthrough occurred in the story we told above. In addition, Mike needed to learn to "hear" what Tanaka-san was saying. He needed to be able to understand "listening" from Tanaka-san's perspective—without forcing Tanaka-san to always adapt to Mike's interpretation of directness.

Using a Metaphor to Understand Communication Styles

Communication style plays a major role in the work that each of us, the authors, does. Basma teaches communication studies at a college in the United States of America and leads many overseas study and service learning trips for students. Barbara designs and implements intercultural communication workshops for U.S. and international faculty, and scholars, and students, as well as for businesses and community organizations. Dianne works as an intercultural effectiveness consultant for multinational businesses. Each of us also volunteers actively in community development. Our jobs involve helping people to collaborate better with one another, to understand themselves and others more meaningfully, and to work together to create stronger communities, companies, and organizations. And, by the way, each of us likes to have fun—which leads us to the reason we chose the circus metaphor we will be using in this book.

We have decided to use the metaphor of a circus for discussing communication for several reasons. As trainers, we find that using metaphors to illustrate new concepts often adds depth and easier retention of meaning for learners, particularly if that metaphor makes sense intuitively. The sense we see in this metaphor is this:

1. There is much going on at a circus—the sounds, smells, sights, feelings, tastes—just as there is a lot going on in any communication. It can be difficult to decipher what makes a circus or communicative experience successful, as so much happens so quickly and there are so many possible definitions of success (captivating discussion, boisterous disagreement, or the resonance of creating shared meaning).
2. There are many discrete components to a circus—the performers, costumes, lights, animals, the tent, the sound system—just as there are many components of communication, including who is communicating, what they say, where they are, the medium of communication, the manner in

which they communicate (such as how loudly or softly they speak), and the flow of the interaction (such as the way they take turns speaking and listening).

3. These components interact with one another to provide a total circus or communicative experience. Just as it can make sense to analyze the discrete components of communication or a circus, we must not lose sight of the overall interaction of these components and the effects they produce.

4. Much occurs behind the scenes, both prior to the circus or the communication, while it is going on, and after the acts are completed. Those who participate in a communication event are not only responding to the current situation, they are responding based on years of previous experience as well as expectations for the future.

We will explain more about this circus metaphor as we go along. Right now it might help to picture communication style—the patterns of how we communicate—as our entry ticket to the Big Top. This ticket to the circus, that is, communication style, provides a window into the differences that make a difference and a pathway to better understanding what is really important to people, so that we can collaborate more productively and enjoyably.

We recognize that the idea of a circus metaphor may feel silly, contradictory to how you want to present your professional work. If that is the case, you will find that you can easily apply the concepts and tools in this book without the metaphor. And yet...we encourage you to consider the power of play and metaphor in your professional lives. In writing about the future of intercultural training, Sandra Fowler and Sheila Ramsey (1999) invite us to reframe our work as a "transformation process" in which we focus much more on the "intrapersonal transformation process because it is evident to all of us that living and working effectively with culturally distinct others and in culturally different systems is an experience that challenges us on very fundamental levels" (353). To reach this goal, they encourage us to use nonlinear training and consider, among other things, the use of metaphor, reflective journaling, dialogue, and appreciative inquiry (355). We encourage you to try the metaphor and see where it takes you.

Naming This Book

Our working title for this book was originally *Don't Make a Fly into an Elephant*—a literal English translation of the Russian expression *Ne delai iz muhi slona*, which is used quite widely throughout the former Soviet nations. The expression originated during the late nineteenth and early twentieth centuries, when circuses were becoming popular in Russia and the elephants imported from India were magnificent and exotic animals that many Russians were excited to see. At the circus, the impressive performances of the elephants added to their grandeur. "Don't make a fly into an elephant" contrasted the elephant's grandeur with the smallness and nuisance of a fly. Its meaning in English would be the equivalent of "Don't make a mountain out of a mole hill" or don't exaggerate something unnecessarily. As you will see in this book, seemingly small differences in communication style can lead to elephantine-sized problems. Paying special attention to such differences and honing our skills can lead us to valuable insights from our team members, colleagues, students, friends, and family. This proverb, "Don't make a fly into an elephant," suggests that we are wise to take things a bit lightly rather than overly seriously. In line with this, Basma tells us that in ancient Egypt, it was believed that a deceased person's heart was weighed on a scale against a feather. If the heart was as light as or lighter than a feather, the person was welcomed into the beautiful afterlife. If the person's heart was heavier than the feather, well, things were not to be so pleasant for eternity. It is our wish for you that your work with communication style might help you to keep your heart light as a feather.

The final title of this book ties in directly with the circus metaphor. "Communication Highwire" illustrates our belief that communication is much like a highwire performance: requiring incredible competence, balance, a great deal of practice, and ultimately, trust in one's abilities. The subtitle, "Leveraging the Power of Diverse Communication Styles," reflects our conviction that individuals and groups can benefit greatly when communication style differences are understood, respected, and utilized appropriately.

Throughout this book we will share with you many stories. Storytelling provides a context that allows us to see and feel how the concepts we describe play out in real life. Let us share with you a second story.

Fourteen

Barbara has a daughter, Annika, who is of course exceptionally beautiful, bright, and charming. She learned to count at a fairly young age. One day Annika stayed with a babysitter, and when Barbara returned the sitter told her, "Wow! Annika is so smart! She counts really well." Barbara asked, "Did you notice anything striking about how she counts?" The sitter responded, "Well, she counts perfectly to thirteen, and after that she randomly repeats the first thirteen numbers. When I tried to encourage and help her to count beyond thirteen, she insisted that thirteen was the last number." Indeed, Annika had no idea that there was a number fourteen in the world. In her world, there *were* thirteen numbers. Annika learned to count because she lived in a two-story house, and each time Mom or Dad carried her up the stairs, they'd count the steps with her. In Annika's house, there were only thirteen steps; when she reached the thirteenth step she was at the top of her world, where her bedroom was and, in her eyes, the place where her day ended and her dream world began. Annika did not know what fourteen was because she had not experienced fourteen.

Undoubtedly we have all had opportunities for discovering our own fourteens—whether we actually experienced a new perspective depended on our awareness and openness to the existence of a new perspective or insight. In Tanaka-san's world, he was being direct, in *his* experience of directness. In Mike's world, he was listening, as per *his* definition of listening. Like Annika's "fourteen," these grown men had no idea that there was a completely different concept of *direct* or *listening* in the world. They were performing in separate rings of the three-ring circus, with no connection to one another. How could we get them to understand one another? While it wouldn't be as easy as teaching the concepts of fourteen and fifteen to Annika, it was possible to help them expand their communication style repertoires. The goal would not be to change their preferred styles, but to expand their abilities to communicate effectively with a wider range of people. We could assist them to see the circus occurring before their very eyes—that there are multiple, effective ways of expressing ourselves verbally and nonverbally, rich dimensions to why we communicate the way we do, and much, much more.

In this book we offer you the same opportunity: to see the communication circus before your very eyes. With this in mind, our goal for this book is to provide several user-friendly, practical tools for understanding and bridging different styles of communication tools that can help you transform communication style differences from hindrances to assets. These tools are:

1. The five factors affecting communication style use presented in Chapter 3.
2. The Star Chart model of these factors' interactions in Chapter 4.
3. The Descriptor Checklist introduced in Chapter 6.
4. The Four-Step method for leveraging communication style differences described in Chapter 7.

So, hang on to your seats and prepare to be entertained, intrigued, amazed, and challenged!

Introduction to Communication Style

We are excited to present to you our approach to communication style. This first section provides you with a definition of communication style and an understanding of why it is important—the benefits of communication style fluency.

Throughout the book we incorporate activities that allow you to practice the ideas from the chapters and enable you to energize, inform, and challenge yourself, your colleagues, your fellow team or group members, or participants in your workshops or coaching sessions, to leverage the power of diverse communication styles.

We trust you will enjoy! So grab your ticket and let us get on with the show!

CHAPTER 1

What Is Communication Style?

Your Ticket to the Circus

Communicating effectively is difficult. Who would have guessed that Mike would be happy that Tanaka-san lost his cool? And who would have thought that this would then lead to a breakthrough for Mike and Tanaka-san? The idea that people from different experiences, genders, and ages—often from diverse cultural, linguistic, and ethnic heritages and a broad range of professional training and education—using varied thought processes and communication styles, can actually understand one another is an accomplishment indeed. When communicating across cultures, it is as if we are on the communication highwire and the safety net is hard to see so far below.

Most of us have worked in teams and lived in communities that did not have a synergistic effect. We may have felt unheard or misunderstood. We may have sensed that others had a lot more they could be sharing, but they either did not speak up or the group was not hearing them. We ourselves may have felt we were not able to contribute our perspectives fully. And sometimes there are so many wonderful ideas, or such opposing ideas, that a group gets stuck.

Let's look at another story to fuel our thinking.

Sherif's Team Meeting

In a meeting with four staff members, the boss, Sherif, turns to Amin, one of the employees, and is soft-spoken when questioning him about the goal of a project. A second staff member, Alexey, interrupts and says he will not work on the project at all. Sherif turns to Alexey and sharply states, "We will not discuss whether or not you will have a role. That has already been determined." The group continues the meeting, seemingly undisturbed by the shift in Sherif's behavior. There appear to be no hurt feelings and no disruptions to the group. In fact, team members seem energized and focused.

What just happened? Is the group dysfunctional? While that could be the case if these exact words were spoken in another group, in this specific situation the boss was extremely effective at managing the conversation and the identities of the individuals involved. Sherif was able to shift his style of communication to effectively interact with his team members, and the team members understood and embraced this shift in his style. Sherif knew that Amin was talented but often quiet in meetings—not a big talker but a deep thinker. Sherif knew from experience that once the group began heated discussions, it would be all too easy to lose Amin's voice. Therefore, he began the meeting by inviting Amin's perspective. He knew Alexey, on the other hand, to be an active, quick, verbal contributor, someone who was more than happy to offer his opinions strongly and directly. Sherif knew that he needed to set clear boundaries for Alexey to focus his energies. He knew Alexey would respond well to a strong, direct statement from the boss. The communication styles Sherif exhibited were successful at bringing out the best contributions of both Amin and Alexey and at steering the team in a productive direction. Sherif exemplifies an excellent ringmaster guiding the performers because Sherif understood individual team members' communication styles and how to manage them.

Effectively grasping the complexity of communication style can offer a way to better understand others and ourselves as well as to enable people to collaborate more productively and enjoyably. Communication style is our ticket to more accurately interpret the sights, sounds, tastes, smells, and feelings of this glorious, chaotic, show-stopping, three-ring circus of communication. So what, exactly, is meant by this ticket—communication style?

Defining Communication Style

Communication style is the way in which we communicate, a pattern of verbal and nonverbal behaviors that comprises our preferred ways of giving and receiving information in a specific situation. If the message content is the *what* and the communicators the *who*, then communication style is the *how*. Communication style includes, for example, how we accomplish the following tasks:

1. Organize and present information and like it to be organized
2. Encourage and like to be encouraged
3. Agree or disagree with others' ideas and prefer agreement or lack thereof to be communicated
4. Build relationships, trust, and intimacy with others
5. Communicate politeness and perceive politeness to be communicated
6. Negotiate and prefer to be negotiated with
7. Establish credibility
8. Approach, manage, and resolve conflict
9. Make decisions and solve problems
10. Interrupt and prefer to be interrupted

Based on our definition and the preceding list, you can see that communication style is broad in scope, and as such it encompasses many specific patterns we engage in every day. Our belief is that these patterns are not universally accepted rules of human interaction; instead, communication style preferences reflect our personal and cultural upbringings.

Even simple nonverbal behaviors that we may consider "natural" are typically learned. People all over the world smile and use eye contact, but they do so in different ways and for different purposes. Answers to the following questions, all about communication style, vary by culture as well as by individual and specific context:

- *How do you show respect to those with whom you are communicating?* One person might look someone directly in the eye to show respect, while another averts eye contact. One person might speak loudly and clearly as a sign of respect, another softly.

- *How do you attempt to establish credibility?* One person may do so by stating her past experiences and citing her credentials, while another might humbly explain that her lengthy experience has given her more questions than answers.
- *Is it polite to answer a question when you are asked directly?* People who value explicit communication may expect a direct answer to a question. People who value implicit communication might find a direct answer to be condescending or patronizing.
- *Is it best to discuss conflict with the person with whom you disagree?* One person may desire to analyze a disagreement giving a specific comment-by-comment replay and paying special attention to the actual words used, while another may prefer to discuss the feelings experienced because of the disagreement, and a third might prefer to overlook the disagreement or to bring it up only after much time has passed and careful consideration has been given.

Communication style—how we express ourselves—reflects our underlying values and beliefs, and those values and beliefs are determined both by culture and personality.

People use and interpret communication styles differently according to these personal and cultural filters. How we communicate (the communication style we use) and how we see others communicating (the meaning we attach to their communication style) depend on many factors. Do we expect interaction to be easy, difficult, enjoyable, or frustrating? Do we believe relationships should be well planned, emergent, explicit, or implicit? Do we think it is smarter to focus first on task or on relationship? A full definition of communication style needs to include these six key points:

1. Communication style is a situational tendency, not a type.
2. The style we use is influenced by many factors.
3. As with culture, everything's relative with communication style.

4. Neutral descriptions are needed, yet those descriptions have their own weaknesses and liabilities.
5. Communication style provides a link between the observable and the unconscious—between our behavior and its underlying motivation.
6. There are advantages and disadvantages to every style.

In the next five subsections we provide more detail about what communication style is and is not, explain each of these six aspects of communication style, and offer additional insights into this amazing phenomenon.

Situational Tendency, Not Type—Sad or Happy Clown?

When discussing communication styles, people often talk about *types,* as if each person or culture were static rather than dynamic and multifaceted. Communication styles are not personality types; they are tendencies or preferred methods of communicating. Tendencies have much more variability and flexibility than types. If I am a clown in the circus, I no doubt have different costumes or different acts that I can use for different situations or even in the same performance.

Most of us demonstrate a variety of communication styles during any given day. We may use different styles when we are happy, excited, angry, sad, or sick; when we are demanding good service, or when we have discovered we are in error. We might use a different style for communicating to a good friend than a style used with someone we have just met, with children than with adults, with native speakers than with nonfluent speakers, and so on. Studying our style tendencies can encourage us to add to our communicative repertoire and can assist us to better understand the values informing our behavior.

You may be thinking, "But when I read about the communication style types, they ring true to my experience." Absolutely! There may well be a great deal of truth to a specific generalization. For example, over the years Barbara has worked with many students from Malaysia. Several Malaysian students have stated, in one way or another, that U.S. Americans are quite direct. Given that the students are speaking from their experiences, this must be true, right? Well, yes, it is true because it is their experience. As a general rule, it could be argued that U.S. Americans tend to be more direct than Malaysians. However, referring to types such as *direct* does not tell us anything about the specific contexts in which U.S. Americans are being direct and the times when they are not. From this cultural snapshot, we may expect all members from a culture to exhibit specific communication styles at all times and within all contexts—expectations that are false.

It is sometimes helpful to associate a particular communication style with a specific culture, yet we make a concerted effort to explore the communication styles as phenomena affected by (and perhaps affecting) culture, but not coupled with culture in a fixed or inflexible way. It is also important to consider the complexity of culture itself. Although there has been a tendency in the literature to label certain nationalities or ethnic groups with certain communication styles, there are regional, familial, and individual differences in style, as well as style differences according to organization, functional role, religious or spiritual background, sexual orientation, age, gender, and other factors.

Influenced by Many Factors—Lights! Music! Action! Adventure!

When we go to the circus, we are amazed at the chaos inside—everything seems to be happening at once, with no apparent rhyme or reason to the events. Upon closer inspection, we realize the events are synchronized and the movement, while chaotic on one level, has a rhythm of its own. Exploring the chaos and synchronized rhythm are integral to understanding communication style. The variables influencing when and why a certain style is used are quite complex and are both individually and culturally based. Factors include context, goals, self-concept, values, and communication style repertoire. We will discuss these factors in depth in Chapter 3. For now suffice it to say that communication style is dynamic and its magic is not easy to capture.

Everything's Relative—The View Depends on Where You Sit

Our perception of communication style depends on our frame of reference. We may hear, for example, that U.S. Americans love to apologize. If I come from Germany, this may be a helpful statement of one aspect of U.S. American communication style. I may have grown up believing that apologies are only given in situations of grave negligence, so I may feel that Americans apologize too frequently. If, on the other hand, I am Korean, a culture in which apologies are often used to create social bonding and harmony, I may feel that U.S. Americans are allergic to apologies, that they rarely if ever apologize. In this case, the statement "Americans love to apologize" is not at all helpful, and in fact may be counter to my experience.

Neutral Descriptions Are Necessary Yet Limiting—To Reveal or Not to Reveal

If we want to perform an illusion, it helps to see the inside of the hat from where we will pull the rabbit. We need to learn the secret behind the tricks. At the same time, knowing the secret somehow takes away the magic. We face a similar dilemma with communication style. To overcome the relativity of communication style, we need to be able to objectively describe behavior. This communication style relativity is similar to cultural relativity, in which communication style preferences are a matter of valuing different choices and tendencies in much the same way that cultures often promote different worldviews.

To say someone demonstrated an assertive style assumes that we share a common definition of *assertive*. What seems assertive to you may be aggressive or even shy to me. But saying the person gave a firm, one-handed handshake accompanied by sustained eye contact and a clearly heard voice might capture the communication style of a given interaction in a more precise way. Yet does it lose something? This latter definition becomes awfully dry and divorced from the feeling and atmosphere of the actual interaction. In some ways, the term *assertive* communicates a lot more, showing that one-word labels can come in handy.

Think about a situation in which you thought somebody from a different cultural background acted rudely. Perhaps you experienced that person's "pushiness," loud speaking voice, concentrated eye contact, and persistent manner, and in that particular context this communicated rudeness to you. Looking back on such situations, it becomes clear that the person involved may not have intended to act rudely at all. Analyzing the experience and identifying specific behaviors can assist you to unlock the secrets of that person's magic hat. In this book, we argue for erring on the side of description for developing a common language to speak about communication style. We have devised a descriptor system to help you navigate the complexities and illusionary effects of communication style. We will reveal more on the secret behind the descriptor tricks in Chapter 6.

Link between the Observable and the Unconscious—Backstage Insights

The performances we see under the Big Top represent a small component of what takes place in the circus. They are a result of behind-the-scenes work by coaches, musicians, lighting and pyrotechnic specialists, costumers, animal trainers, and the performers themselves. Communication style can give us a glimpse into what goes on backstage in our unconscious selves. It provides insight into our own motivations and assumptions—as well as others'. Here is a personal story that illustrates some of the tendencies frequently discussed about gender differences in communication.

Calling to Say "Hello"

In high school Basma called her good friend Mark one day. After several minutes of catching up on the news, he started asking questions about how her math class was going and if she needed his help, if her car was functioning properly, if she needed a ride somewhere, or if her family wanted assistance with a house project. Basma said no to all of his inquiries. Puzzled, he finally asked, "Well, if you don't need my help with math, your car, or your house, then why did you call?" When she replied that she had called simply to say hello, he still pushed for the underlying reason for the call. It was difficult for Mark to understand that there didn't need to be a more tangible purpose for calling.

The salient communication style differences in this case included what topics were seen as acceptable for a phone call and how the call should proceed. Mark's communication style indicated his perhaps unconscious, perhaps conscious, focus on achieving a goal or accomplishing a task. Basma's communication style indicated a focus of which she may have been equally unaware—connecting with and supporting her friends. Communication style is the very important link between the behavior we are able to observe—surface-level culture—and the often-hidden values and beliefs that comprise deep-level culture. We can think of communication style as a window into a person's most basic intentions, feelings, psychological state, and priorities. Recognizing and understanding a person's communication style can give us a very quick "read" on how the person is feeling and what she or he is thinking, much as couples of many years know without asking how their partner is responding in a given situation. An ability to correctly interpret communication style provides us access to the contributions people have to offer. Inability to correctly interpret communication style blocks our ability to benefit from those contributions.

Advantages and Disadvantages to Every Style—Variety Makes the Circus Go Round

One of the beauties of a circus is that no matter where you focus your attention, you are sure to find something fascinating. The elephants, horses, tigers, acrobats, and mimes each offer their own unique talents and their individual shortcomings. The same is true with communication styles. Communication styles are not inherently good or bad, and they each have distinct advantages and disadvantages. One style may be more appropriate in certain interactions than in others, but none is inherently better than another. The following story indicates how one style can be advantageous in one environment and detrimental in another.

Two Different Jobs, the Same Style

Eola was familiar with sharing her thoughts and feelings fairly immediately upon experiencing them. When she came to the Midwest of the United States from Northern Europe, she first worked for a liberal magazine where she received many compliments for her effective communication. In her second position, with a liberal radio program, she assumed that the way she had communicated at the magazine would work well in her new position. Much to her surprise, she was actually barred from meetings and could not figure out why until finally a colleague confided, "You don't know your place and how to keep your reactions to yourself." Eola was soon thereafter "downsized" when the radio station faced budget cutbacks.

It is important to remember that an effective style in one environment may be counterproductive in another. In this story, the corporate culture of the magazine supported Eola's explicit and immediate expression of her thoughts and feelings. They viewed her communication style as collaborative, creative, and respectful. The corporate culture of the radio station equated collaboration and mutual respect with a communication style that was carefully considerate of others' feelings and opinions, one in which all employees thought things through and expressed themselves diplomatically with attentiveness to their relationships with others. Eola's attempts to express collaboration and respect by sharing her thoughts and feelings were immediately seen by her radio station colleagues as disrespectful and inconsiderate. Her style worked in one corporate culture but not in the other, just as some styles of communication may be more appropriate for certain purposes or a particular medium (telephone vs. e-mail vs. face-to-face) than others. Using communication style effectively requires that we be able to self-observe and adapt our behavior to the situation in order to achieve our desired outcomes. In summary, any definition of communication style must go beyond one-word, type-like terms and into a more descriptive, situational, yet easy-to-use vocabulary that allows us to communicate the richness, depth, subtlety, intention, and variety of communication style.

Communication and Communication Style

Communication and communication style represent rather large, ambiguous concepts. A standard dictionary's definition of *communication* is "the exchange, transmission, or sending and receiving of thoughts and messages. To communicate is to have an interchange, to express yourself so that you are clearly and readily understood." It is our belief that this last part of the definition of communication is culturally relative. Although some cultures give a high priority to clarity and efficiency of communication, in other cultures these are lower priorities. Some cultures emphasize lengthy and elaborate messages; others find that this level of detail detracts from the communicative message. Even the beginning part of the definition has cultural implications. One variation is whether you believe you communicate a message or thought to another (a rather individualistic definition), or whether, through communication, you mutually create or discover meaning (a more collectivistic mentality).

Communication has many parts, depending on the model used for analysis and is often said to include four components:

1. The medium or channel (face-to-face, telephone, television, mail, e-mail, and language, e.g., English, French, Japanese).
2. The communicators (sender and receiver, speaker and listener, writer and reader, performer and audience, or group of people discussing).
3. The message (content). What is tricky is that the message people receive is often not the message that was sent. Therefore, most models of communication also include a fourth component.
4. Filters or interference, mechanisms that distort intended and perceived meaning. Edward T. Hall introduced one of these filters in the 1950s. He asked whether people perceive meaning in what is actually said—the *words*— or whether they perceive meaning in the body language, the intonation, the place, or who is present—the *context*. It is when we start thinking in this way that the difference between communication and communication style becomes murky.

If, as we have premised at the beginning of this chapter, the message content is the *what*, the communicators the *who*, and communication style the *how*, communication is then the composite of all of these. Perhaps analyzing an example will help clarify this.

Let us say you telephone an acquaintance, Carlos, to invite him to a party. He responds by saying, "I'm really busy . . . but I'd love to be there." Does this mean Carlos is coming or not? Since Carlos' words do not explicitly tell us this, we need to look beyond the words themselves. Does he sound excited? Torn? Confused? Does Carlos typically respond to invitations in this way? For our purposes, *communication style* is how he communicates—the pattern of words Carlos chooses, the volume and pace of his speech, his use of pause; *communication* is the entire process of your speaking with Carlos and trying to create shared meaning. In short, communication is broader than communication style. And communication style is broader than one specific behavior. Communication style encompasses a wide range of verbal and nonverbal behaviors that represent an individual's preferred way of giving and receiving information.

You have now purchased your communication style ticket, which is your entry to understanding the communication circus. In the next chapter we invite you to explore the benefits of communication style fluency.

The following are two activities you can do on your own, with teams, or in a training setting to work with the concepts of communication style as presented in this chapter. Activity 1, "What Would You Do?," enables group members to see the diversity, complexity, and importance of communication style preferences. Activity 2, "Who's the Boss?," shows participants that every communication style has inherent advantages and disadvantages.

ACTIVITY *1:* What Would You Do?

Objectives: To discover a broad range of "appropriate" responses in given scenarios—the diversity of communication styles within the group.

Assumptions/Theory Inherent in the Activity: The basic notion that a wide range of communication style differences exist within every culture and that minor communication style differences can have major effects on interactions and relationships.

Time Frame: 15 to 30 minutes.

Parameters: This activity works well as an introduction to communication style. It can be used as a "think piece" to get a group of participants to consider possible responses to the situations you describe. It can also be used for more in-depth analysis. This activity is particularly useful with homogeneous audiences or with people who do not have a lot of intercultural contact because it can help participants see how many communication style differences exist even within their own circles of interaction and influence, and even among people who are culturally similar to one another.

Materials, Supplies, Handouts: Various situations (see the following suggestions) written on cards to be passed out to participants; at least 4 pieces of poster-sized newsprint.

Situation 1: You have been asked to prepare a one-hour presentation. The day before your presentation, your colleague says you have just 10 minutes to present. You are frustrated about the change. What would you do?

Situation 2: One of your co-workers comes to your office frequently and interrupts your work. What would you do?

Situation 3: You are at an important social function and an acquaintance at your table makes a comment that offends you. What would you do?

Situation 4: You are at a meeting and a colleague compliments the work you have done, so much so that you feel embarrassed. What would you do?

Source: Communication Highwire: Leveraging the Power of Diverse Communication Styles (Intercultural Press).
© 2005 Dianne Hofner Saphiere, Barbara Kappler Mikk, and Basma Ibrahim DeVries. All rights reserved.

How to Facilitate:
1. Ask participants to form small groups.
2. Pass out the cards describing the situations and ask participants to think about potential responses.
3. Ask participants to discuss their reactions in their small groups.
4. Hang up a poster-sized paper for each of the situations. As a large group, ask volunteers to share, one by one, how they would react in the different situations. Record their reactions on the paper.
5. Debrief in a large group and point out the wide range of responses—even within a given culture and with a fairly homogeneous group—to the same situation. Discuss the factors that contribute to this variety of responses as a means of introducing the complexity of noticing, understanding, and working with different communication styles.

Tips: Keep in mind that this activity is meant to generate a wide range of possible responses. To accomplish this goal, we recommend that you keep your selected situations short and simple. Some situations you might use, however, may not elicit a wide range of responses. You can use such situations as examples to discuss some of the more socially sanctioned expectations and responses in particular situations. In such cases, it might be useful to discuss how and why such situations seem to call for particular responses.

ACTIVITY *2:* Who's the Boss?

Objectives: To gain familiarity with the advantages and disadvantages of various communication styles and to practice using different styles while discussing an important (yet hypothetical) issue—the size of a pay increase. This activity also highlights that there are multiple ways to be direct, indirect, circular, person-centered, and so on, and as a result, the labels used with communication styles are very subjective.

Assumptions/Theory Inherent in the Activity: Highlights notions of persuasion and how communication styles affect our perceptions of persuasive messages; demonstrates the effects of power in interactions.

Time Frame: 15 to 30 minutes.

Parameters: This activity works well in showing the effects and implications of using different communication styles or as a more advanced means of demonstrating communication style differences in a negotiation setting. It is critical to highlight in the facilitation that not all participants share the same exact idea of what a particular style constitutes (e.g., direct, indirect) and that they do not share the same view of when it is appropriate to use various styles in a particular context. It is helpful if participants know one another prior to working together on this activity, but it is not necessary.

Materials, Supplies, Handouts: Communication style images—one per participant (see page 20 for images). Pass out only the image and label to each participant. We do not recommend giving a handout with a description of each label, as this can limit the participants' insights about what these labels mean and how they are enacted. If you have many second-language participants, it might be helpful to have the negotiation scenario available as a handout.

Trainer Preparation: Before the training, choose the communication style labels you will use. Be prepared to define the goals of the communication style and some specific behaviors associated with the style. Also, be prepared to share examples of when this style has worked well and not so well. Note that it is easy to come up with negative examples. The goal here is to help participants see

Source: Communication Highwire: Leveraging the Power of Diverse Communication Styles (Intercultural Press).

that there are advantages and disadvantages to every style. If you do not focus on the advantages, it may be difficult for participants to do so and they may spend valuable time stereotyping and conceiving of only the disadvantages of a particular style. For the images and labels we have included, consider these goals and behaviors:

- **Direct.** The point is to get to the point. "Don't beat around the bush." Brevity and being linear are often rewarded.
- **Circular.** The goal is to tell a story or provide enough information so that the point "speaks for itself." Typically, a great deal of information is included, allowing the listener to reach the conclusion on his or her own.
- **Indirect.** The purpose is to bring up a point or respond to an issue, while preserving face and maintaining positive feelings. The goal of harmony in relationships is a higher priority than exactness and speed in communicating.
- **Person-centered.** Communication is a vehicle for building personal relationships. Verbal and nonverbal communication have the power to enhance or damage these relationships because meaning and message are often closely integrated with the identities of the communicators.
- **Idea-focused.** Communication around ideas involving critical thinking or passionate discussion is essential for showing commitment to the ideas and to the people involved. Lively debate between friends, family, or co-workers is satisfying and can positively impact relationships.

How to Facilitate:

1. Tell participants that they must pay attention because they will have to be able to act out the style that their symbol represents.
2. Using behavioral descriptions, explain the different communication styles and their goals as represented by the symbols you have selected.
3. Pair the participants and assign one to be the supervisor and one to be the employee.
4. Explain that they will be meeting for their annual review. The supervisor offers a 2 percent raise, but the employee was expecting a 5 percent raise. Both must use their assigned style to conduct a conversation.

Source: Communication Highwire: Leveraging the Power of Diverse Communication Styles (Intercultural Press).

5. Discuss observations with the large group. Suggested debriefing questions include the following:
   - How comfortable or uncomfortable was the communication style assigned to you?
   - How well were you able to follow the communication style assigned? What affected this?
   - How successful did you feel in the negotiation?
   - What strategies did you use to negotiate in your assigned style?
   - Have you experienced this style before with co-workers?
   - In what situations would you feel comfortable using the style assigned to you?
   - What behaviors did you use to enact a particular style? Ask this question for each of the styles—indirect, direct, circular, person-centered, and idea-focused.
   - How able were you to follow and respond to your partner's style?
   - What strategies did you observe your partner using during the negotiation? How did this affect your enactment of your own assigned style?
   - How would you assess your partner's success in the negotiation based on the communication styles used?

Tips: Sometimes participants need encouragement and coaxing to effectively enact their assigned styles.

Adaptations: Depending on your goals, you may choose to use many different communication styles or you may choose just two or three. You may also give the same styles to partner participants and different styles to other partner participants, and then compare their experiences in the debriefing session. You can adapt this activity to be about any relevant challenge facing your participants. For example, for front-line staff at a health clinic, the client is late. The staff want the appointment rescheduled and the client still wants to be seen. They have a conversation using their assigned style.

Note: The explanations are adapted from William Gudykunst and Stella Ting-Toomey (1988) and Janet Bennett and R. Michael Paige (1996), the training materials are from Barbara Kappler Mikk and Rhonda Davy (1999). *Source: Communication Highwire: Leveraging the Power of Diverse Communication Styles* (Intercultural Press) © 2005 Dianne Hofner Saphiere, Barbara Kappler Mikk, and Basma Ibrahim DeVries. All rights reserved.

SUGGESTED IMAGES AND LABELS

Direct

Circular

Indirect

Person-centered

Idea-focused

Source: Communication Highwire: Leveraging the Power of Diverse Communication Styles (Intercultural Press).

CHAPTER 2

Benefits of Communication Style Fluency

What Does This Ticket Get Me?

Your ticket to the circus is an understanding of communication style. Hopefully you see that communication style is about tendencies and that it can link what is seen and what is unseen. You can probably think of plenty of your own life experiences that have revealed at least some of the advantages and disadvantages of various communication styles. So here you are with your ticket in hand, but have you thought about why this ticket is so valuable? In other words, what are the advantages to competence on the communication highwire?

We have already discussed the most obvious benefit of communication style competence or fluency: to improve our ability to communicate with people who use styles that are different from our own. When given a choice, many people find it easier to avoid interacting with people who are different because they find it stressful or frustrating. The resulting human cost to organizations and communities by those who do not share the dominant communication style is enormous in terms of lost motivation, lost contribution, and turnover. The ability to manage communication style differences has a huge impact on productivity and relationships.

In addition to this obvious benefit to communication style competence or fluency, we see three other major advantages:

1. **Authenticity.** Communication style fluency enables us to know others and ourselves as individuals and as group members, and it helps us to see how we are influenced by many social and cultural factors.

2. **Intentionality.** Communication style fluency enables us to make conscious choices about how we want to express ourselves rather than being limited by the habitual ways we have done things. If circus performers did not discover new ways to accomplish their intended outcomes of bringing the audience thrills and joy, clowns would all dress alike and acrobats would repeat the same moves over and over.

3. **Critical mass.** A circus is fun when it is an ensemble of talented performers and behind-the-tent specialists. It is not a circus if there is only one main event. Communication style fluency enables a family, team, or organization to coordinate their actions so that everyone's authenticity is valued and their best performances are achieved.

Authenticity—Understanding Others and Ourselves

"I just don't seem to understand what she is saying."
"He always takes too long to make his point."
"It's a waste of time to talk to her."
"I don't like the way he always attacks my ideas."

Comments like these are frequently heard in cross-cultural interactions. They reflect the fact that people are not able to connect across a cultural or personal divide. Our view is that it is precisely such communication style disconnects that provide an entryway into knowing others and ourselves in deeper and more meaningful ways.

Ashu

Ashu, who grew up in India, was interviewing for a position in the U.S.A. and was asked, "Can you tell me a little bit about your experience with groups?" Taking the statement quite literally, Ashu pointed to his resumé and said, "Like it says here, I have a great deal of experience organizing groups." Ashu did not realize that this was a request for him to elaborate on his background and offer details about his experiences. The U.S. American interviewer did not understand what else he needed to say to prompt

Ashu to explain more about his competencies. Ashu did not get the job precisely because, as the interviewer said, "He could not defend the experience he had on paper."

The gap—or disconnect—between Ashu's style of communication and the interviewer's expectations prevented the interviewer from discovering Ashu's true work experience. Perhaps Ashu was not the right person for the job; perhaps he did not have the required job competencies. In this case, however, the only competence that was definitely lacking was the ability of the interviewee and interviewer to communicate across their style differences. If Ashu had recognized the misunderstanding, he might have said, "I'm sure I am qualified. What do you need to hear from me to understand my credentials?" Or if the interviewer had said, "This interview, not your resumé, is your chance to tell me everything I need to know to hire you and not someone else for the job," then the style difference might have been bridged.

Communication style allows us a glimpse into who we are as cultural beings. Anyone who has grown up in a community with other people is a cultural being. Most of us have learned multiple cultures: we grew up in a family, with a spiritual tradition, in one or more places, speaking certain languages, with ethnic traditions and, as adults, with professional training. Understanding communication style can enable us to understand ourselves in all our complexity, as an amalgam of personality and the various cultures of which we are or have been members.

Most of us are unaware to varying degrees of our underlying cultural values, beliefs, and expectations. They seem to us "natural" ways of being and often the only "correct" assumptions about the world. Say, for example, that you have just declined a social invitation due to work commitments, and the friend who invited you tells you that you do not value your relationship with him. One response is to become defensive, and another is to use the opportunity to learn. You might reflect on how you made your decision and how often you have chosen work over relationships. Perhaps your choices depend on how long it has been since you have seen your friend, how much you want to see your friend, how pressing your work is, and the firmness of your job situation. You might wonder what in your experience has caused you to prioritize the way you do; what has made you who you are. You might also reflect on these same aspects in your friend. You might use this opportunity to talk with your friend to help both of you understand each other better.

Reflecting on styles of communication can help us to clarify what is personally important to us—our core values. If we only interact with those who are similar to ourselves, we never have the opportunity to realize that there are other ways of thinking or behaving. Knowing the alternatives, that there *are* alternatives, helps us understand the ways in which we are unique as individual persons and in which ways we are culturally influenced. And in today's increasingly complex world, the need to interact across cultures is occurring more frequently in our work, communities, and schools.

Communication style allows us to get past stereotypes and to get to know others as the complex individuals or cultural composites that we are. This is a valuable tool, particularly in the workplace. So often when people say *culture*, what they mean is *nationality*. Yet from our experience and those of many of our intercultural colleagues, nationality is often not the strongest cultural influence on people. In the workplace it is often professional affiliation (finance, research, production) that produces the strongest commonality or cultural pull, followed by organizational culture, gender, and age. Especially in this era of migration, global travel, and expatriate assignments, birth or passport nationality may be one of the lesser influences for some people. Communication style analysis allows us a window into who people really are, beyond some national or ethnic label that may be placed on them. The following example shows just how powerful communication style differences can be in interpersonal interactions.

Two Friends

Ingrid is German-born but has lived in the U.S.A. for most of her adult life. Julie is U.S.-born but lived in Japan for a major portion of her adult life. The two women have been friends for fifteen years. Ingrid and Julie are having an early-morning conversation at a weekend getaway. Julie shares her experience of the weekend so far; Ingrid expresses a contrary view-

point. Julie says she does not want to argue. Ingrid says she is not arguing; she is discussing the weekend. Julie apologizes and says that what
she meant is she was sharing her perspective; she did not want to debate.
Ingrid explains that she is not debating; she is sharing her viewpoint. Julie
gets up and walks away, upset. Her walking away really upsets Ingrid. A
fifteen-year relationship faces a serious test from mere seconds of miscommunication.

The strong feelings that often accompany communication style disconnects
can take us by surprise. As we have seen repeatedly, communication style disconnects are often emotionally charged and are sometimes based on cumulative experiences. We may seek to avoid discussing such disconnects with the people with
whom we are communicating, viewing the differences negatively rather than positively and fearing that such discussions will be unpleasant or tense. It is important
to recognize that emotion often points the way to the differences that do truly
make a difference. These communication style disconnects can help us to discover
what is truly important to us and why—enabling us to be more authentic in our
interactions.

Whether at work, as in Ashu's story, or in our personal lives, as in Julie and
Ingrid's story, communication style disconnects can cause confusion, frustration,
anger, and pain. Communication style disconnects can send us the wrong message—that others are wrong, rude, and so on. Yet Ingrid and Julie could use this disconnect as an opportunity to reflect on what is important in their friendship and to
consider ways in which they can adapt to each other. In short, they could use it as a
chance to get to know themselves and each other better, and to bring the friendship
past the painful event and back to a respectful place. One way to have such a conversation is to use the Four-Step method that we present in Chapter 7.

If we can enhance our abilities to communicate across style differences, we will
be better able to be fully ourselves and to allow others to be fully themselves. The
goal of communication style fluency is not to make everyone the same; it is to
allow everyone to bring forth the best of who they are, in a way that is comfortable,
understood, valued, and utilized.

Intentionality—Making Conscious (Rather than Habitual) Choices

It appears to be human nature to see what we expect to see. We often look for only enough information to corroborate our hypotheses. If we believe people raise their voices when they are angry or upset, then when we hear people speaking loudly in what is to them an enjoyable, animated discussion, we will assume that they are fighting. A robust communication style repertoire enables us to better see what is really happening (e.g., that loud could mean enjoyable) rather than what we are used to seeing or accustomed to expecting (e.g., that loud means angry).

Communication style fluency can allow us to discover our habitual, unconscious behavior and then make conscious choices about whether to continue, modify, supplement, or delete certain behaviors from our communication style repertoire. It can be a good way of discovering that what we intend to communicate is often not what another perceives us as communicating. Once we realize that gap, we can make conscious choices about how we want to behave.

May I Interrupt You?

Years ago, two very good friends, Sarah and Elise, were working on a new product. Sarah, the supervisor, was working on several projects at the time, while Elise, the subordinate, was working only on this one. When Elise would get an idea, she would interrupt Sarah to see what she thought of it. Sarah was happy to talk about the ideas because it kept her in the loop with Elise's thinking, clarified her own vision for the project, and in general helped the project along. One afternoon Elise seemed very upset. When Sarah asked what was up, Elise said, "You act as if my being here is such a bother. I'm here to help with the project. I need your help, yet you seem to resent it."

"Oh, I'm sorry you feel that way. Nothing could be further from the truth! I'm thrilled to have you here. What is it I'm doing that causes you to think that I feel you're a bother?" Sarah asked. "Every time I interrupt you, you look at me with this grimace on your face, as if you're really put out that I'd bother you," Elise replied, exasperated.

The light bulb went on for Sarah, the friend in the supervisor's role. She knew that she was very good at focusing and that she found it difficult to "pull her mind" away from whatever she was working on. While she welcomed discussions with Elise, it took her a moment or two to "switch" her mind. Sarah did not realize, however, that she grimaced during the switching process! Since that day she has done her best, whenever interrupted from deep thought, to put a smile on her face before looking up. This interaction enabled Sarah to look at her communication style and make an intentional rather than a habitual decision about how she wished to communicate in similar situations in the future. She has not been able to change the hardwiring of her brain to "switch" more quickly, but she has been able to expand her communication style repertoire so that she can more effectively communicate her intended meaning.

As complex individuals and cultural beings we have emotional "hot buttons," areas in which we are especially vulnerable and prone to anger or defensiveness. Very often these hot buttons are dismissed as "personal issues," and therefore they are usually off-limits for discussion. Such dismissal can result in people feeling that their opinions, experiences, and even they themselves, do not matter. Frequently what is labeled "off-limits" takes on a power of its own that is out of proportion to its real weight. The communication style descriptors presented in Chapter 6, the factors affecting communication style use introduced in Chapter 3, and the Four-Step method discussed in Chapter 7 are all tools to help us use emotion and personal hot buttons to promote mutual understanding and productivity.

The misunderstanding and frustration that result from communication style disconnects are often cumulative. After repeated misunderstandings, some people will become more adamant while others will give up. History is powerful. The irony is that the person who is offended, hurt, or emotionally charged is often the one pressed to facilitate resolution of the misunderstanding. With communication style, as with communication in general, *we are all responsible*. It is important that each of us develop the ability to promote mutual understanding and generation of solutions, so that we do not by default give those who are feeling defensive the additional responsibility of having to structure a resolution discussion. Communication style fluency can enable us to make purposeful choices about how we wish to engage.

Individuals vary in their perceptual acuity in recognizing and making positive use of communication style differences, but all of us can become more adept at making intentional choices about the communication styles we employ in different contexts and for different purposes. This is not meant to suggest that what we learn about communication styles should be used in a manipulative manner; rather, our continually expanding knowledge level and skills can allow us to become more effective communicators across various contexts as we understand a person's comfort level with communication styles and adapt to them. The following story emphasizes the commitment that is often necessary to understand and connect with another person's style. It also illustrates how worthwhile the investment—the intentionality—can be.

The In-Laws

When Rosa's sister, Anna Maria, announced that she was going to marry Paul, Rosa was ecstatic. She had really grown to admire Paul and was happy that he would be officially joining her family.

Over the next couple of years, however, Rosa became increasingly frustrated every time she called her sister and Paul answered the phone. Paul is a man of very few words, particularly over the phone, and the slow pace of his side of the conversation made Rosa impatient. Sometimes when she asked a question, Paul would take what seemed like an entire minute to respond to her simple inquiry, and his answers were typically two- or three-word phrases with little elaboration or explanation. A few times he did not respond at all, even though she knew he had heard the question clearly.

Prior to her relationship with Paul, Rosa had not been accustomed to this style. When Rosa thought about why Paul communicated the way he did (intentionality), she began to find some clear connections between his values, his personality, and his family's communication patterns (to discover who Paul really was, his authenticity). She started to notice how he communicated with his family of origin, and she observed that his parents used very similar communication styles. This new knowledge helped Rosa understand her brother-in-law and his family better, and in turn allowed her to adapt her own communication style with them so that communication seemed to flow more smoothly and comfortably. When she called Anna Maria's home and Paul answered the phone, Rosa engaged him in conversation by being careful to ask just one question at a time and by mirroring his style. This approach seemed to encourage Paul to converse more. He became more invested in his interactions on the phone with Rosa and in their relationship in general. Over time, Rosa has been able to apply these observational techniques and her new insights to many other communicative situations.

Rosa's intentionality enabled her to connect with Paul despite their communication style differences. She did not change who she was, but she did expand her communicative repertoire, her skill base. The extra work paid off; Paul himself has commented that he feels very comfortable talking with Rosa and noticed that she changed her behavior to adapt to him. While he is not changing any of his own behaviors right now, he appreciates the effort Rosa has made and realizes it has made a difference in their relationship.

Think back to the introductory story about Tanaka-san and Mike. The point is not simply that Tanaka-san spoke explicitly about how he felt—it is also something much more. In that pivotal moment, Mike and Tanaka-san were able to reach a level of understanding that neither one had thought would be possible—they were able to see beyond their habitual behavior and traditional worldviews to obtain a glimpse of the other's reality and experience. Both began to see how the other's interpretive frames functioned and how much they both were affected by the other's communication style. They were then freed to make a conscious choice about how they wished to communicate, rather than remain trapped in habitual communication styles.

Do you remember looking into those amusing distorted circus mirrors? Some made you look much larger than you were, some made you very thin, some stretched certain parts of your body, and some multiplied your image. In a sense, Mike and Tanaka-san found themselves standing in front of each other's mirrors, exposed to images that took on new meaning and helped them understand what was behind their previously distorted images of one another. Standing there next to each other also affected how they felt about themselves and, in turn, how they decided to express themselves. They were able to use communication style to better understand themselves and to make intentional choices about how they wanted to work together.

Critical Mass—Productive and Satisfying Workspaces and Communities

Increased attention to communication style differences leads to greater understanding, satisfaction, and productivity. Just as negative relational effects may result from communication style differences, so too can positive and productive outcomes. The following story explains how differences can be successfully leveraged.

Two Colleagues

Barbara and Basma worked as co-chairs to plan a national conference. Barbara typically responds to e-mail messages with as little text as possible, while Basma provides more background information. When one participant e-mailed that the conference fee was too high, Barbara drafted a quick reply stating that the conference fees were set and not negotiable. She did not send her response to the participant, however; she sent it to Basma for additional text. Basma perceived emotion in the participant's request and supplemented the e-mail message with empathy for the participant, acknowledging that it can be quite difficult to find funds to cover conference costs and explaining in detail that the conference fees also included meals and receptions.

Barbara is making it clear that fees were not to be negotiated freed Basma to focus on the relationship with the participant. When the e-mail was sent to the participant with comments from both Barbara and Basma, it was effective—the participant attended the conference and commented on her appreciation of how her inquiry was handled.

It would have been all too easy for Barbara to send the quick response, making the participant and Basma feel it was too abrupt and alienating. Had Basma sent her text alone, the participant may have felt the door was open to negotiate, which was not Basma's intended outcome. Different communication styles, when used properly, can indeed supplement one another. Basma and Barbara found many ways to utilize their different styles throughout the conference planning process. They discovered that understanding their style differences allowed them to divide some jobs quite naturally and to leverage their communication styles for optimal outcomes.

When individuals understand the communicative approaches of others, they often learn to more effectively interpret and adapt to the other person, to the situation, and to the goals of the interaction. The constructive synergy that emerges from a clear understanding of and ability to work with communication style differences can create positive feelings about the interaction, the task, the organization or community, and the relationship itself.

In this example, it would have been all too easy for Barbara and Basma to rub each other the wrong way and work at cross-purposes. Either person operating alone would not have achieved the optimal result. In fact, they effectively dovetailed their different communication styles in their interaction with the conference participant to achieve positive results—the participant felt listened to and was able to attend the conference, they represented the sponsoring organization well, and they both felt respected by the other and proud of their teamwork.

Lion tamers and unicyclists undoubtedly have more than a few stories to tell about their "near misses." Any act made to look easy takes hundreds or thousands of hours to perfect and, even more important, it requires a commitment to succeed. The same can be said for apparently "seamless" communication. Yes, some individuals seem to dance effortlessly together and may have found that their path was fairly easy. However, for many daily interactions, success takes a commitment to truly understand one another and to work together effectively.

Communication style competence is a cornerstone for developing organization-wide intercultural competence—systems, structures, capacities, and spaces. It is one of the fundamental skills underlying people's abilities to develop themselves and others, as well as the systems and structures that will facilitate intercultural effectiveness in the organization or community.

The creation of communities in which all are able to contribute and feel valued requires discussion about shared values and practices—a common language and rules for working or living together across differences. From our experience, effective intercultural dialogue is most frequently accomplished in a spirit of inquiry, honesty, and respect, with an approach of seeking to listen, understand, and create new and more effective solutions. Such an approach will, of course, require personal and cultural adjustments by all parties—broad and deep communication style competence.

Let us share with you another story.

Lisa

Lisa is a Chinese woman whose father was in the diplomatic corps. While growing up, she attended international schools in five countries, and she speaks Chinese, English, German, and French. She is what many people call a "global nomad." About two years ago, Lisa found what she thought was her ideal job: acting as a liaison between her corporation's operations in Beijing and Geneva. She was thrilled with the opportunity. But now, two years later, she is ready to resign. She tells us she loves working with the Chinese and she loves working with the Swiss at the home office, but she is very tired of having to "carry the weight" of the cultural gap on her own. She tells us that she can't be the only one explaining Chinese business and communication style expectations to the Swiss and vice versa. She needs people to take responsibility, but they see bridging cultures as her expertise, not as their responsibility.

Lisa's experience, similar to that of so many others, demonstrates the need to educate a critical mass of people within the organization or community with the requisite ability to bridge communication style differences. Such education and training involves learning on cognitive, affective, and behavioral levels.

We must be able to use a communication style that can encourage one person without discouraging another and enlighten someone without confusing someone else. These are, of course, very advanced communication style competencies. Communication style involves balance. How do we point out and promote understanding of differences without appearing to threaten or criticize? How do we share common ground without seeming presumptuous or naive?

By increasing our own skills and making intentional choices about communication style, and by facilitating the learning of others, we can positively affect the environments in which we work, live, and play. As more people join in, we can begin to transform previously negative communication spaces into more enjoyable and productive spaces. This is obviously no small order. Each of us is only one performer in a very large circus, but we each have our roles to play: we each have our audiences that we can mesmerize.

The following three activities help people realize the benefits of communication style fluency. Activity 3, "Messages I Heard," allows people to bring some habitual behavior to intentional levels of understanding, while Activity 4, "Teach Me How to Convince You," encourages us to know ourselves well enough to be able to teach others how to persuade *us* effectively. Activity 5, "Team Membership and Task Effectiveness," helps a team to know the styles and strengths of team members well enough to be able to plan how they might dovetail to better accomplish the team's goals.

ACTIVITY *3:* Messages I Heard

Objectives: Participants have the opportunity to better understand their own communication style by reflecting on what they learned about it while growing up, which messages they have internalized, and how and when those messages manifest in behavior. Participants will better understand the advantage of a broad communication style repertoire.

Assumptions/Theory Inherent in the Activity: Focuses on communication style, culture, and social learning.

Time Frame: 30 to 45 minutes.

Materials, Supplies, Handouts: Index cards or sticky notes; a flipchart. No handouts required.

Trainer Preparation: Write down a few examples of messages and consider if/how they have influenced your communication style, and how you have internalized those messages into communicative behavior. Print the list of questions used in step 4 on a flipchart.

How to Facilitate:

1. Introduce the objectives for the exercise as described above.
2. Present a few messages you heard as a child that have influenced your communication style. For example, you might say, "My father often told me to 'Get to the point,' so I tend to be conscious of stating my opinion or request fairly quickly. Friends often called out 'Last one in is a rotten egg,' and I think that's taught me to contribute verbally and assertively in a group setting. Teachers often reminded us to 'take turns,' and even today I find I'm very conscious in conversations or meetings about ensuring everyone the opportunity to speak."
3. Ask participants to think about the messages they heard or learned as children and young adults that may have influenced how they communicate today. Instruct them to write one message per index card, ideally recording several messages on several cards.
4. Display the following list of questions on the flipchart:

- What messages did you hear and how have they affected your communication style?
- In what situations do you use the style?
- What do you like about it?
- What do you dislike about it?
- What are its advantages and disadvantages?

5. Ask participants to form small groups and to read their messages to each other, using the questions on the flipchart to guide them.

6. After the small group discussion, ask participants to report on some of the more frequent messages of the group members—messages they shared. Discuss if the common messages resulted in similar communication styles for different participants, or if there are personal and cultural differences on the effects of some messages. You may ask participants to expand on how the messages make a difference in how they communicate today and how the messages fit (or not) with the broader culture in which participants grew up. Ask if there were any unique messages—messages that others had not heard as children or young adults, and how those have translated into our communication styles as adults.

7. Ask participants to summarize for you the advantages and disadvantages of different communication styles. Ask them if they believe one style is inherently better than another. Ask them if they think it is better to have a broader or narrower repertoire of communicative style. Finally, ask them about steps they might take to expand their communication style repertoires.

Tips: Participants can prepare their cards as homework before the exercise.

Adaptations: This activity can be done with different cultural groups as a comparative communication style activity.

Source: Communication Highwire: Leveraging the Power of Diverse Communication Styles (Intercultural Press).
© 2005 Dianne Hofner Saphiere, Barbara Kappler Mikk, and Basma Ibrahim DeVries. All rights reserved.

ACTIVITY *4:* Teach Me How to Convince You

Objectives: Participants have the opportunity to better understand their own and others' persuasion styles, and to adapt their styles for maximum team effectiveness.

Assumptions/Theory Inherent in the Activity: Listening, decision making, problem solving, and style switching.

Time Frame: One hour or more depending on the number of participants or subgroups.

Parameters: A work team or group, or a group of people attempting to learn about the persuasion strategies of another culture (another nationality, profession, gender, age group, and so on).

Materials, Supplies, Handouts: A video camera to tape the role play for later playback; a flipchart or whiteboard; paper and pens for participants to take notes if desired. Prepare copies of the situation and instructions for each phase if desired.

Trainer Preparation: Prepare, ideally in writing, the situation for step 4. Decide how to divide team members or subgroups, and the time you will allow for each stage of the activity.

How to Facilitate:

1. Explain that to make the best decisions, team members must learn to hear one another fully, and learn to weigh the information provided by each team member appropriately to the decision at hand.

2. To get participants thinking, lead a discussion of common methods of persuasion. It might be best to put the persuasion into a context that will be meaningful for the participants—if you are working with a sales team, you might discuss what would convince them to make more sales calls; with a group of students, you might ask what would encourage them to develop a more efficient study plan; with a community group you might discuss what would convince the participants to start and follow an exercise program.

Sample answers to the community group situation would include the following points:

- Some people are convinced by data. Showing those people statistics on death due to heart disease, high blood pressure, and how exercise can lower disease rates would help convince such people.
- Others are most convinced by personal experience. Surviving a grave illness would convince people to pay more attention to their health.
- Some people are convinced by people they respect or love. Having someone talk to them about an exercise program or volunteer to partner with them in an exercise program might be the best way to convince them.
- People can be convinced by what they consider tangible evidence: the physical (getting a sense of how much better they will feel if they exercise regularly), the visual (picturing themselves healthier and more in shape), or the intuitive (perhaps they meditate or write a journal to convince themselves to continue their exercise regimen).

Note: If you would like to read more about different styles of persuasion, we recommend Barbara Johnstone's descriptions of three different styles—*quasilogical* (preferences for statistical and factual information and using expert, objective witnesses as evidence); *presentational* (preferences for emotional appeals in persuading, focusing on a person's presentation style and ability to "move" listeners as convincing, even beyond the information itself); and *analogical* (preferences for using stories, parables, or analogies in making connections among claims). Her work discusses what counts as evidence within each style and some of the underlying assumptions of these styles.

3. Explain that you are going to allow team members to describe their preferred persuasion strategies to the others in the group, and then allow the others to practice convincing them. You can arrange for this to be done by individuals or subgroups (for example, a group of Brazilians and a group of Romanians, or a group of salespeople and a group of researchers).

4. Describe a typical situation in which team members would need to persuade one another in a convincing manner.

5. Ask each team member (or subgroup) to prepare an explanation, with examples, of how other team members might most effectively convince him or her in this situation. Participants might include how they are influenced in a discussion, what method of listening and explanation they prefer, what most bothers them, what type of supporting information they like, in what venue the conversation is best conducted, who could most effectively persuade them, what questions they might want answered, what would feel pushy or out of line, and so on. Allow sufficient time for team members to prepare (30 minutes, or homework if overnight).

6. Ask for a volunteer team member or subgroup to deliver a prepared explanation to the others (maximum ten minutes each). The listeners should summarize what they have heard *to the satisfaction of the speakers.* This may take multiple iterations and rewordings.

7. Next, have the listeners role-play a meeting in which they try to convince the speakers using the persuasion style that the speakers just explained to them. Have some participants act as observers who will provide feedback.

8. Ask role players how they feel they did. Ask the observers what they saw. Play the videotape of the role playing, highlighting any particularly positive or difficult moments. Discuss what worked well and what could have been better. Allow participants to summarize their learning and apply it to everyday life.

9. Switch places, and have another team member or subgroup present, following steps 6–8.

Tips: If this activity is conducted with an actual work group, the facilitator must take care to balance truthfulness and real-time learning with the potential for hurt feelings or misunderstandings. A constant focus on continuous improvement for the future rather than dwelling on possible past mistakes can be important. Often a key insight is that neither "side" understands itself as well as it may have thought it did.

Adaptations: This activity could also be done with a group of participants with a common interest. It could teach financial people, for example, how to interact with other staff members. Or it could help those relocating to a new country to learn the predominant persuasion style(s) of the new national culture.

ACTIVITY *5:* Team Membership and Task Effectiveness

Objectives: Participants have the opportunity to discuss and agree on how they can utilize the communication styles of each team member to best accomplish the team's objectives. This works best with an intact work team that has been working together for enough time to know one another's styles and tendencies, and is a good activity to have a team revisit at intervals during the lifecycle of the team.

Assumptions/Theory Inherent in the Activity: Advantages and disadvantages of diversity on a team, third cultures/intercultural spaces, project management.

Time Frame: 1 to 2 hours, depending on the discussion style of the group.

Materials, Supplies, Handouts: Forms, flipchart or whiteboard, and markers. Make a copy of the "Analysis of Team Membership and Task Effectiveness" form (at the end of this activity) for each participant.

How to Facilitate:

1. Lead a team discussion of the team's objectives and clearly record the group's consensus.

2. Conduct a discussion of the tasks that the team must be able to achieve to be successful, the communication styles that will be required to accomplish those tasks effectively, and when/why that style will be needed. For example, if the team's objective is to host a customer event successfully (or for a college admissions office, hosting a student recruiting event, for example), tasks would include reserving the venue, organizing the program, securing the speakers, promoting the event to customers to ensure attendance, and paying the bills. Regarding the styles for different tasks, when reserving the venue it would be important to use a communication style that is precise and detail-oriented, and to ask lots of questions to minimize surprises. Inviting the customers and ensuring solid attendance would require a communication style that is motivational, perhaps involving storytelling, to help customers understand how happy they will be to

have attended the event and how much they will benefit from the event. On a flipchart record the answers to question 1 from the handout.

3. Next, have participants spend some individual time reflecting on questions 2 and 3 on the handout—his or her own style as well as the communication styles of team members. Participants should complete the handout, describing what communication styles are represented on the team and how the team might best use those styles appropriately, which needed styles might be missing on the team, and strategies for compensating for that lack.

4. Lead a group discussion of questions 2 and 3 on the handout. Note styles the team will require that are represented on the team and those that are underrepresented. Brainstorm ways to utilize the styles needed at appropriate times and how to avoid using inappropriate styles at inappropriate times. Also brainstorm how to compensate for any necessary styles that are not strongly represented by individuals on the team.

5. If you are working with a team on an ongoing basis, revisit group agreements frequently, or urge the team to do so on its own, to ensure that plans are followed or modified as appropriate. This will also help the team focus on skill development and reflect on ways they have expanded their communication style repertoires and choices.

Tips: Attempt to get the group to be as specific as possible about actions they will take and behaviors they will demonstrate, when, and how.

ANALYSIS OF TEAM MEMBERSHIP AND TASK EFFECTIVENESS

1. Given the objectives of this team, describe some of the tasks that you as a team are going to need to be able to accomplish, and the styles/approaches most useful in accomplishing them.

TASK	STYLE NEEDED	WHEN/WHY

2. List the styles your team has and how you as a team can best ensure that the styles are used at appropriate times.

STYLE	HOW TO USE	WHAT TO AVOID

ANALYSIS OF TEAM MEMBERSHIP AND TASK EFFECTIVENESS *(continued)*

3. List the styles your team is missing and how you as a team can best compensate.

STYLE	HOW TO COMPENSATE	WHAT TO AVOID

Source: Communication Highwire: Leveraging the Power of Diverse Communication Styles (Intercultural Press).

The Motivators of Communication Style

In this section we introduce you to the first of the tools that you can use to analyze and learn about communication style. In Chapter 3 we explain five key factors that affect the communication style used in a given situation. In Chapter 4 we illustrate how these five factors interact and fit together (the Star Chart), and in Chapter 5 we give you the opportunity to practice using the factors to learn from your interactions and become a more effective communicator.

CHAPTER 3

Factors Affecting Communication Style
Starring Acts in the Circus

Come one, come all, to the greatest show in communication! You have your tickets, and it is time to enter the seemingly chaotic yet highly synchronized dynamic of the Big Top!

In the Introduction we told you the story of Mike and Tanaka-san, the two company presidents, one working primarily in the U.S.A. and the other in Japan, who just could not see eye-to-eye. Mike felt he could not trust Tanaka-san because he was too indirect and poker-faced. He felt Tanaka maintained the appearance of agreement, hid his real opinions, and in reality went off and did as he pleased. Tanaka felt that Mike was primarily concerned about his own career and objectives, not the success of the subsidiary. He felt Mike did not listen and was inflexible. After months of facilitated interaction, an exasperated, angry outburst finally enabled them to gain some respect for each other and to work together more productively.

Why? Communication style was obviously a major impediment to their ability to work together effectively. What caused it to be such a problem? What was actually going on in each of their minds? Despite the frequent references people make to communication style, we realized that there was not an integrative theory or tool that would help these two to better understand all that communication style is and its impact on their interaction, trust, and productivity.

We knew that such a tool would need to be flexible and interactive enough to be applicable to specific contexts, because communication style is situation-dependent.

We also knew that the tool must be useful for understanding not only a specific interaction, but also for improving our understanding of the overall dynamics of communication style. We ventured to create a tool that people can use to decipher everyday conversations, and we present this tool in this chapter.

We continue with the circus metaphor to introduce the factors affecting communication style use, and begin this chapter with a bit more background on why we have chosen this metaphor. It is our sincere hope that you will work with and build from this metaphor, and that it will serve as a stepping-stone to bring forth a deeper and more meaningful understanding of communication style.

The Circus Metaphor

Part of what makes the circus metaphor so rich is its applicability to so many aspects of the communication style process: complexity, the need for constant revision based on what is happening in the interaction, the responsibility of each participant, and the importance of a leader.

Amazing Complexity

A key aspect of the circus metaphor for us is its complexity. Once you begin to really focus on it, you may start to wonder how anyone on earth could manage all aspects of the multisensory circus experience, assemble and use props, lighting, and music to best effect, and accomplish such incredible feats of dexterity. We feel this is quite analogous to intercultural communication in general. It is quite an amazing feat that communication occurs with any amount of frequency and accuracy, particularly across cultures. Communicating effectively across cultures is similar to the process of perfecting a circus performance in that mistakes, miscommunications, and other misses are to be expected.

Interactivity and Constant Revision

A second important aspect of the circus metaphor is its interactivity. All performers are influenced by their own and the others' performances, as well as by audience reaction and the input of the coach or trainer. If the music is too loud, too soft, or perhaps does not play at all, performers adjust their acts accordingly. If the popcorn popper breaks or the props trunk is lost in transit, circus staff regroup and figure out alternatives. When we are communicating, we constantly reassess our communication style and adjust it in response to the reactions we observe, the goals we want to achieve, and the values and intentions we feel.

Every Performer's Responsibility

Although every circus act may have a leader, each performer is crucial to the overall success of the act. If one trapeze artist is blamed for not jumping far enough, the other in turn can be blamed for not reaching out far enough. The reality is that each performer has a role, and we all need to be able to dovetail with one another to make the performance as stellar as possible. Likewise, all communicators in an interaction bear multiple responsibilities for the success of the communication and the trust in the relationship.

Need for a Coach or Facilitator

Even though the performers all bear a sense of responsibility for their acts, there is often a ringleader or trainer, someone who coordinates the multiple efforts of the circus performers. This "behind the scenes" coach or facilitator encourages the performers to look at themselves and analyze their individual actions as well as the overall outcome in order to improve the effectiveness and "wow" factor of the act. At times, the intercultural facilitator or coach is figuratively making a video so that the performers can "rewind" or "replay" the performance, experience it from a different perspective, with the clarity of hindsight to focus on details. The coach also demonstrates the power of the "pause" button—the importance in intercultural interactions of taking a mental step backward, taking a deep breath, and calling for a break from the discussions at hand to better understand where each performer is coming from, what they are intending, and how to refocus on desired outcomes.

In Chapter 1, we mentioned the five factors influencing when and why a certain communication style is used: the context, goals, self-concept, values, and communication style repertoire of each person in the interaction. These factors are complex and are individually and culturally based. These key factors and their applications will help us to figure out, in retrospect, what happened with Mike and Tanaka-san. If used during the actual work relationship, they could have possibly saved these two men several years of frustration and negativity, and given their organizations enhanced productivity.

We first explain each of the five factors—what they are and how they fit into the communication process—and then apply the factor to the Mike and Tanaka story introduced in the Introduction and highlight the role of that factor in their interaction. We also offer additional stories and examples that illustrate and emphasize the importance of that factor in effective communication. Finally, we provide a list of questions to consider in determining the role of that particular factor in analyzing your own communication incidents. We hope that the Mike and Tanaka reprise helps increase your understanding of the breadth and depth of these communication style factors, and that the additional stories, examples, and lists of questions to consider provide you with useful material you can apply in your training, teaching, coaching, and facilitating.

Mike and Tanaka Revisited

Mike was based on the West Coast of the U.S.A. and Tanaka-san was based in Tokyo—locations with a seventeen-hour time difference between them. Thus, they communicated primarily by e-mail and met one another in person only two to four times a year. Both men found it difficult to discuss complex business issues via e-mail, but they also struggled with phoning one another due to the time difference. When they met in person, they usually met in one or the other's office in California or Tokyo. When they met in Tokyo, Mike was a bit uncomfortable and unsure of himself; the same was true for Tanaka when the two met in California.

Mike saw himself as an action man, energetic and vigorous. He tended to speak straight to the main point without spending a lot of time on background information. He saw himself as powerful, quick, and dynamic. Mike was very focused on achieving quick profitability from new ventures in the Japanese subsidiary. He spoke only American English, and since he was a senior executive traveling as a representative of the head office abroad, he had the fortunate position of rarely having to question the validity of his style or approach. He did adapt his English when talking with nonfluent English speakers by speaking a bit more slowly and by using simpler sentence structure and more standard vocabulary.

Tanaka learned to speak English as a working adult, and though he was fluent in the language, he often struggled with Mike's use of slang expressions, sports metaphors, and quick pace of speaking. Tanaka saw himself as highly disciplined and persevering. He arose at 4:00 every morning to meditate, read, and exercise. He was a man of few words and frequent long pauses, a man who valued contemplation. He tended to explain the context in detail so that his supervisor, Mike, could understand Tanaka's recommendations. Having worked for decades in a Western company in Japan, Tanaka recognized the home office's desire for quick profitability, but Tanaka was convinced that the only way to achieve profitability in Japan was to take a longer-term approach and build market share. His tenure in a Western company had taught Tanaka-san to be forthright, persuasive, and verbally assertive, or so he thought. Tanaka used a fairly broad repertoire of communication styles with Mike, but none of these styles seemed to connect in a way that Mike found meaningful or trustworthy.

The two men had not spent much time talking about their respective roles, and they had very different expectations of their supervisor–subordinate relationship. Tanaka-san was conscious of the hierarchy, of demonstrating respect to Mike, and of preserving Mike's face. He expected Mike to watch out for him and protect the Japan operation. In contrast, Mike expected Tanaka-san to speak up and advocate for the Japanese subsidiary, and saw his own role as one of balancing the competing needs of the various subsidiaries in the Asia–Pacific region.

Now that you have a bit more background on the story, let us look at our model of communication style—the factors that we see affecting which style is used in a given interaction.

Introducing the Factors

Context—The House of Mirrors

A favorite aspect of many circuses or carnivals is the house of mirrors, that wonderful attraction where as we attempt to walk through it we cannot tell which way is forward and which way is backward. We look at ourselves in the mirrors, yet we do not look as we expect—we may be taller, thinner, or there may be 33 of us! We walk into what we think is a passageway and find ourselves walking straight into a mirrored wall that is blocking our way and forcing us to turn around.

The house of mirrors illustrates that while one communicator means one thing, the other may experience something completely different. As we frequently discover when miscommunication occurs, participants often seem to be living in alternate realities. Thus, the context is important for understanding any communicative endeavor; it sheds light on the alternate realities. Who is communicating? Where are they? How well do they know one another? How do they feel about each other? Who else is present? What language are they speaking? How is each of them feeling at the moment? Have they had similar discussions before, or is this the first? The communicators choose their style of communication depending on how they perceive the context of the communication. We define *context* as the circumstances in which an event occurs, that is, the aspects of the communication situation that can typically be readily identified and described.

Returning to our Mike and Tanaka story, let us take a quick look at the contexts—the house of mirrors—in which they were operating.

Mike and Tanaka—Context

Because Mike and Tanaka both were performance-driven individuals who found it difficult to work via e-mail, and because one or the other of them was inconvenienced by the 17-hour time difference to participate in a telephone call, the context (virtual communication) meant that they tended to approach their communication with a sense of irritability.

When Tanaka and Mike were able to meet face-to-face, it was never "neutral" ground. When they met in Tokyo, even though Mike was very well traveled, he was not completely sure where to sit, how to acknowledge the person who served tea, or how to establish credibility with the staff. Restaurants and evening activities brought more questions. When they met in California, Tanaka felt a bit tentative about such things as where to get coffee and where to phone internationally. He found it rather insulting that someone of his status would have to navigate his own way through the maze of office cubicles, and that he was often left to entertain himself in the evenings. Thus, the physical context affected how the two men communicated with each other.

Mike and Tanaka-san each had different perceptions of their roles and were thus seeing different things. Tanaka expected his boss to look out for him and make sure subsidiary needs were adequately met. Mike saw Tanaka as more than able to take care of himself, and as subsidiary president Tom felt Tanaka was responsible for subsidiary operations. Mike saw a clear separation between his and Tanaka's roles, and saw their relationship as purely professional. Tanaka saw a lot of overlap in their roles, and expected an intertwining of their personal and professional relationships.

The two men communicated in English, and though they both spoke the language fluently, Tanaka struggled with Mike's slang expressions, sports metaphors, and quick pace. The contextual factors of language usage and fluency therefore created a power imbalance and caused difficulty in achieving mutual understanding. All of these different views of context greatly impacted how each of these men communicated—their communication style.

We have identified seven components of context that impact communication style interaction—seven mirrors that reflect or skew our view of the interaction itself, and thus affect how we communicate. These are:

- **Physical context.** Where we communicate (a conference room, our office via e-mail, restaurant) affects the style of communication we employ in the interaction. As mentioned earlier, the lack of "neutral" ground for face-to-face meetings caused discomfort and a lack of surety for Tanaka-san and Mike that kept their communication style consistently out of sync with each other.

- **Roles.** Perception of our own role (as customer, supervisor, friend) and the roles of other communicators affect how we interact. Mike and Tanaka-san had different expectations of their own roles and that of the other person, and thus frequently talked right past each other.

- **Historical context.** History affects the here and now of any interaction. History between nations, spiritual traditions, companies, and communities can easily affect how we perceive each other, and thus can influence our style. For Mike, the histories between Japan and the U.S.A. left him feeling that the U.S.A. was a superior country. He never openly spoke of this superiority, but ultimately he believed that the U.S. approach to business was the best model, and as a result he did not see it as necessary to truly understand the Japanese models for conducting business. For Tanaka-san, who was very proud of his Japanese heritage, history affected his communication style with Mike in that he strongly expected to be listened to and have his opinion and expertise with the Japanese marketplace elicited and valued.

- **Chronology.** How this interaction fits into a series of interaction events affects our choice of communication style. It makes a difference if this is the first time we have talked about something or the tenth, and whether our past interactions have been successful or unpleasant. Tanaka and Mike had a pattern of miscommunication that, over time, became more difficult to change.

- **Language.** The language that we use, the "version" of the language that we speak (e.g., Aussie, British, or American versions of English), and our fluency with the language all play a part in the style with which we communicate. Mike's communication style in English meant that Tanaka did not fully understand him, and this limited Tanaka's ability to fully participate and influence the direction of the conversation.

- **Relationship.** How well we know the other person, and how much we like or trust him or her, will also affect how we communicate. Additionally, the patterns we develop over time within specific relationships often have a cumulative effect on future interactions between relational partners. Mike had learned to expect Tanaka to be difficult and obtuse; Tanaka had learned to expect Mike to be a poor listener, focused only on his own agenda. Beginning a discussion with expectations like that did not encourage constructive communication.

- **Constraints.** The method we use to communicate (e.g., some people hate e-mail or phone calls) and the time we have available for the interaction are examples of the types of constraints that affect how we communicate. Communicating virtually or across a seventeen-hour time difference irritated Mike and Tanaka and thus influenced the style with which they communicated.

STORIES ILLUSTRATING THE EFFECT OF CONTEXT ON COMMUNICATION STYLE

A few quick examples might be useful to demonstrate the different ways context can influence communication style.

Arabic and English

When speaking in Arabic with her extended family or Egyptian community members, Basma feels that the conversation is often more lively, animated, and louder than when she is speaking in English. These conversational style differences sometimes seem even more pronounced when she is in Egypt, whether speaking English or Arabic, and whether among Egyptians only or among a mixed group of Egyptians and U.S. Americans. Whether in the U.S.A. or in Egypt, when her non-Egyptian friends or U.S. American students who travel to Egypt with her observe these conversations, they often think that the Arabic speakers are arguing or being overly assertive or even rude. Basma *feels* different when communicating in Arabic instead of English. She often feels free to use a more aggressive communicative approach and finds herself speaking more loudly in Arabic.

The affective experience of an interaction highlights the importance of language in influencing the communication styles employed and in assessing the experiences of the communicators. These differences in experience and perception help illuminate the intricate relationship between language and culture. The preceding example also reveals the possible interplays between the language used and the physical context of an interaction. People who move freely between different linguistic and cultural worlds often shift styles so naturally that they are unaware of the adaptations they are making.

Unanswered Questions

Barbara, a U.S. American, and her husband, Tonu, from Estonia, were having dinner with their two kids, Annika and Oliver. Barbara asked Tonu a question and Tonu did not respond. Annika noticed the lack of response, and being a diligent four-year-old, she was quick to point out a communication rule infraction, noting, "Mama, Papa did not answer your question. That's rude." To this, Barbara explained, "Papa does not always answer Mama's questions." Before Barbara could explain further, Annika chimed in "Yeah, and that's rude." Barbara replied, "Not in Papa's culture. In Papa's culture, when you ask a question and the person knows you know the answer, you don't have to say it out loud." Annika's response? "Hmm, that's interesting, isn't it Mama?"

This example helps us understand that chronology can influence our behavior (for example, Barbara's previous experience with Tonu's silence prepared her for silence in this situation), emotions (again, having learned to understand that the silence was not intended to mean "your question is unimportant," Barbara was able to respond in a calm voice to Annika's comments), and choices (Barbara chose to use the situation to highlight different communication style patterns—that silence can be interpreted in different ways). Context definitely affects the style with which we communicate!

I've Enjoyed Working with You

Dianne, a U.S. American, tells the story of working virtually with an Irish colleague. She was enjoying their joint project, and at the end of an e-mail wrote, "Robert, I've really enjoyed working with you on this project." During their next phone conversation, Robert's voice became a bit hesitant, and he asked Dianne what she had meant by "I have really enjoyed working with you." When he read it, he thought it read like something one would put on a tombstone! He thought she was trying to say that their relationship on this project and future professional endeavors was finished. This was not Dianne's intended meaning at all and she was rather shocked and amused at Robert's interpretation!

Linguists and others schooled in strict adherence to grammar rules might note that the use of "have enjoyed" in the example above is the present perfect tense and implies an action has been completed. This use of the present perfect is common in day-to-day U.S. American English. In short, to Dianne, it was an emotional action completed—the enjoyment and not the process of working together. It is precisely this use of U.S. American English that demonstrates that the Irish and U.S. Americans *are* speaking a different language!! This story illustrates how another aspect of context—the communication medium, in this case e-mail—affects communication style and how it is perceived. Robert's initial interpretation of Dianne's comment was influenced by the fact that he read it on e-mail rather than in another format. Had he heard it from Dianne over the phone or in a face-to-face conversation, he would have had more nonverbal clues (for example, vocal cues if over the phone, and eye contact and facial expressions if communicating face-to-face) on which to base his analysis and, likely, would have come to a very different conclusion about her intended meaning. The seemingly clear and concise nature of Dianne's comment, her simple feeling that she enjoyed working with Robert, was understood from a completely different perspective that led to a very different conclusion (a rather definitive one concerning the future of their working relationship). This small difference—with potentially major consequences—was based primarily on the medium with which it was communicated, a constraint that hindered communication.

QUESTIONS TO CONSIDER ABOUT CONTEXT

The following are key questions to consider when determining whether context is a key issue in a communication style interaction:

- **Physical context.** What is the place and time? Who is present? What is the medium (phone, e-mail, face-to-face)? Is the physical context more familiar or comfortable for one communicator than another? Does the physical context itself cause any assumptions to be made by the communicators ("This is my office, so I am responsible for determining the agenda.")? Does the physical context lend advantages or disadvantages to one communicator over another? Does it indicate any power dynamics to the communicators?

- **Roles.** What do the communicators perceive their roles to be in this situation? What do they believe people in each of these roles should and should not do? What responsibilities do they equate with their roles? What are their expectations of someone in these roles? What power do they associate with these roles? What power dynamics do they see among these roles?

- **Historical context.** What is the shared history between the cultural groups to which the communicators belong? What perceptions do they have of each other's cultural groups? Is there a larger historical context underlying the topic about which they are communicating? How does such experience affect the current interaction?

- **Chronology.** Have the communicators discussed this topic previously? What was the process? What was the outcome? How are these past experiences affecting the current interaction?

- **Language.** What language are the communicators using? Are all of the communicators fluent in this language? Is the language used native to one or all of the communicators? How do the communicators feel about using this language? Do they speak the same dialect of the language? How does the language used affect the way in which the topic is discussed? Does the language used significantly affect power and influence in the communication?

- **Relationship.** How long have the communicators known one another and in what capacity? What is each communicator's status? What perception do they have of each other's competence? Do the communicators like and respect one another?

- **Constraints.** Are there any limits that constrain the interaction? How do the communicators perceive the time allotted for this interaction? Does the medium interfere with someone's ability to fully participate? Are there distractions (such as someone knocking on the office door during the interaction) or pressures (such as an impending deadline) affecting the interaction?

Goals—The Smell of Circus Snacks

As soon as we enter the circus tent we are surrounded by delicious smells, and in such variety—popcorn, peanuts, cotton candy, and, depending on locale, corn on the cob or grilled octopus—very tantalizing smells. But we also want a front-row seat for the best view of the circus action. How do we accomplish both our goals—securing a good seat and a delicious snack? We define *goal* as the outcome we intend to accomplish.

The approach (communication style) we use to reach our goal will affect whether we are able to achieve our goals. In turn, the goals we have and how we hold (that is, rate or value) them affect how we communicate. Should we wait for our first choice of snack even though there is a long line, or go to the shortest line and get whatever that vendor sells? Or should we skip a snack altogether? We may use a very different communication style depending on whether our goal is to enjoy ourselves, get a job done well, get a job done quickly, consider if we want to develop a relationship with someone, or accomplish multiple goals.

Mike and Tanaka—Goals

Mike's goals included having profitable operations in Japan; he and his bosses had to keep quarterly returns-conscious investors in the U.S.A. happy. Tanaka's goals were for profitable operations in Japan over the long term. He saw a need for the company to invest now to build market share.

Goals might be shared or divergent, they might dovetail or hinder one another, yet they very much affect the communication style we choose to use. In this case, Mike held his goal solidly in his hands and focused on accomplishing it. He felt that communicating in a particular manner would best help him achieve his goal. He focused on communicating his main point—the need for quick profitability—and did not complicate it with background information such as investment procedures in the U.S.A. Tanaka heard Mike's objective and did not like it. However, he felt that questioning the logic behind his superior's goal would be disrespectful. He therefore never fully understood that the company needed quick profitability in order to maintain funding, and Mike misread Tanaka's silence as acceptance of Mike's goal.

Likewise, Tanaka-san held his goal solidly in his hands and focused on accomplishing it. He felt that explaining the situation rather than the main point would best help him achieve his goal. By explaining the Japanese market and economic climate, he believed that Mike would reach the same conclusion that he had. If Mike understood, the goal would be obvious. And then Tanaka would not have to tell Mike what to do; Mike would figure it out on his own. Thus, Mike's face would be preserved.

Both of these gentlemen were so intent on achieving their objectives that they didn't step back far enough to see that their communication styles were actually interfering with the achievement of those very objectives!

We can see from this example that our goals and how we hold them affect how we communicate. We need to take the time to understand one another's goals. This can be done by being open to hearing others' goals and by sharing our goals and the logic or realities driving them with one another, so we can agree on shared goals. We can also use more indirect methods, such as having intermediaries speak directly to each party or liaisons help each person understand the goals of the other.

Communicating in a flexible manner allows us to adapt appropriately to the situation and accomplish what we desire. In this manner, we can accomplish the dual goals of securing a front-row circus seat and enjoying a delicious snack!

STORIES ILLUSTRATING THE EFFECTS OF GOALS
ON COMMUNICATION STYLE

Female Bonding

Keiko from Japan, Kelsey from the United States, and Olga from Hungary enter a conversation during a break from their educators' conference. Each woman is interested in bonding with the others to solidify their relationships and possibly connect on future professional endeavors. Keiko uses apologies to accomplish this goal; the others perceive her apologies as indicating she lacks self-confidence. Kelsey uses compliments to bond; the compliments make Keiko a bit self-conscious and cause Olga to question Kelsey's intentions. Olga "nags" the others to show her concern and build relationships; this behavior irritates Keiko and Kelsey.

This story shows three women attempting to build relationships using the communication style they had assimilated from their cultures of origin. In this case, they shared a common goal, but their use of different patterns of communication and mutual failure to recognize the intent or goals behind those communication styles caused them to fail to bond in the way they had hoped.

Disconnected Phone Call

Ted called a friend, Xavier, with whom he had not talked in a long time. Ted was in the middle of a very important project deadline, and he was sure that Xavier would know the answer to a question he had, saving Ted a lot of time and research.

When Xavier answered the phone, he was overjoyed to hear from Ted. He asked Ted about his family, his life, his job. Ted interrupted to explain that he did not have time to talk right then—he was facing a work deadline and had one quick question for Xavier. Ted asked Xavier the question, received the answer he desired, thanked Xavier, and said, "Let's talk soon to catch up."

Xavier hung up the phone with distaste in his mouth. How could Ted, a friend, not have ten minutes to spare for a conversation? He guessed that Ted did not really consider them friends anymore. On Ted's end, he hung up feeling grateful for his friendship with Xavier, whose expertise had just helped him significantly.

This example demonstrates a very different effect of goals compared to the "Female Bonding" story. In this one, Ted and Xavier actually have opposite goals—Ted's is get his question answered quickly, counting on the fact that his friend Xavier will understand his rush. Xavier's goal is to reconnect with and enjoy his friend, even for a few moments. The different goals result in very different communication styles, which again result in a misunderstanding. In this case, Ted is mistaken in thinking that all went well, and Xavier is frustrated. Undoubtedly, their next conversation will be affected by this interaction.

QUESTIONS TO CONSIDER ABOUT GOALS

Key questions to consider when determining whether goals are a key issue in communication style interaction include the following:

1. What are the communicators trying to accomplish for the long term? What are the communicators trying to accomplish in this conversation? At the end of the conversation, what do they hope the other will understand about why they were talking?
2. Are all communicators aware of their own goals? Are they aware of the others' goals in this particular interaction?
3. Are the communicators verbally explicit about their desired outcomes? Are the communicators nonverbally explicit about their desired outcomes? Is it difficult to find any verbal or nonverbal clues about the desired outcome?
4. How are their goals and intentions influencing the communication process?
5. How is the communicators' interaction affected when they share the same goals and intentions?
6. How is the communicators' interaction affected when they have different or even opposite goals and intentions?

7. Is it possible in the given situation for the communicators to arrive at one or more common goals?

8. What is the sequence over time of reaching one's communication goals? For example, how might the goal of an initial conversation differ from the goal of a conversation one month from now?

Self-Concept—Circus Music

One of the joys of most circuses is auditory: the music. The music fills our ears, our minds, and our bodies. Circus entry music, that deep "oompah" marching sound, helps us to feel energized and joyous. The dangerous circus acts with their accompanying music stimulate us to feel fear and breathless anticipation.

The music—the rhythms, the tones with which we resonate—is a wonderful metaphor for our self-concept. Some of us see ourselves as high, light, quick little notes. We may tend to communicate in that way—softly, tentatively, quickly, in and out of a conversation. Others of us may see ourselves as heavy bass notes. We may frequently set the pace of a conversation, steering the choice of topic and helping to determine what gets discussed and what is dropped. Some of us may see ourselves as players in a dramatic opera that is life; we might communicate expressively, with effusive gestures and facial and verbal expressions. Others of us may see ourselves as performers in a lyrical ballet—expecting others to give their rapt attention, to listen and interpret what is communicated. How we see ourselves—our self-concept, the music in our heads—strongly impacts how we communicate.

Mike and Tanaka—Self-Concept

Looking at our now-familiar Mike and Tanaka example, Mike's self-concept was that of a go-getter, the guy who gets things done. He saw himself as taking charge, effective and efficient, a well-oiled machine. He saw himself as energetic and vigorous. His theme music might have been "Mission Impossible"—powerful, quick, and exciting.

Tanaka-san saw himself as very much of an aesthete, driven by discipline with his early morning ritual of meditation, reading, and exercise. He saw himself as a man of few words, a man who could cut through the unnecessary to reveal the core truth. His self-concept was that of a man able to tolerate and rise up in the face of adversity. His theme music would be strong yet slow and contemplative, perhaps traditional Japanese *shakuhachi* (bamboo flute) music.

We're sure you can see how Tanaka's and Mike's self-concepts affected their communication styles. Mike frequently made strong, clear statements and expected a quick response. Tanaka-san explained Japanese market realities, consumer preferences, buying patterns, and distribution routes, expecting that Mike was putting all the pieces together and reaching the same obvious conclusion that he had reached. Their styles were much like their theme songs.

In theory it should be possible for each of these men to be fully themselves and yet perform effectively together. And herein lies the power of the music metaphor. We all know how difficult it can be to maintain a melody or tune when someone else is playing or humming a very different one in our ears. It can be similarly difficult to maintain our sense of self in the presence of obvious difference.

One common reaction, as with goals, is to cling to our sense of self. We refuse to change or adapt and become stuck in our ways: "My way or the highway"; "I'm right and you're wrong." A second common reaction is to give in, give up, or fit in.

The music metaphor can provide some valuable clues as to how to manage self-concept and communication style. If we think of a symphony, all the musicians must play from the same score, yet each instrument has its own voice, its own uniqueness. The individual instruments are distinct yet synchronized. In jazz music there may be less of a score and more improvisation—more of the unique, spontaneous voices, yet in good jazz these voices blend and build on one another.

Intercultural communication brings us into contact with unfamiliar situations—situations that have no clear right or wrong answers. A frequent reality of intercultural interaction is that we inadvertently offend someone, fail to communicate what we intend, and make mistakes. Particularly if the mistakes happen frequently, it can be easy to question our self-worth, our intelligence, and our capabilities. We must learn to distinguish between the music in our own minds and the music that we hear coming in from the outside. Such distinguishing requires mindful attention, being "in tune" with our surroundings and ourselves.

Our goal with communication style, therefore, is to maintain our self-concept while enhancing our collaboration. The goal is not necessarily to change our style, but to be able to express ourselves in a variety of ways with a diversity of other musicians—to be both more strongly and uniquely ourselves and more flexible and responsive to others.

A STORY ILLUSTRATING THE EFFECT OF SELF-CONCEPT ON COMMUNICATION STYLE

Thirty Participants?

Jane, from New Zealand, was working at a Japanese company in Tokyo. She was fairly fluent in Japanese and had been working in the country for six years. She saw herself as a well-intentioned person, strong and clear yet amenable and cooperative. Her job was to train Japanese managers in a heavily skill-based program. The maximum number of participants per workshop was twelve. One afternoon, Jane's Japanese boss, Mr. Ohashi, approached her desk. Mr. Ohashi was director of the department, and he saw himself as caretaker of the department and as a substitute workplace father to this young foreigner. He saw himself as a strong, authoritative, and kind person.

Jane's desk was one in a row of desks in a large, open office space. Ohashi-san informed her (in Japanese) that next week she would have 30 participants in her workshop. Her first thought was that the participants would not get a lot of skill practice if there were so many of them, so she asked her boss (in Japanese), "Why will there be 30 people?"

Ohashi-san backed up half a step, got a stern look on his face, and reiterated that she would have 30 people in her workshop. Still oblivious to the communication dynamic, Jane explained her concern, "But Ohashi-san, if we have 30 people in the class, I'm afraid the participants won't be satisfied. They won't get individual skill practice." Upon hearing this, Mr. Ohashi, still looking stern, switched to English and responded, "Okay, you'll have twelve people in your class next week."

At this point Jane realized that she had upset her boss. She realized Ohashi-san was "lying," telling her what she wanted to hear so that she would stop arguing with him and stop embarrassing herself, him, and everyone nearby. She knew she would have 30 participants next week. While she had been intending to be respectful and responsible, he'd experienced her as rude and insubordinate, as arguing with him in front of the other employees. Ohashi saw her as disrespecting his ability to take care of the department and reach the appropriate conclusions, and as not appreciative of all that he had done for her.

The irony in a situation like this is that both people were unable to express their self-concept in a way that accurately communicated to the other. When Jane first realized that Ohashi-san was lying to her, she did not at all feel him to be kind or caretaking! As Ohashi perceived Jane to be acting insubordinate, he did not at all feel her being well intentioned or amenable! Thus, while communication style is closely linked to our self-concept, we can clearly see that a repertoire of styles can enable us to more accurately communicate that self-concept to others.

In this case, fortunately, both Ohashi and Jane were mindful enough to see their own role in the miscommunication. They were able to return to their self-concepts, she of being well intentioned, he of being kind. Shortly after the initial exchange, Jane apologized to Ohashi-san and asked him if they might have a private meeting. He agreed that they could meet the following day.

At the meeting Jane apologized for offending him and listened as he explained animatedly why he was upset. She apologized again, summarized what she heard him say, and explained that her intention was not to be insubordinate but to understand the situation more fully. She again apologized, and explained that she was willing to work on the weekend to redesign the course to be sure that the client would be happy. She explained that for her, it was motivating to understand the reason for a change in schedule or any out-of-ordinary practice. He explained that he was happy to tell her that, but that she must not question his authority, particularly in public. Finally, she asked a few background questions, phrased positively, about next week's workshop: Would it be a new client? Were they a large client? Were there any future plans for business partnerships?

There are many factors that lead to the successful resolution of this story. The two people had a strong relationship and respected each other; they realized how easily cross-cultural miscommunication could happen and that neither person had bad intentions; they were able to explain their own cultural preferences and assumptions and to hear those of the other person; and they were amenable to finding solutions that would make the situation work for each of them. Additionally, clear yet flexible self-concepts helped in this resolution as well.

In this story it is important to recognize that while making an apology in some cultural contexts may be considered a sign of weakness or lack of confidence, the opposite was the case here.

QUESTIONS TO CONSIDER ABOUT SELF-CONCEPT

There are five key questions to consider when determining whether self-concept is a key issue in communication style interaction:

1. How do the communicators seem to view themselves?
2. How do the communicators' nationalities, ethnicities, race, gender, sexual orientation, religion, age, or other aspects of self-concept seem to affect their communication style?
3. Do the communicators seem to define themselves independently or in relationship with others? If the communicators differ in how they define themselves, how does this influence the interaction? If they define themselves similarly, how does this influence the interaction?
4. How do the communicators see the interaction? Do they discuss it as something personalized and part of them, or do they see the interaction as something separate from but influenced by them? Do any communicators see the interaction as separate from themselves and feel that they have no influence in the interaction?
5. Does the interaction appear to influence how the communicators feel

about themselves and their own competence? How so? Does the interaction appear to influence how the communicators feel about the others' competence? How so?

Values—The Performances

Any circus, of course, revolves around the thrill of the performances, whether the performance is taming the big cats, eating fire, clowning, or swinging on the trapeze. One trapeze artist may value risk taking, and her performance and style will reflect that. Another trapeze artist may value beauty, technique, and precision, and his style will reflect those values. Values are those things that are in our hearts—those things that are near and dear to us, things we consider worthy of our time and energy, the priorities in our lives. Values motivate how we attempt to achieve our goals and manifest who we are. Our values influence our behavior and focus our priorities and attention. Values are often unconscious—they include our assumptions and common sense. In short, *values* are our priorities and the principles that guide our behavior. As such, they are important determinants of the communication styles we exhibit. And the use of an appropriate communication style can help us to communicate our values in ways in which they will be understood.

Mike and Tanaka—Values

How did values affect the communication styles of Tanaka and Mike? Tanaka-san valued respect, contemplation, and truth. His speech was rather slow and thoughtful. He was generally soft-spoken, but he tended to speak with a feeling of authority. He paused frequently to think about what had just been said. He became aggravated when people were in a hurry. And Mike was usually in a hurry. Mike valued action, results, and honesty. His communication was fast, often fragmented, and usually to the point. He maintained direct eye contact, stated his opinions clearly, and expected others to do the same.

Our values have a direct influence on our communication style, but there are many different ways to express every value. What is "honest" to one person is "brutally honest" to another and may be "treading lightly" to a third person. While we may seem to value the same things, everything is in the perception.

STORIES ILLUSTRATING THE EFFECTS OF VALUES ON COMMUNICATION STYLE

Drafting a Policy

Renee, in preparing to leave the office for a trip of several weeks, sent Janika, her employee, an e-mail detailing that Janika should draft a written policy that had been under much discussion. Renee explicitly stated, "The policy should be drafted prior to our next meeting and be circulated for all to review and critique." Janika e-mailed back that she was unsure of how to draft the policy, specifically stating, "How should I put this into words at this point?" Renee replied that Janika should use her notes from previous meetings to guide her writing of the draft of the policy.

Renee was very frustrated to find out upon returning from vacation that Janika had not drafted the policy. She felt that she could not have been more clear in her directions and very much believed that Janika was revealing a weakness in her work—based on Janika's apparent hesitancy and seeming inability to draft the document. She directly confronted Janika. Janika knew Renee was upset, and explained that she had asked Renee for assistance. This further frustrated Renee, because she felt that she had given advice ("use your notes from the meetings").

Renee could have simply remained frustrated and noted how Janika did not seem to take enough initiative. Instead, Renee called a meeting, brought copies of the e-mail exchanges, and encouraged them both to look at the e-mails and ask themselves, "We had a misunderstanding; how and where did it occur?" This led to an open conversation in which Janika said that she could not conceive of how to put into writing herself what she saw as a task involving a group needing to come to consensus. She felt it was too confrontational to force the committee members to read her words and then comment on whether they agreed. This felt to her like forcing a debate, and she valued the process of the group reaching the policy decisions via consensus. Upon hearing these views, Renee realized that Janika valued developing decisions via open discussion. Renee could not envision drafting the policy without someone first committing initial ideas on paper. Once Renee understood that the underlying difference was not about work ethic but rather was about values, they worked out a plan to set some guidelines for the upcoming meeting and drafted the policy during the meeting via consensus.

The two women's communication style differences provided a window into deep-seated values differences. The different communication styles and values affected their productivity and relationship. With the new insight they achieved by examining communication style differences, Renee and Janika were able to learn more about themselves and each other and to improve their team effectiveness. This approach of talking to each other about the differences worked well because there was a history of having these kinds of conversations. In situations where a direct approach may be viewed as too confrontational, asking another coworker or confidante to provide insight could also lead to a breakthrough in understanding one's own and another's values.

Service Learning

Svetlana and Marianne were co-leading a student service–learning travel course to Guatemala. As faculty colleagues, they thought they knew each other fairly well and shared the same visions for the course: that the students gain a better understanding of Guatemalan culture, and that they experience how fulfilling it can be to actively participate in the house-building project in the village. Throughout the two-week trip, Marianne consistently attended the optional community breakfasts, assisted the students with their daily tasks, worked alongside the students in their service projects, and involved herself in the host Guatemalan community. Svetlana chose to skip breakfast most days, kept more to herself, and only occasionally participated in the same activities with the students. Both travel course leaders held shared values of exemplifying a cultural learning approach, respecting their hosts, fostering a sense of accomplishment and independence in their students, and building positive rapport with their students.

Marianne's idea of "living these values" literally meant that she "lived" like the students—getting right there in the action with them, interacting every chance she got with the hosts, and modeling what she considered to be good service behavior. In short, she viewed that the quantity of talk and time spent together was critical in that more was better. Svetlana's idea of reflecting the same values caused her to adopt a more "hands-off" approach to the students and to Marianne, to reduce her interaction with them to allow them to fully experience the culture on their own, and to not interfere with the hosts' or the students' experiences unless necessary. In short, she felt that to talk and interact as little as possible was best.

The two weeks in Guatemala were difficult for Marianne and Svetlana; neither could understand how her co-leader could act so differently and their communication be so strained given their shared values. It wasn't until their return that they both realized that there was considerable difference in *how* their values manifested themselves in the communicative and behavioral choices they made.

In this example, although Marianne and Svetlana had spent many hours planning the trip and meeting with each other and the students, they discovered in retrospect a fundamental oversight in their conversations about their vision for this trip. Both thought that their shared values implied certain things about how they would communicate and behave with the students and each other during the trip. It seemed clear to both of them that their values, in a sense, dictated some obvious things about how involved to be with the student experience and with the host community—indeed, it was their mutual values on expanding student learning and increasing intercultural understanding that brought them together to implement this trip in the first place. Value differences often play out this way, sometimes leading to confusion, because it seems so "natural" to us to live our values in certain ways that it often does not occur to us that someone might act on the same value in a very different manner. A key learning from this experience for them was realizing how helpful it would be to talk ahead of time, during the trip planning phase, about how they would like to behave with the students when in the host country.

If talking openly about your values would feel too revealing or against your norms of discretion, use the following values questions to challenge *yourself* to reflect upon your own values and how the values of the others involved could also lead to a breakthrough in communication.

As with the other factors, shared values may result in different communication styles, or different communication styles may prove to be a window into different underlying values. Either way, communication style provides insight and a tool to help us synthesize our differences.

QUESTIONS TO CONSIDER ABOUT VALUES

The following are some key questions to consider when determining whether values are an important issue in communication style interaction:

1. What core values lie beneath the surface in the communication event? (To get to the multiple layers of values, keep asking the question, "Why might she or he do that?" when assessing the choices communicators make.)
2. What values seem to motivate the communication styles used? (Be sure to consider the values that motivate both what messages are communicated and how the messages are received.)
3. How do the communication styles employed perpetuate certain cultural values? In what ways does a deeper understanding of the relationship between communication styles and their affiliated values inform the analysis of the communication situation?
4. Does the communication style used in the interaction empower or sanction certain values and disempower or disenfranchise others?

Communication Style Repertoire—Props

Finally, no circus is complete without the props—the glittering costumes, the flaming swords, and the jugglers' balls. In communication, some of us have a treasure chest full of props from which to choose; we have large communication style reper-toires. We can gauge our audience and the situations in which we find ourselves, and choose which prop or style might most effectively enhance our performance. We may use many gorgeous props, or we may simplify. We might explain the back-ground first or the main point first; we might actively interrupt and engage, or listen until our partner is finished speaking. We may hold an opinion firmly and strive to persuade others of its merits, or we may maintain an open mind and talk with others to build shared meaning. If we have a chest full of options, we are better able to choose how to respond and tailor our performance. As the saying goes, if you only have a hammer, everything looks like a nail! We define *communication style repertoire* as the number of diverse approaches one has for communicating and the ability to tap into this diversity in order to be more effective in an interaction. Lack of a sufficient communication style repertoire limits our choices and can impede our competence.

Mike and Tanaka—Communication Style Repertoire

Let's look again at Tanaka and Mike. What were their communication style repertoires? What were the props they each had available to them? Tanaka was a native speaker of Japanese and proficient in English. He'd worked for decades in a Western company in Japan, and as a result was more forth-right, persuasive, assertive, and verbally interactive than what the norms of Japanese culture had taught him. He tried different style strategies to com-municate with Mike—he tried active listening, clarifying Mike's points as he spoke; he tried more passive listening, quietly taking notes and then summarizing. Tanaka-san, with some coaching from Dianne, was able to explain his proposed strategies clearly and explicitly, verbally linking the points to reasons. None of these communication strategies ever quite reached Mike—until the blowup. Thus, Tanaka had a fairly good stock of props and used them, but the props alone were not enough to enable him to communicate effectively with Mike.

Mike's repertoire of props was more limited. He spoke only U.S. Amer-ican English. While he had traveled the world extensively, he had always worked for Western companies. Because he worked at the home office, he was usually traveling in the fortunate position of guest or boss. Thus, he had never really had to question the validity of his communication style and hadn't developed much breadth or depth with alternative styles. He was not able to fully comprehend what Tanaka-san was saying, and thus he did not attach credibility or trust to Tanaka's proposals. Tanaka's proposals just did not make sense to Mike. Mike did make some adjustments in his communication style with Tanaka-san, for example, speaking more slowly and using simpler and more standard vocabulary. But overall, he still spoke quickly and used slang and sports metaphors, to the extent that Tanaka-san did not feel Mike was credible as an international executive. Mike was not able to listen in a way that helped Tanaka to feel heard, and the two were not able to find a way to mesh their communication styles to actually coordinate their actions and develop a rapport.

What we can see from this example is that, as is so often the case, the person with a large repertoire of styles constantly tries out new ways of communicating in order to make a connection, and the person with a small communication style repertoire is not able to be of much help. Here, Tanaka-san adjusted to Mike, but effective communication still did not happen. We trust that this example will make it clear that the larger, more varied communication style repertoire that people can develop, the larger and fuller the suitcase of props they have at their disposal, and the more styles people can develop fluency in, the more effective they can be cross-culturally. But a strong communication style repertoire alone is not enough to ensure effective communication.

The prop metaphor highlights two problematic aspects. We have all seen performers whose clothes do not quite seem to fit, and performers whose clothes seem the perfect expression of what they are trying to do. We have seen jugglers who are at one with the balls they juggle, and jugglers who are still perfecting their performances. This reminds us that at many junctures as we develop our communication style repertoires, we will still not have made the new style our own. It is important to keep practicing and tweaking, so that we are able to improve our performance. Working on our act takes time until the new behaviors become internalized.

As we continue to expand our communication style repertoire, another "bump" becomes apparent: we can become confused or overwhelmed. You may have so many props at your disposal that you are not sure which style to use. Or your prop suitcase may be so full that you cannot find the item you need. Perhaps you have lived in several cultures and are comfortable with different styles of communication, but find it difficult to decide which style to use when. Expanding our communication style repertoires, continuously practicing various styles to maintain the fluency and accessibility of our skills, and internalizing the styles to make them our own, all enhance our intercultural effectiveness.

STORIES ILLUSTRATING THE EFFECT OF COMMUNICATION STYLE REPERTOIRE ON COMMUNICATION STYLE

E-mail Adaptations

Liz is quite concise and explicit in e-mails. It's her least preferred form of communication. Linda, one of her students, knew this. So the day of a scheduled meeting, Linda, who was preparing to go to France, sent an e-mail saying, "I am sorry Liz, but I have to cancel today's meeting. I know your schedule is busy but I need to talk with you before I leave about my research proposal. I have it all done and just need to meet with you and get your permission." By making an explicit request, Linda adopted the explicit style she had previously observed Liz using.

Liz felt she was in a bit of a dilemma. While she wanted to help the student, she felt she could not reschedule the appointment without sacrificing other programs. Since they had had several conversations, Liz felt it would be rude to simply suggest to Linda that they no longer work together. However, at this point Liz felt she needed to release herself from further commitments. She decided to reply by focusing on their relationship and communicating in a more roundabout manner. She responded to Linda in an e-mail saying, "I am very sorry that we are not able to meet today. I've really enjoyed talking with you and know that you are going to do very well in France. We have both been so busy lately that I don't believe that I have told you that I will be going on maternity leave part of the time that you will be gone, and I want to make sure you don't get stranded on this project. I wonder if you would like me to suggest an additional faculty member to work with you."

Linda correctly interpreted the message as a request to end working together and responded in a way that honored the relationship and demonstrated that she understood Liz's intent. "Congratulations! I leave tomorrow and appreciate all the help you have given me. I can find a faculty member while I am in France and keep working on this during your leave. I will let you know how things go!" While Linda may not have been satisfied with this outcome, she did understand Liz's earlier explicit and then roundabout messages and was able to adapt her own style to match Liz's.

This story illustrates two women who were able to use a diversity of communication styles from their repertoires according to circumstances. What made the communication successful is that they were both able to make adaptations, especially Linda who now needed to find a new adviser. You may feel upon reading this example that you make adaptations like this all the time—and that is our point! We are often savvy about reading cues from others and can shift how we communicate in many situations. Our goal in examining communication style repertoires and the effects of the other factors is to make us aware that we can make these shifts even more often than we realize.

The Storyteller

Every organization has a storyteller. In his office, Mukhtar is the resident storyteller. The challenge for storytellers is that listeners are required. Mukhtar, having been in the organization for several months, is well aware that not everyone is willing to take the time to be recipients of stories.

At meetings in this particular office, the time is watched very carefully and it is up to presenters to be brief and select information that they believe is appropriate for the group to know. Mukhtar presents his items as "information-only," knowing that others are not always interested in taking the time needed to hear his ideas fully in order to generate the discussion he would prefer. A typical presentation includes Mukhtar giving an abbreviated synopsis of the issue and announcing what he wants others to do. In this manner, he is using his skill repertoire to be succinct. However, he is also clever enough to realize that once the issue is introduced to discussion, he will be invited to give more information. He then uses this invitation as an opportunity to tell his story.

The key aspect to Mukhtar's skill is that in the end, the typically noninterested listeners are now the ones asking for the story because they want to know the background details. Clever, isn't it? There are times, however, when Mukhtar is so enthusiastic about sharing his story that he just jumps right in, without this same kind of setup that often eases his listeners into his stories. When this happens, his colleagues often become frustrated and impatient with Mukhtar's seeming lack of consideration for the time and the energy it takes for them to follow his stories.

Mukhtar is very talented at "style switching"—adapting his communication style to his audience and his purposes—although he clearly has a preferred style of communication. In being able to gauge when to approach the issue in a certain way and how to engage his colleagues, Mukhtar is better able to accomplish his goals and to influence the meeting agenda. He is not changing who he is or his persona, he is simply using different communication styles from his skill set and adapting to the situation. Most of us can think about the effective "storytellers" we know and perhaps work with, and can identify key aspects of how they use their communication style repertoires to make their stories more meaningful, engaging, and intentional.

QUESTIONS TO CONSIDER ABOUT COMMUNICATION STYLE REPERTOIRE

The following are important questions to consider when determining whether communication style repertoire is a key issue in communication style interaction:

1. What experiences have the communicators had that would enable them to switch among various communication styles?

2. If the communicators speak more than one language, how might this influence their style repertoire?
3. Have the communicators lived in another culture or had experience as a member of a nondominant culture?
4. What communication styles do the communicators have at their disposal?
5. Do the communicators have clear preferences for one style over another?
6. Have the communicators demonstrated the desire and ability to modify their communication style in order to accomplish their objectives?
7. Does the communicator's switching of styles appear appropriate to the situation and desired outcome? If so, how? And if not, why not?
8. Do the communicators seem to self-observe and adapt their behavior as they proceed with the interaction? How do they accomplish this? What do you observe as contributing to these self-adaptive abilities or lack thereof?

How Could the Factors Help?

We have seen how these five factors affected the communication styles of Mike and Tanaka. That is all well and good for analytical purposes. But, in the end, how does the analysis help us in our goal to ease their frustration, improve their productivity, and strengthen their relationship?

The mirror of context tells us that Mike and Tanaka both feel limited and frustrated by virtual communication. One way to enhance their communication, then, would be to schedule regular teleconferences at pre-appointed times, rotating who is inconvenienced time-wise. Since they seem to prefer modes of communication in which they can more easily discuss matters, they could also schedule regular face-to-face meetings and perhaps regular remote discussions using videoconferencing and remote meeting technology. These two might find it worthwhile to meet in "neutral" territory; we are sure neither would mind a rendezvous once a year in Hawaii or at another central location that is a bit foreign to both of them. Language is a more difficult issue, but we are confident that any attempt by Mike to speak a few words of Japanese, even simple words of greeting and acknowledgment, and to recognize the effort that Tanaka-san is making due to their need to use English, would go a long way toward improving the climate in which these two work. Mike and Tanaka have a long history in their work relationship and have developed patterns of interaction over time. Developing deeper awareness of the effects of their chronology and how they can use it to their advantage will further assist Mike and Tanaka in finding satisfaction in their work together. Finally, a discussion about role relationships and expectations might allow both of them to become more conscious of their own assumptions and to agree on the roles that will make their relationship most rewarding and productive.

The role of goals may mean that both Tanaka and Mike need to synthesize a bit, or, if they take the time, they may find a way to accomplish both of their goals. Once they get beyond working at cross-purposes, Tanaka and Mike may be able to bridge their communication styles to truly collaborate. The first step for both of them will be to hold their individual goals loosely enough to hear, accept, and more fully understand each other's goals. Mike, as the boss, may need to be the one to begin this discussion by providing more context to his main points and inviting questions of Tanaka to check for Tanaka's understanding and to learn his perspective. If Mike wants short-term profit, he may learn to believe that by investing in market share the business will more quickly be able to turn a profit. He can learn this by expanding his ability to listen to and comprehend what Tanaka-san is saying, accepting what he hears as temporarily credible, and withholding his judgment until he fully understands the concept. Mike may learn that a focus on short-term profit might prevent meaningful return on investment. In contrast, Tanaka might learn that his subsidiary must return profit to investors if there is to be any longevity for the business. Tanaka can learn this by asking Mike focused questions to understand the background information and the reasons for Mike's instructions. Like Mike, he needs to temporarily accept what he hears until he fully understands it. Then, together, they can take the pieces of the whole truth, the pieces of the larger picture that they each hold, and piece them together like a puzzle to form an effective business strategy. In this way, communication style differences can enable these two to see the complementary nature rather than the cross-purposes in their different goals. The music in their heads, their self-concepts, is significant to their working relationship. These two gentlemen are two incredibly different people. The window of communication style helped us discover this fact. By observing Mike's communication style, we were able to discover that his self-concept was action-oriented and productivity-driven, and that he viewed it as his responsibility to keep things moving. He did not feel that he needed to adapt—even though he was working with a Japanese counterpart. By observing Tanaka's style, we were able to see how his self-concept reflected underlying emphases on effectiveness, strong loyalty and commitment to his work, and a diligence in trying out different communication styles that were consistent with how he viewed himself and his role.

How can two such different people possibly work together effectively? *Vive la différence!* We believe in the power of diversity, do we not? Two heads are better than one. Opposites attract. If Tanaka and Mike can learn to connect their styles so that they can effectively communicate, respect one another for the strengths and insights they each contribute, and work toward dovetailing their assets rather than trying to change the other, there is no doubt that productivity will soar. And, paying attention to communication style is the impetus, the window to discovering their differences, and the method for learning to link or leverage their differences through collaboration.

Their communication performances based on values in this case is tricky. Mike's values led to a communication style that was quick, brief, and focused on immediate results. Tanaka's values caused him to communicate more slowly, with frequent pauses for thought and contemplation. How can they communicate without one giving in to the other? If they openly discuss their values and communication styles with an aim to improving their productivity, to bringing out the best that each of them has to offer, no doubt Mike will learn that providing Tanaka a bit of time to think things through will result in more action and honesty (which are near and dear to Mike *and* Tanaka). Tanaka will realize that when Mike speaks quickly, loudly, and assertively, it is not that he does not want to hear what Tanaka has to say. On the contrary, Tanaka will learn that by speaking out clearly, Mike is encouraging him to speak up as well (and Tanaka values respect and truth; he wants to be heard). Again, using the window of communication style, something that is observable, we are able to learn more about others and their values, and figure out how to use our differences to mutual benefit.

Finally, we look into the props chest of communication style repertoires and see what Tanaka and Mike can use to more effectively work together. This one seems fairly easy. Ideally, both of the gentlemen will take steps to continually expand their communication style repertoires. Tanaka can push himself to become more comfortable with asking questions to get the context he needs, so that he can better understand the reasons for Mike's recommended strategy. He can learn to state his own perspective explicitly and explain the reasons that lead him to his conclusions. Tanaka can figure out the link between new communicative behavior and the values he holds dear; in this case, he can experience how assertiveness can help him to achieve respect and truth. Mike can learn that silence and reflection can be excellent managerial tools to add to his repertoire. He may learn new, more nonverbal and contextual ways of obtaining meaning in a discussion, rather than limiting himself to finding meaning in the words that are used. Mike can gain a deeper understanding by seeing beyond the words used, and he may learn to appreciate more what is not stated directly in addition to what is more explicit.

We hope that you have enjoyed the circus metaphor in this chapter and, more important, have found value in the five factors influencing communication style: context, goals, self-concept, values, and communication style repertoire. It is important to remember that each of these five factors overlap with and affect one another; they are interactive rather than discrete and separate. In the next chapter you have an opportunity to explore the interaction of these factors, to play with the ideas and gain understanding of their importance in our everyday communication circuses.

QUESTIONS TO CONSIDER WHEN ANALYZING THE FACTORS

CONTEXT—MIRRORS	CONTEXT, continued	GOALS—SNACKS	SELF-CONCEPT—MUSIC	VALUES—PERFORMANCE	COMMUNICATION STYLE REPERTOIRE—PROPS
The circumstances in which an event occurs		*The outcome we intend to accomplish*	*How we see ourselves*	*Priorities and principles that guide our behavior*	*Amount of and ability to use diverse communicative behaviors*
1. **Physical context**—What is the place and time? Who is present? What is the medium (phone, e-mail, face-to-face)? Is the physical context more familiar or comfortable for one communicator than another? Does the physical context itself cause any assumptions to be made by the communicators ("This is my office, so I am responsible for determining the agenda.")? Does the physical context lend advantages or disadvantages to one communicator over another? Does it indicate any power dynamics to the communicators? 2. **Roles**—What do the communicators perceive their roles to be in this situation? What do they believe people in each of these roles should and should not do? What responsibilities do they equate with their roles? What are their expectations of someone in these roles? What power do they associate with these roles? What power dynamics do they see between these roles? 3. **Historical context**—What is the shared history between the cultural groups to which the communicators belong? What perceptions do they have of each other's cultural groups? Is there a larger historical context underlying the topic about which they are communicating? How does such experience affect the current interaction?	4. **Chronology**—Have the communicators discussed this topic previously? What was the outcome? What are these past experiences affecting the current interaction? 5. **Language**—What language are the communicators using? Are all of the communicators fluent in this language? Is the language used native to one or all of the communicators? How do the communicators feel about using this language? Do they speak the same dialect of the language? How does the language used affect the way in which the topic is discussed? Does the language used significantly affect power and influence in the interaction? 6. **Relationship**— How long have the communicators known one another, and in what capacity? What is each communicator's status? What perception do they have of each other's competence? Do the communicators like and respect one another? 7. **Constraints**—Are there any limits that constrain the interaction? How do the communicators perceive the time allotted for this interaction? Does the medium interfere with someone's ability to fully participate? Are there distractions (such as someone knocking on the office door during the interaction) or pressures (such as an impending deadline) affecting the interaction?	1. What are the communicators trying to accomplish for the long term? What are the communicators trying to accomplish in this conversation? At the end of the conversation, what do they hope the other will understand about why they were talking? 2. Are all communicators aware of their own goals? Are they aware of the others' goals in this particular interaction? 3. Are the communicators verbally explicit about their desired outcomes? Are the communicators nonverbally explicit about their desired outcomes? Is it difficult to find any verbal or nonverbal clues about the desired outcome? 4. How are their goals and intentions influencing the communication process? 5. How is the communicators' interaction affected when they share the same goals and intentions? 6. How is the communicators' interaction affected when they have differing or even opposite goals and intentions? 7. Is it possible in the given situation for the communicators to arrive at one or more common goals? 8. What is the sequence over time of reaching one's communication goals? For example, how might the goal of an initial conversation differ from the goal of a conversation one month from now?	1. How do the communicators seem to view themselves? 2. How do the communicators' nationalities, ethnicities, race, gender, sexual orientation, religion, age, or other aspects of self-concept seem to affect their communication style? 3. Do the communicators seem to define themselves independently or in relationship with others? If the communicators differ in how they define themselves, how does this influence the interaction? If they define themselves similarly, how does this influence the interaction? 4. How do the communicators see the interaction? Do they discuss it as something personalized and part of them, or do they see the interaction as something separate from but influenced by them? Do any communicators see the interaction as separate from themselves and feel that they have no influence in the interaction? 5. Does the interaction appear to influence how the communicators feel about themselves and their own competence? How so? Does the interaction appear to influence how the communicators feel about the others' competence? How so?	1. What core values lie beneath the surface in the communication event? (To get to the multiple layers of values, keep asking the question, "Why might she or he do that?" when assessing choices communicators make.) 2. What values seem to motivate the communication styles used? (Be sure to consider the values that motivate both the messages that are communicated and how the messages are received.) 3. How do the communication styles employed perpetuate certain cultural values? In what ways does a deeper understanding of the relationship between communication styles and their affiliated values inform the analysis of the communication situation? 4. Does the communication style used in the interaction empower or sanction certain values and disempower or disenfranchise others?	1. What experiences have the communicators had that would enable them to switch among various communication styles? 2. If the communicators speak more than one language, how might this influence their style repertoire? 3. Have the communicators lived in another culture or had experience as a member of a nondominant culture? 4. What communication styles do the communicators have at their disposal? 5. Do the communicators have clear preferences for one style over another? 6. Have the communicators demonstrated the desire and ability to modify their communication style in order to accomplish their objectives? 7. Does the communicator's switching of styles appear appropriate to the situation and desired outcome? If so, how? If not, why not? 8. Do the communicators seem to self-observe and adapt their behavior as they proceed with the interaction? How do they accomplish this? What do you observe as contributing to these self-adaptive abilities or lack thereof?

Source: Communication Highwire: Leveraging the Power of Diverse Communication Styles (Intercultural Press).
© 2005 Dianne Hofner Saphiere, Barbara Kappler Mikk, and Basma Ibrahim DeVries. All rights reserved.

CHAPTER 4

How the Five Factors Interact
Combining the Starring Acts

Get ready! Now is your chance to take what you have learned so far about communication styles and put your knowledge and experience into practice. In Chapter 3 we introduced the five factors (context, goals, self-concept, values, and communication style repertoire).

In this chapter you will be asked to combine these starring acts by learning to use the five-factor diagram, or *Star Chart*. By playing with the factors in this chapter, you will see that the intention is not to peg somebody as a "type" and label him or her with a particular communication style (e.g., "She's direct"), but to show how multiple factors interact and choices are made. Examining these choices helps to uncover what is important to us so that we can get at deeper levels of meaning about who we are and how we move through this world.

Creating a Star Chart

One way we have found to conceptualize this idea is with a Star Chart. We provide a version of this chart that you can copy for your team members or training participants at the end of this chapter. Figure 4-1 shows a Star Chart. To fill in a Star Chart, determine the tip of each point of the star according to the influence that particular factor plays in a communication scenario. If a factor has a major influence on communication style used in the interaction, use that factor's outermost dot on the Star Chart as the tip of that point. If a factor is of high importance, choose the third dot of that factor's point on the Star Chart. If a factor has some

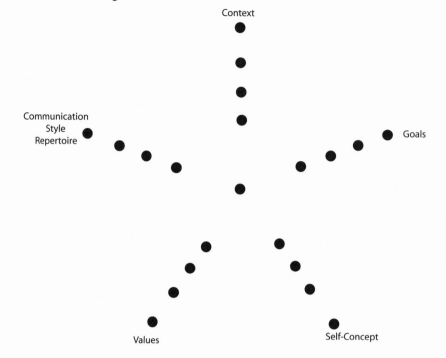

Figure 4-1 Star Chart

importance, choose the second dot and if a factor has a minor impact on the communication style in the interaction, choose the lowest dot on the corresponding point of the Star Chart. Then connect the dots and color in the center portion, so that you can easily see and discuss the star's shape.

Let's consider an example from the previous chapter and spend some time examining how the factors influence the communication styles that are used. Refer to the Star Chart in Figure 4-2 to help in your analysis. Let us take the last example from Chapter 3, involving Mukhtar, the storyteller (see pages 76–77). Now let us add a few twists to the story.

The Storyteller Reprise 1

First, let's say that Mukhtar is at a staff meeting with colleagues. There are ten minutes left in the scheduled meeting, and Mukhtar begins leading into one of his stories in an effort to introduce a new issue. Some colleagues appear visibly frustrated with Mukhtar for bringing up a new topic that could potentially prolong the meeting. Celia, one of seven team members present for the meeting, who is often quick to jump into conversation and does not hesitate to speak her mind, is feeling that people do not fully listen to Mukhtar and that they are missing his point. She sees herself as a positive and responsible member of the group, and she makes the decision to speak up and is comfortable doing so. She speaks loudly and clearly, sustains eye contact with the others, and has a calm facial expression. She says, "On several occasions, Mukhtar has wanted to share examples with us and we have asked him to be brief. Today, I think we should listen to his story so we can fully consider his ideas." She also makes a suggestion as to how the process of the meeting might be improved.

What factors influenced the communication style Celia used?

The goal of using star charts is to better see the link between the factors and what actually happens in a communication situation. We provide a sample analysis in order to demonstrate the thought process that goes into a star chart analysis.

A major factor in this example is Celia's *goal* of changing behavior in the staff meeting to become more inclusive and tolerant. Also contributing to her communication style is the fact that she *values* the equal opportunity of all staff to contribute at the meeting. She values an action orientation and explicit communication, which motivates her to speak up. Thus, values are also a primary factor in the interaction. The *context* was of high yet secondary importance—without the history of past staff meetings, Celia would not have been concerned about this issue. Her *communication style repertoire* played a lesser role in the interaction. Celia did not tap into a wide repertoire of communication style, because she delivered her message in a manner that was most comfortable to her and was thus utilizing her preferred style. It was of some importance, however, because, given the negative reaction of some other staff members to Mukhtar's approach, Celia needed to consider how to make her point in a manner that could satisfy all parties. She was able to use her communication style skills to balance the situation. Celia's communication style allowed her to accomplish her goal while adhering to her values. Finally, her *self-concept* was of some importance in that she saw herself as a positive, responsible

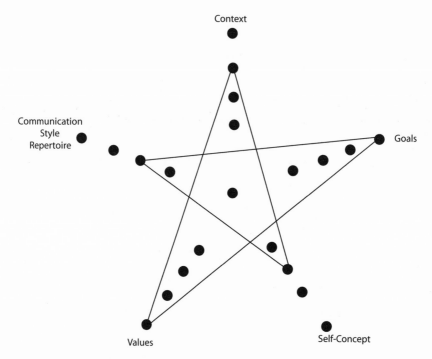

Figure 4-2 Celia's Star Chart for Storyteller Reprise 1

contributor in this group, who was able to influence the interaction. Thus, our Star Chart for Celia's communication style in this interaction might look something like Figure 4-2 (note that we are using dots in the Star Charts to make the amplitude of each of the factors clear).

It is important to realize with this exercise that there is not one definitive "correct" answer (Star Chart configuration), unless you have the advantage of talking with the actual people involved in the interaction. This exercise is designed to encourage us to think about the factors, to see how they interact with one another, to understand how they impact communication style, and to practice putting ourselves in the shoes of other people. Let us change the example again.

The Storyteller Reprise 2

In this case, Celia has an extremely busy schedule and really does not have time for the staff meeting. She wants the meeting to finish as quickly as possible so that she can get back to her work. During the meeting Mukhtar has spoken at length several times, and now, just as the meeting is about to finish, he begins another one of his stories. Celia can tell it's going to go on for a while. She also feels that Mukhtar is talking about something that is not on the agenda. She has a telephone call to make in five minutes. She fidgets a little to gain attention and demonstrate that she wants to speak. She makes direct eye contact with everyone around the table, and especially with Mukhtar, and explains that she needs to leave the meeting and that she has a phone call to make. Her brow is wrinkled as if she feels sorry. She apologizes for interrupting, explains why she has to leave, stands up, and leaves the meeting.

What were the factors affecting Celia's communication style?

In the first scenario, Celia was defending Mukhtar's storytelling. In this one, she is aggravated by it. Surely these two scenarios indicate very different communication styles and factors motivating that style, right? Again, use the Star Chart to help you interpret this interaction.

In this second example, Celia's *goals* are again the major factor, this time because Celia is on a mission to be finished with that staff meeting and nothing is going to get in her way! Based on these two examples, her communication style seems to be primarily determined by her goals. *Context* is also a major factor. Celia has been extremely busy recently, and she feels that she has a strong enough relationship with Mukhtar and the others that she can interrupt and leave the staff meeting a bit early. A main constraining factor for her is that she needs to be available for her phone call in a few minutes. This becomes part of the context in that her other responsibilities are a distraction and she cannot fully participate at the end of the meeting. These contextual elements and her *values* (task focus) lead her to feel it is acceptable to interrupt Mukhtar in the middle of his story in order to get up and leave the meeting. Her feeling sorry about this reflects a values conflict in that she also values appreciating the differences on the staff and realizes that in this scenario she is placing a value on task over a value on appreciating differences. Thus, values are also significant. The overall relevance of her self-concept is consistent with Reprise 1. Celia is again explicit and assertive in her communication style, and

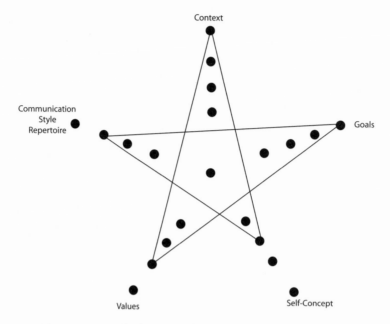

Figure 4-3 Celia's Star Chart for Storyteller Reprise 2

yet taps into her repertoire somewhat as she utilizes a broad range of nonverbal behaviors and also makes an apology before leaving, rather than calling the entire meeting to an end. Thus, while she does not access a wide *communication style repertoire,* she is accessing her repertoire more so in this example than in the first. Regarding *self-concept,* Celia seems to be defining herself in this situation as a person responsible for her work rather than as a person responsible to fellow staff members. Self-concept thus influences her communication style, but to a minor extent. The Star Chart for Celia in this scenario might look like Figure 4-3.

Let us look at one final hypothetical scenario with this Celia–Mukhtar story.

The Storyteller Reprise 3

This time, Mukhtar is just finishing one of his long stories in the staff meeting, and no one seems to understand its relevance to the topic under discussion. However, Celia senses that what Mukhtar is saying is very important. She again speaks up (another trend), thanks Mukhtar for his story, and explains that it sounds very important and she wants to be sure that she understands. Trusting her previous successes in asking Mukhtar questions in one-on-one situations, she goes ahead and asks several questions about the story and about Mukhtar's concern and main point. This interaction takes a good ten minutes of the staff meeting. At the conclusion, the team leader speaks up, thanks them both for bringing out this information, and asks the group how they want to deal with it. Through teamwork, Celia and Mukhtar have made sure something important to the topic they are discussing was not neglected.

What were the factors impacting Celia's communication style in this interaction?

Use the Star Chart in Figure 4-4 to look at an interpretation of what happened in this interaction. We would venture that *self-concept* was the key factor here— Celia sensed something important, trusted her instinct, and saw herself as someone to take responsibility for acting on her instinct. She saw herself as a cultural or style bridge person, an interpreter. Her *communication style repertoire* proved crucial. Celia had a wide enough repertoire of communication styles to realize that something in the way Mukhtar was telling this story indicated it was heartfelt, important, and relevant. She was also able to connect with Mukhtar's storytelling in a way that helped Mukhtar himself to realize what his main point was and to state it more clearly. By serving in this role as a direct encourager, Celia's approach helped Mukhtar be more effective in his communication style with the team. Thus, communication style repertoire was also a key factor influencing the interaction. *Values* played a significant role, because hearing Mukhtar's perspective was important to her. As in "The Storyteller Reprise 1" story, Celia values the opportunity for all staff members to contribute, and thus she feels the need for everyone to hear Mukhtar's point. Her values motivate her to use a communication style that will make that possible. *Context* was also of significance in two ways. First, Celia was obviously at ease and able to be fully herself in the context of the staff meeting. Second, the chronology of Mukhtar and Celia's previous interactions played a role in that they had had success

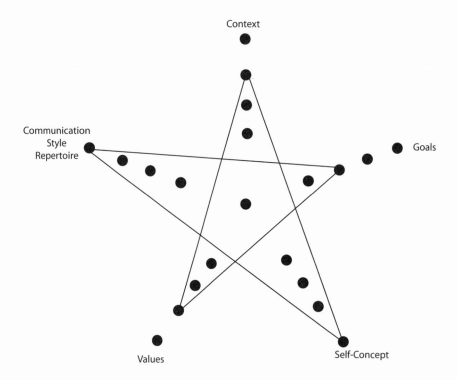

Figure 4-4 Celia's Star Chart for Storyteller Reprise 3

with these kinds of interactions before. Celia's *goals* were of more mid-level importance, as she wanted to be sure all relevant information was understood and
included in the discussion.

The Star Chart is one tool we can use to analyze the factors affecting communication style and how they interact. The emphasis should not be on what "ranking"
of the factors is right or wrong, but that the process of analysis and discussion promotes a deeper understanding of the complexity and richness of the interaction
and the communicators. By using this technique over time, we believe it might be
possible to gain significant insight into others and ourselves regarding conscious
and unconscious decision-making processes used in our daily lives.

Taking time to analyze and learn from communication by using the Star Chart
can greatly enhance your understanding and effectiveness. As you focus on the
process and analyze different communication situations using the five factors, we
encourage you to discuss your insights with your interaction partners. In doing so,

you can assist one another in gaining deeper meaning and understanding about the effects of communication styles.

． ． ．

We would like to encourage you to spend a few weeks reflecting on your communication style in different situations. To ensure you make the most of what can be gained from the material in this section, we encourage you to keep a journal about typical, comfortable, and challenging or uncomfortable interactions you have. Then, use Activity 6 to reflect on your own interactions and Activity 7 to reflect on the interaction of a team or group of which you are a member.

Take time now to make a copy of the Star Chart on page 95 to begin learning more about yourself and your interactions. After all, joining the circus is more exciting than sitting in the audience!

ACTIVITY 6: Using the Star Chart to Keep a Journal

Here are some ideas for using the Star Chart to analyze yourself:

1. Record your observations and findings in some way: Use a paper journal, send yourself e-mails, or speak your thoughts and record them.

2. Transfer the ideas from your notes or recordings onto the Star Chart by using different color pens, markers, or crayons to indicate the importance of a particular factor. Remember that if you make a star's point longer (by choosing dots farther from the star's center), you are indicating its importance as an influence on communication style; a shorter point indicates less importance on that factor. Using colors and markers will help make your charts more visually appealing, and assigning a color to each factor can help you more quickly see trends or patterns in your own communication style.

3. Keep records for several days.

4. Note the factors that seem to be dominant and those that are less prominent. It can be interesting to discover your own internal decision-making or habitual style—which factors have the strongest influence on how you communicate with those around you.

5. Consider ways to focus on the factors receiving less attention and how these may be impacting your interactions. For example, if the *communication style repertoire* points seem to be quite limited, what can you do to stretch your styles (we recommend beginning with activities in this book!)?

6. Keep in mind that it is not necessary to rank order the factors, as several factors can be weighted to have equal importance.

7. Note that in some situations one factor may really stand out as having a primary influence on your communication style within an interaction. Or multiple factors may be interacting to influence the outcome, such as having a value that you should be humble interacting with a desire to be recognized for a recent accomplishment (goal) interacting with a self-concept of wanting to be viewed as a professional.

Source: Communication Highwire: Leveraging the Power of Diverse Communication Styles (Intercultural Press).
© 2005 Dianne Hofner Saphiere, Barbara Kappler Mikk, and Basma Ibrahim DeVries. All rights reserved.

ACTIVITY 7: Team Star Chart

Objectives: Participants will be able to better understand which factors most affect their own and their team members' communication styles in specific interactions.

Assumptions/Theory Inherent in the Activity: Advantages and disadvantages of diversity on a team, the importance of creating third cultures/intercultural spaces, project management.

Time Frame: one to two hours, depending on the discussion style of the group.

Parameters: An intact work team that has been working together for enough time to know one another's styles and tendencies.

Materials, Supplies, Handouts: Star Chart(s)—if participants make a chart for each teammate, you will need multiple copies for each participant; flipchart or whiteboard and markers.

Trainer Preparation: Careful consideration of the participants' "hot spots" (Star Charts or team discussion that may stimulate emotional reactions in team members) and how you will facilitate discussion of these hot spots.

How to Facilitate:
1. Introduce the factors and explain how the factors interact.
2. Ask the partners or team members to identify a situation in which their team encountered communication style differences that had a negative impact on the group's interaction.
3. Using the Star Chart, instruct each participant to make a diagram of how he or she sees the factors impacting his or her own communication style and the communication style of every other participant. They might use a different color to mark the factors they see influencing each team member. Alternatively, they can use one Star Chart for each team member, and label the charts accordingly. Make sure to inform them that they will be asked to share these diagrams with each other.

Source: Communication Highwire: Leveraging the Power of Diverse Communication Styles (Intercultural Press).

4. Once the participants have completed the Star Charts, post them around the room and have the participants examine the charts others have made about themselves and about others.

5. Begin the debriefing by asking participants why they scored the star charts as they did and to note what differences and similarities they saw and experienced while making and viewing the charts. Continue the debriefing by asking what insights have been gained from the charts.

6. Once the differences and similarities have been noted, it might be helpful to have the participants create a team Star Chart. Pose the questions "What is the Star Chart of our ideal team communication?" and "What factors do we want influencing the communication style we use with one another?" The team may find they can agree on a preferred pattern of factors, or the team may discover that they want to be open to diversity.

Tips: Attempt to get the group to be as specific as possible about actions they will take and behaviors they will demonstrate, and when and how.

Adaptations: If you are working with teams with little or no history together, or if you are not comfortable with issues that may come up from the team's real experiences, you could prepare some fictional but plausible team communication situations and have the participants discuss their ideal responses. They could then compare their ideal responses; your role would be to summarize the similarities and differences uncovered. Possible situations include:

1. You are preparing mandatory training for your staff. How do you communicate this to your staff?

2. Your unit will merge with another unit. How do you communicate this to your staff?

3. There will be a reduction in health benefits coverage. How do you communicate this to your staff?

4. All open office space will be converted to cubicles. How do you communicate this to your staff?

STAR CHART

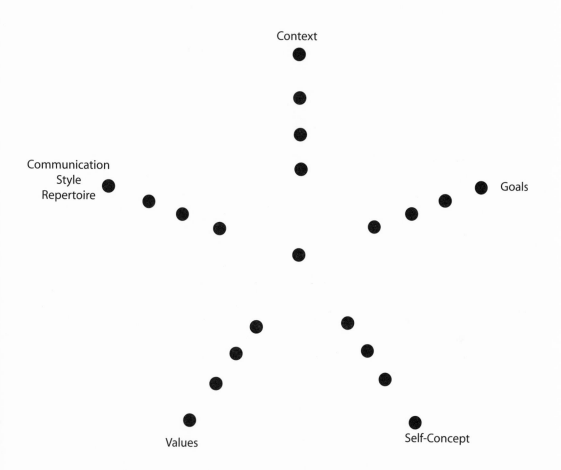

CHAPTER 5

Practicing Star Chart Analysis

Looking Deeper into the Magician's Hat

By now you have enjoyed quite a bit of what the circus has to offer—the house of mirrors, some spectacular performances, delicious snacks, thrilling music—and you have seen a variety of circus props. One of the most enticing props is perhaps one of the most mysterious: the magician's hat. What is inside? How does the magician create the magic? Understanding what is "inside" the hat and how the hat works, and practicing to gain fluency in the use of the hat, are crucial to a successful performance. In this chapter we dig deeper into the magic hat of communication style and examine what can easily be missed when we are not mindful of the power of communication styles.

Chapters 3 and 4 presented the five key factors involved in analyzing communication styles and discussed how those factors interact with one another. In this chapter we describe in depth two actual experiences of communication style differences. We tell two stories and give you a chance to reflect on and interpret these stories using the factors from Chapter 3 and the Star Chart analysis format from Chapter 4. Using these factors will help you become more skilled at interpreting communication style.

Drum roll, please, as we set the stage with our first story . . . .

You Are Such a Star!

The setting: A meeting room following a panel presentation at an annual conference for training professionals. The only people remaining in the room are the five panelists who did a presentation on the ABC Program they designed and implemented, and they are debriefing their presentation.

The players:
- Thorunn, one of the two main coordinators of the ABC Program; she had been responsible for creating the visual aids for the presentation, organizing parts of the overall presentation, and delivering the theoretical aspect of the presentation.
- Basma, a panelist who had worked with the ABC Program for several years, but was much less involved this particular year and was added to the panel to give her perspective.
- Barbara, the other main coordinator of the ABC Program; she assisted with coordinating the panel presentation.
- Kentaro, an international graduate student who had worked with the ABC Program for two years and was presenting at a national conference for the first time.
- Holly, a graduate student who had also worked with the ABC Program for two years; she had taken much initiative in organizing the panel and preparing outlined descriptions of each person's role on the panel.

The background: This team of five had worked together on the ABC Program for at least two years. Thorunn and Barbara work in the same office and coordinate the ABC Program each year. They hire orientation leaders each year to help implement the ABC Program. This "train the trainer" structure helps orientation leaders gain training and/or culture-specific experience. The purpose of the presentation at this national conference with other training professionals in the field was to share their experiences of designing, planning, and implementing the

ABC Program and to explain their unique program training structure. All five had met the day before to go over their presentation plan and were equipped with the detailed outline that Holly had put together indicating who would speak when and for how long.

During the actual presentation, Barbara and Thorunn, who were scheduled to talk for the first twenty minutes about the background and structure of the ABC Program, spoke for much longer. This resulted in part from audience questions and requests for clarification or more information on certain aspects of the program. Additionally, during this presentation segment, Thorunn was explaining one of the hand-outs, which was a bit complex and required more elaboration than the scheduled time allowed. Because Holly and Kentaro had worked hard to help prepare the conference presentation and because they were looking forward to the opportunity to present at this national confer-ence, Basma kept her comments very brief and left the remaining time for Holly and Kentaro to cover their planned remarks.

The interaction: After all the audience members had left the room, the five panelists began informally discussing their presentation. They all shared the perception that it went well, and they were energized by the audience's enthusiasm for their work. Individual panelists then asked the others for feedback on their particular parts of the presentation, and in general they affirmed everyone's abilities to explain such a com-plex program in a one-hour session. At one point during the debrief-ing, the following conversation took place.

Holly noted how well she thought Thorunn had explained the complex handout. She had found it very understandable. Basma enthusiastically agreed with Holly's comment and, with a raised voice and proud smile, added, "Thorunn, you are such a star!" Barbara and Kentaro chimed in, noting that they thought this part of the presenta-tion went especially well. Thorunn sat silently.

Source: Communication Highwire: Leveraging the Power of Diverse Communication Styles (Intercultural Press).

As the other four continued the debriefing in an animated manner, Thorunn sat there rather contemplatively. After about ten minutes, Thorunn asked, "Can I ask you something, Basma? What did you mean by your comment that I am 'such a star'?"

Basma explained that she was impressed how Thorunn had managed to explain complex material to the audience, and that she was proud to be affiliated with the ABC Program and on this panel with such great colleagues. Basma, sensing Thorunn's confusion about her comment, emphasized that she meant that Thorunn was a "star" in the most positive way.

Thorunn commented, "Ever since you called me a 'star,' I have been sitting here thinking about it and all I could think of was that you thought I stole the show. I keep thinking that you are upset that I took so much of the presentation time for my part and that I was trying to be in the center of the stage, you know, drawing attention to myself like a 'star' and away from other people."

Basma was dumbfounded by Thorunn's interpretation. She exclaimed, "Oh my goodness, Thorunn! I did not mean it that way at all! When I call someone a 'star'—and it is rare that I do—I mean it as only positive; that you were really impressive and that you shined in a very good way. I meant it as a compliment."

Thorunn replied, "I did not interpret your comment positively like that. Even though I know you and know that you would not say something mean like that, I was just really confused by that comment."

Basma replied, "I am so glad that you brought this up because I never would have known that you took my comment that way. I really appreciate that you shared your perceptions and reactions about this, Thorunn. I am sorry that my comment upset you—that was not my intention at all. This was really eye-opening for me to discover how such a seemingly simple comment could be interpreted so oppositely of how it was intended."

ACTIVITY *8:* You Are Such a Star!

Please fill out the Interaction Debriefing Worksheet to help you analyze which factors most affected Basma's and Thorunn's communication styles.

After completing the worksheet for this activity, read on to find out how others have reacted and to gain deeper insights about how the Star Chart can help explain the miscommunication. Don't peek!

THE INTERACTION DEBRIEFING WORKSHEET

A. Initial Reactions:

Based on the information provided in the story, take a moment and consider these two questions.

1. What did you observe in this scenario?

2. What, if anything, went wrong in this scenario? Why?

B. Considering the Five Factors . . .

From Person A's Perspective	From Person B's Perspective
Context:	*Context:*
Goals:	*Goals:*
Self-concept:	*Self-concept:*
Values:	*Values:*
Communication style repertoire:	*Communication style repertoire:*

Source: Communication Highwire: Leveraging the Power of Diverse Communication Styles (Intercultural Press).
© 2005 Dianne Hofner Saphiere, Barbara Kappler Mikk, and Basma Ibrahim DeVries. All rights reserved.

C. Using these small stars, indicate which factors seem to be most important for Person A and for Person B.

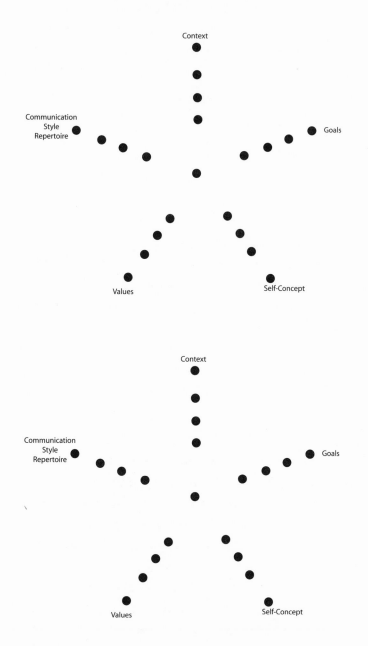

Source: Communication Highwire: Leveraging the Power of Diverse Communication Styles (Intercultural Press).
© 2005 Dianne Hofner Saphiere, Barbara Kappler Mikk, and Basma Ibrahim DeVries. All rights reserved.

Reactions We Have Collected

When others hear this story, they are most often surprised at how Thorunn interpreted Basma's intended compliment. Communication style expectations affect how compliments are interpreted; it relates to the contextual factors in which compliments are appropriate and the manner in which we prefer to give and receive them. People note that the interaction took place in a warm, collegial setting, that it was clear the presentation had been a success, and that the panelists were affirming one another's parts in that success. It seemed logical then that Basma's comment to Thorunn would be interpreted in a positive manner and that this was clearly implied. Basma was, in fact, praising Thorunn above the others for her particular role in the presentation's success.

A few people have noted that, thinking about it further, they could see how Thorunn could have interpreted Basma's "star" statement as a subtle commentary on how the time ended up being divided between the various presenters, and that audience members might have perceived Thorunn as the "star of the show" or as the main player simply because of "talk time" differences. After all, Thorunn had the stage longer than any of the other presenters.

In processing this example more deeply with the communication styles factors, we discover that there is more going on than this surface analysis suggests. What else led to Thorunn's interpretation of Basma's comment?

Authors' Insights—What Else Can Be Pulled from the Hat?

In discussing this incident with Thorunn later, Basma learned that Thorunn had in fact been a little nervous before the presentation and was concerned that everything go smoothly. After all, Thorunn was presenting at this particular national conference in front of her professional colleagues for the first time, and although she is very fluent in English, it is her second language. Thus, for Thorunn, language and physical context were important elements of the context factor. Basma, on the other hand, had been heavily involved in this national organization in the past and had presented during two other sessions at this particular conference. She saw her participation on this panel presentation as a kind gesture by her colleagues to include her, but had focused her preparation for the conference on her other presentations in which she had a much larger role. Basma had faith in her colleagues, was impressed by their planning and organization for the presentation, and was confident that this panel would go smoothly. It did not occur to her that her fellow panelists would feel differently. Basma had not considered how Thorunn might be approaching this presentation. For this interaction, their roles and history were not the key elements of context: the two do not interact a great deal outside of this program, and while Basma has more experience presenting, Thorunn was technically Basma's boss during this program. As Barbara is Thorunn's boss, Thorunn felt some pressure in presenting with her boss, but the relationship between these two—as well as the one between Basma and Thorunn—has always been extremely friendly, and professional power dynamics did not play a major role in this interaction. The discussion in this paragraph is all part of the *context* of the five-factor star diagram, helping to frame the level of importance of this presentation for each communicator.

These differences in how Thorunn and Basma approached the presentation and the effects on their debriefing afterward relate to both the goals and self-concept factors. Basma's *goal* on this panel was simply to have a good time with colleagues she enjoyed working with and to share her perceptions of the ABC Program in a rather informal manner. Her *goal* in the debriefing was to casually discuss how the presentation went and to express her praise for her colleagues' efforts. Thorunn's *goal* was to effectively "perform" during her first public appearance at this national organization's conference and to present, in an organized and professional way, her experiences with a program in which she had invested a great deal of time and energy over the past several years. Thorunn's *goal*, therefore, during the debriefing was more serious than Basma's in that she wanted to gain important feedback about her performance so she could improve her presentation style.

Because Basma saw her role on this panel as a minor one, she was relaxed and confident about her part in it, and knew she had already gained some positive visibility within this organization. It makes sense that Thorunn was feeling less confident as a relative newcomer to the organization and as someone who had a much larger stake in this particular presentation. These aspects of their *self-concepts* affected their perceptions of the debriefing interaction, even though they may not have realized it. As a result, Basma casually made her "star" comment to Thorunn not realizing that it might require more contextualization or explanation.

When Basma and Thorunn spoke after the conference, Thorunn explained how her *values* on equality, utilitarianism, and receiving flattery and feedback—values she considers to be Icelandic—greatly impacted this interaction:

- **Equality.** I spent a lot of time developing the presentation and was sure Kentaro and Holly had as well. So when I realized that I had taken more time than agreed on, I was mortified that I had somehow communicated to my colleagues and the audience that I mattered more and that my part of the presentation was more important. I was extremely embarrassed and uncomfortable with this fact. Then when Basma said, "You are such a star!" this confirmed my fear that I had not only taken too much time, but I had also stolen the attention away from my colleagues who had worked just as hard as I had and valued this opportunity as much as I did—to do a wasteful and superficial thing—sparkle like a star. To me this presentation was a package; my part was only one part, and the others' presentations mattered just as much as mine. So here I had "stolen the show," made people think of me first, and had taken over and disrespected my colleagues' need to be part of this presentation as well. This had broken my value of equality and in a way I was ashamed that this had happened.

- **Utilitarianism.** I was expecting a critical evaluation of this presentation—something I could use in the future when I prepare for other presentations. I wanted to hear about the content of the presentation: Did I manage to pull out for the audience the substance of the ABC Program? Did I do so clearly and with good use of language? I wanted to hear what kind of effect I had on the audience and what I could change about it. And I wanted to hear how the overall package was perceived—how the presentation as a whole worked: my bit, Barbara's, Holly's, Kentaro's, and Basma's. As a group we were talking about these things when Basma said "You are such a star!" and it just hit me in the wrong way. I also think it is important to this situation that I was stressed and really wanted to do a good job. I believe that when we are stressed we revert even more to our cultural programming—so in the moment I was operating as an extreme Icelander—and interpreting things from a very narrow window.

- **Feedback and flattery.** The difference between feedback and flattery probably comes out of the utilitarian value that Icelanders operate from. In Iceland compliments are very rarely, if ever, given. So in a way, compliments are taken as flattery and only fools are moved by flattery—their heads expand, and they forget the most important thing is still the content. So to me, "You are such a star" meant that I outshined the others with sparkle and pretense, not with content and substance.

Basma *values* flexibility and being in the moment, and as a result she was very comfortable with the presentation and in how the presentation varied from the initial plan. In addition, Basma values harmony and attentiveness to others, so Thorunn's initial reaction of silence and then her expression of confusion deeply affected Basma. Rather than walk away from the situation and assume Thorunn was overreacting, Basma was sincerely interested in what had gone wrong.

In examining *communication style repertoire*, it was significant that Thorunn decided to speak up and address her concern during the debriefing session. Thorunn initially participated in the debriefing discussion, then became contemplative after hearing Basma's "such a star" comment. After thinking about Basma's comment for a few minutes, Thorunn asked for clarification, which led to a group discussion about the misinterpretation. Thorunn's ability to shift her communication style during the debriefing in response to her emotional reactions was pivotal in moving the group to greater understanding. Basma maintained her typical, engaged discussion style until she realized that Thorunn had interpreted her "such a star" comment quite differently from what she had intended. Upon discovering this difference, Basma adopted a more inquisitive style and began asking questions for clarification and providing explanations concerning her own experience of the interaction. Basma's ability to step back and shift her style to a focus on information gathering and on attentive responding shows how their communication style repertoires could work in complementary ways. Although the direction the discussion was going felt risky, both Thorunn and Basma had a wide enough range of communication style experiences that they could appropriately engage and facilitate a learning moment for their whole ABC Program group.

Ultimately, although it caused some initial discomfort and confusion, it was a good thing for the whole group that Thorunn spoke up during this debriefing session and shared her reactions. Everyone walked away from the discussion with a much better understanding of how differently seemingly simple comments can be interpreted and with increased sensitivity to cultural and individual differences in the use of compliments. Can you imagine Basma and Thorunn's future working relationship if nothing had been said or processed about this difference in interpretation?

Thorunn explains just how important addressing the confusion was for her:

> Since I brought this discomfort up right away—in the few moments after it happened—I got this confusion and discomfort out of my system. I was able to hear Basma and how she meant it, and I could move on and take the compliment as it was meant. So to me this element of checking to see if your interpretation is what the person you are talking with intended it to be became a big "aha" moment, and I moved out of my discomfort to enjoy the rest of the conference. I know that if I had not asked for clarification, I would have been uncomfortable for the rest of the conference and perhaps even longer.

Explanation of Star Charts for Activity 8

Figure 5-1 shows the Star Charts with our assessments for Activity 8. For Thorunn, *all the factors played a significant role* in this interaction, with 4 of the 5 factors (context, values, self-concept, and communication style repertoire) being ranked at the farthest point of the star and goals nearly at the end of the point. The "You are such a star" comment primarily challenged her self-concept and values, especially because she was so stressed about the context (including her relationship with the others on the panel) and goals (representing the ABC Program in the best way possible). Without an incredibly rich and accessible communication style repertoire, Thorunn would not have been so able to initiate and fully discuss the comment, and the learning would not have occurred.

For Basma, her goals, values, perception of context, and self-concept were important, yet they did not greatly impact her communication style in this interaction. Thus, the most influential factor for Basma was her ability to shift her behavior, reflecting strong skills in utilizing her communication style repertoire.

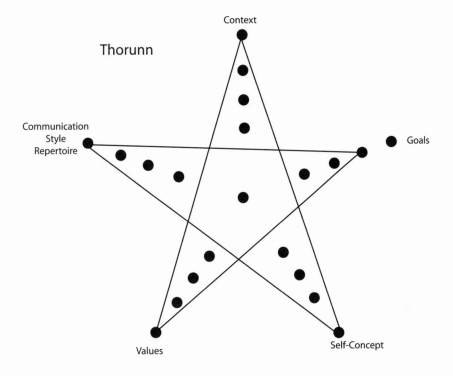

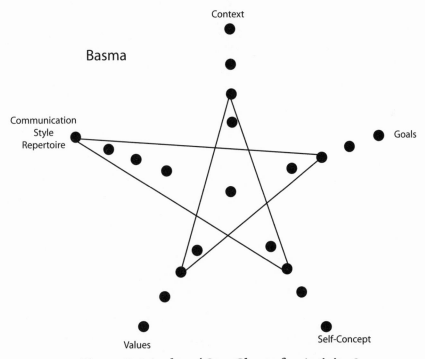

Figure 5-1 Authors' Star Charts for Activity 8

Why It Is Important to Look Deeper Inside the Hat!

Exploring this situation in greater depth and examining what really is sometimes hidden with such subtlety shows how a deeper analysis can be so insightful. It would be easy to stop at the surface interpretation and to conclude, for example, that Thorunn is just overly sensitive and that she should just learn to hear and accept compliments—and too often we stop there. If we do so and do not delve deeper, we fail to recognize that there might be other, equally valid, interpretations of even seemingly simple statements. We lose an opportunity to learn and to practice intercultural communication effectiveness. It is like the magician's hat—there is so much more than a rabbit and scarf!

Summarizing the "You Are Such a Star!" Scenario

In this interaction, one simple comment led to a half-hour group discussion and a later discussion between just Thorunn and Basma. These discussions resulted in increased understanding among the whole group, and between Thorunn and Basma especially, about how easily our intended meanings can be misinterpreted. How does this new learning affect how you think about giving and receiving compliments and about the complexity of group dynamics when public presentations are involved?

This first story offered you the opportunity to practice analyzing the factors affecting communication style. Let us further develop your facility with the factors by analyzing a second story.

The Engineers

The setting: Corporate offices in The Hague, Netherlands, of a major multinational corporation. Both Dutch and English are used in the offices. Employees come from all over the world.

The players:

- Shehu, a Nigerian expatriate engineer who has been in The Hague for three years
- Ronald, a Dutch engineer who works with Shehu on a project
- Erik, a Dutch engineer who is not affiliated with this project, but whom Shehu has called in for his technical expertise
- Gert and Martijn, Dutch business managers affiliated with the project

The background: Shehu has been charged with generating possible solutions to an engineering and business issue in Nigeria. He has invited the four other players described to a meeting to obtain their perspectives on the issue and to make a decision.

The interaction: Shehu is the first to enter the meeting room. He sits and readies his notes and papers. The others join one by one, and Shehu stands to greet each one, thanking them for coming and shaking their hands. They talk casually in English until all five members are present. When they are all there, Shehu says, "Thank you all very much for coming. As you know, this is a crucial issue requiring a quick decision and response. I'm hoping that today we can all share our insights into the issue in order to more fully understand it, and leave here today with a decision about how to proceed."

At some point not long after Shehu's comments, the language of the discussion shifts from being in English to Dutch. The four Dutch men interact actively and animatedly. Shehu does not say much, if anything. After about an hour, Gert says, in English, "Well, that settles it then. It sounds

Source: Communication Highwire: Leveraging the Power of Diverse Communication Styles (Intercultural Press).

like we're all in agreement." The men stand up, ready to leave the room. At this point Shehu says, "What is it you've agreed to?"

The Dutchmen look at him incredulously. "You mean you haven't understood us? Don't you speak Dutch?"

"No, I don't," replies Shehu.

"Well, why didn't you say something? We could have spoken English! Why in the world didn't you say something?"

Shehu looks at them but does not really respond. He has a slight smile and a rather proud look on his face that puzzles the others.

"Why didn't you tell us?" the men ask again.

"I expected you to ask me," says Shehu. "I called you all here, this project is my responsibility, and I started the meeting in English. I can't believe you call yourselves international managers!"

Martijn then speaks up. "You've been here several years already. We expected you'd have learned Dutch by now. If you didn't understand us, you should have said something."

ACTIVITY *9:* The Engineers

Please fill out the Interaction Debriefing Worksheet included with Activity 8 (page 101) to help you analyze which factors most affected Shehu's and the Dutchmen's communication styles. As with the previous example, we have inserted our assessments in Star Charts for both later in this chapter, along with a few notes. We trust you again not to peek!

Source: Communication Highwire: Leveraging the Power of Diverse Communication Styles (Intercultural Press).

After completing the worksheet for this "The Engineers" scenario, read on to find out how others have reacted and to gain deeper insights about how the Star Chart can help explain the miscommunication.

Reactions We Have Collected

When we have introduced this story in our workshops, participants (usually Westerners) tend to quickly and loudly accuse Shehu of misbehavior. They agree with the Dutchmen: Shehu should have spoken up! How unprofessional he was. He wasted his own and everyone else's time. Why would he sit there quietly for an hour without understanding? It does not make sense. Either the guy is an egotist, overly proud, or he lacks the assertiveness and confidence needed to succeed in a multinational business. They tend to see Shehu as meek, weak, arrogant, or unreasonable. Sometimes we have participants, most frequently non-Westerners, who empathize with Shehu. They understand that it is difficult to speak in such situations; they know that they would hesitate as well. And a few, of course, feel that Shehu was right and the Dutchmen should have been more attentive.

Usually, however, participants will defend the Dutchmen. They are in their homeland, so it is natural for them to speak their native language with each other. Yes, it would have been nice if they had checked their assumptions and asked Shehu if he spoke Dutch, but they were a team of people in a meeting room, working on a task together. They all shared a common goal: to solve the problem in the best and quickest way possible. To do that required collaboration and communication. Shehu should have spoken up so that they could all have made the best use of their time and resources by speaking a common language.

In an ideal world, perhaps that is what should happen. But jumping so quickly to a solution, a judgment, circumvents the process of learning more about these players and this interaction, and prevents us from generating alternative and perhaps more creative or sustainable solutions.

Authors' Insights—What Else Can Be Pulled from the Hat?

Again, we see that communication styles and patterns are a valuable window into deeper culture. Let us consider the *values* factor first. By looking at what happened and thinking about it, we can see that the Dutchmen valued individual responsibility and forthrightness. To them it was common sense that Shehu should have spoken up about not understanding Dutch, directly and honestly. They believed in egalitarianism, and saw Shehu and themselves as on equal footing for this project. All were free—in fact responsible—to contribute their ideas and opinions openly and actively. They had a pragmatic approach to the business at hand—communicating in Dutch allowed them to share more information more accurately and faster than had they been communicating in English, assuming, of course, that all present at the meeting spoke Dutch. They also valued consensus, and they thought that they had heard everyone's perspectives and that an obvious conclusion had presented itself. The trouble was that although they valued consensus, they had not noticed that Shehu had not spoken. Probably because speaking up was such a matter-of-fact manner of interacting to them, it did not even enter their radar screen that his lack of participation might indicate a lack of understanding. That is the trouble with communication styles, common sense, and cultural filters: while there is power in diversity, these can all blind us to seeing what is actually occurring. Instead, we see what we expect to see.

In contrast to the egalitarianism of the Dutch, Shehu valued status and roles on the project. Shehu was the project leader, and he expected to be treated as such, with a bit of deference or at least what he would see as some minimal polite consideration for his status as leader. He probably approached this meeting with a more relaxed sense of time than did the Dutch and with more of an emphasis on human relations. His agenda probably included a few moments at least to get to know one another before jumping into a discussion of the specific task. This value on human relations and more relaxed time also contributed to the Dutchmen's unknowingly taking power and influence away from Shehu.

In terms of *context*, Shehu no doubt expected the others to thank him for arranging the meeting and to wait for him to take the lead and structure the meeting. He did not expect what he perceived to be a free-for-all discussion. Given Nigeria's colonial history, the history of slavery and racism, and its economic situation, Shehu very likely saw the Dutchmen's behavior as colonialist or racist. The context that the Dutchmen were working in was that of a typical business meeting in the Netherlands:

they looked at one another as equal contributors, they expected to discuss the subject at hand in a forthright and independent manner and to generate a consensual decision, and they assumed that discussion could occur in the Dutch language.

As for *self-concept*, Shehu felt pride in his professional training and education. When the Dutchmen switched from speaking English to Dutch, he may have seen this as a move on their part to take the meeting away from him—as a personal insult to his status as a skilled engineer, a Nigerian on a Nigerian project, and as a project leader. Like Shehu, the Dutchmen felt pride in their professional training and education as well. Their self-concepts led them to expect that everyone in the meeting would be able and willing to speak up for himself.

The *goals* in this case were fairly similar. Both Shehu and the Dutchmen wanted to share information and make decisions that would be best for the business. They were not working at cross-purposes. *Communication style repertoire* was an important issue in this story, however. Neither side demonstrated willingness or ability to be flexible with communication style; they wanted the "other" to communicate in the ways each preferred (the Dutch wanted Shehu to speak up, and Shehu wanted the Dutch to be more considerate).

The result of the meeting was that Shehu was unable to exercise his leadership, hear the expert input of his colleagues, or participate in the group process that he had organized; the Dutchmen did not benefit from Shehu's insights and guidance; the parties were not able to make a joint decision; and both parties left with severe doubts about the competencies of the other. Communication style mismanagement, in this case as in others, resulted in incredible lost opportunity.

Explanation of Star Charts for Activity 9

As you can see in Figure 5-2, our Star Charts for both Shehu and the Dutchmen are very similar. The one difference is regarding context, which is of major significance for Shehu given his history with colonialism. Neither Shehu nor the Dutchmen exhibited much breadth of communication style repertoire, and their limited repertoires had a major impact on their interaction. Their values very much influenced how they communicated, followed by context and self-concept. They had shared goals, and though they were both very goal-oriented, this factor had only minor impact on the styles used in the interaction.

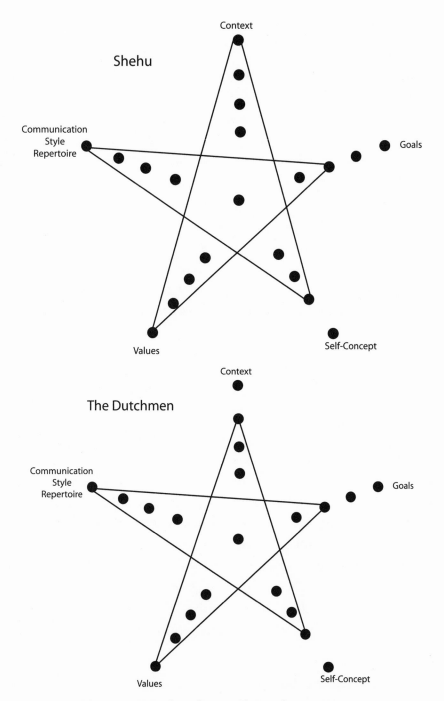

Figure 5-2 Authors' Star Charts for Activity 9

Why It Is Important to Look Deeper Inside the Hat!

We trust that you see a major difference between the initial interpretation and this second analysis. Very often it is human nature to take sides or to judge right and wrong based on very limited data. While this can feel good—and in a group we often get caught up in heated discussions at this level—it does not provide us information or insight into the situation in question. It often completely disregards history, the emotions of the people involved, and their communicative abilities. And it does not lead to a true strengthening of our cross-cultural collaboration.

Summarizing "The Engineers" Scenario

Given what you have learned in this analysis, think about what this group might learn from this interaction. What steps might they take to prevent such future miscommunications? Is the only answer that Shehu should speak up, or do you see a greater breadth and depth of alternative approaches—approaches that might benefit all the players?

Take Some Time to Think

The five core factors provide a framework for understanding communication style choices and for revealing deeper aspects of individual and cultural influences. As authors of this book, we have had years to ponder our own communication style encounters, examining them from our multiple perspectives and seeking additional information from the parties involved to understand their perspectives. This has been an enormously helpful process, not simply in solidifying the content for this book, but also in developing our own skills in understanding and ultimately leveraging communication style differences. Activities 8 and 9 helped you to use the core factors to analyze communication. In Activity 10 we encourage you to take a few moments and ponder your own encounters. You may use both the list of questions that follows it and the Interaction Debriefing Worksheet.

ACTIVITY *10:* A Bit of Self-Reflection

Consider a situation in which you personally experienced a communication style difference. Think through how you came to realize the difference was a communication style difference. Use the Interaction Debriefing Worksheet to analyze your situation and then consider the following questions:

1. Did you know it was a communication style difference intuitively?
2. Did you guess it was a communication style difference based on specific behaviors involved, and if so, what were those behaviors?
3. Did you speak with others about the situation? If so, what insights or affirmation did you receive from others?
4. What questions do you still have about the situation? How can the factors help you gain more insight? What resources do you have to pursue support in getting your questions answered?
5. Did you or others eventually adapt your behaviors? If so, was this comfortable for those adapting? If you did not adapt your behaviors, how did this affect the situation and your future relationships/interactions with those involved?

Source: Communication Highwire: Leveraging the Power of Diverse Communication Styles (Intercultural Press).

Communication Style Behaviors

In this section we introduce two additional important tools: (1) a way to be less judgmental and more objective in your analysis and discussion of communication styles (the Descriptor Checklist in Chapter 6), and (2) a new method for interpreting communication style disconnects (the Four-Step method in Chapter 7). We are confident that with increased awareness and a little practice, the descriptors and Four-Step method presented in this section will enhance your ability to leverage the benefits of diverse communication styles.

Finding the Differences That Make a Difference

Behind the Scenes of the Big Top

Being invited backstage to an event affords us the unique opportunity to experience all that is really necessary to make the event take place. When we slip behind the backstage tent flap and enter the circus backyard, we see an even more chaotic scene than that in the Big Top itself. Dozens of roustabouts (circus stage-hands) shuffle and reshuffle scenes and props at an amazing speed, acrobats stretch wherever there is an open space, managers yell out orders, and performers whisper with each other excitedly. Everywhere you look there is movement and energy. As you relax and let your senses focus, you realize there is a cadence to what initially appeared as chaos.

Our goal in this chapter is to help you more closely observe what is behind the scenes of communication style—the actual behaviors that comprise communication style in our daily interactions. The *Communication Style Descriptor Checklist* will help you develop a vocabulary that can be acceptable (not feel judgmental) to the communicators in an interaction—neutral terminology that can help us meaningfully discuss differences in communication style and link these to differences in deeper culture. Because there is rarely a term or word that is truly "neutral" or that means identical things to different people, we may never strictly accomplish the goal of developing a neutral terminology; nevertheless, we can progress in that direction.

As we have previously discussed, defining someone's style as direct or indirect can be generally helpful, yet can give us a false sense of confidence that we fully understand what is happening in the interaction. These labels inhibit us from deeper understanding because they do not help us identify the specific *behaviors* that lead to misinterpretation, misunderstanding, or mistakes in effectively communicating with others. In this chapter we present categories of descriptors and specific descriptions of the behaviors that comprise communication style. As depicted in Chapters 3, 4, and 5, understanding the impact the factors have on an interaction is critical for building a broader communication style repertoire and for building relationships with others. We posit in this chapter that knowing the actual behaviors that make a difference in our communication styles is one of the keys to leveraging differences.

The following example demonstrates the power of knowing the behavioral difference that is making a difference.

Antonella

Barbara was facilitating an intercultural communication workshop for U.S. American staff to help them understand common challenges international students encounter in the U.S.A. During the break, her coworker, Antonella, approached her and requested that Barbara "tell the participants that they really need to understand the value of time and how time is so important to Americans." Barbara said, "Tell me more about what you want me to say." Antonella repeated her request and added that U.S. Americans often don't know how much emphasis they place on time. Barbara jokingly stated, "Well, the break is almost over and I don't have much time to hear your ideas." However, the look on Antonella's face told Barbara that the issue was very important. Barbara asked if there were certain behaviors that seemed most bothersome to her, as a non-American, and then Barbara suggested some of the behaviors from the descriptor list. When Barbara mentioned differences in how conversations are ended, Antonella said, "That's it! That's it! People focus so much on time that they don't even take time to say good-bye!" Barbara then asked directly, "Does it bother you that when I am talking to you I often walk away when I think we are done, without any leave-taking behaviors?" "Yes!" Antonella replied.

This breakthrough in discovering a specific difference that was making a difference enabled them to consider how they might then adapt their behaviors to better meet the needs of the other. This small difference was part of a larger communication style pattern (around the value of time). While it may not be possible—or even wise—for either Barbara or Antonella to adapt her entire communication style pattern, this small behavior is one area both can modify: Antonella can bring up again that she would like Barbara to end the conversation differently, joke about the difference, and accept the difference. Barbara also has more options, such as to change her behavior, explain her behavior to Antonella, or use humor.

Barbara's and Antonella's abilities to reflect upon the specific behaviors involved in their interaction and to discuss the behaviors bothering Antonella about the perception of time in the U.S.A. led them to broaden their communication style repertoires and bridge a difference that was making a difference. They were able to *leverage* their communication style differences to enhance their productivity and pleasure in working together.

Leveraging is the ability to use specific information to accomplish a particular goal. In terms of communication styles, leveraging is the ability to understand the differences that make a difference and to use this information to enhance your effectiveness for responding to that difference. Leverage actions could include using the specific knowledge to find humor in the situation, educating others about your own actions, informing others about how their actions are perceived, requesting that others adapt their behavior, adapting your own behavior, or developing a third way of interacting.

Overview of the Descriptors

The descriptors highlight common areas of challenge we have witnessed in our work in the field of intercultural communication training and education. Our intention is to balance the enormous amount of detail that can be portrayed with our desire to present a list that is useful for everyday interactions. Please note that these descriptors are intended to work in tandem with the factors that were introduced in Chapter 3: context, goals, self-concept, values, and communication style repertoire. In combination with the factors, the descriptors are a first attempt to create a vocabulary and mental model for looking at communication style that is an alternative to typologies. The factors help you understand the bigger picture of how someone is communicating, whereas the descriptors reflect specific behaviors that can be of enormous importance in an interaction. Thus, combining the descriptors with the factors provides you an opportunity for understanding the breadth and depth of communication style.

In the following pages we define descriptors, set out a framework for them, and explain what each of the descriptors means. Chapters 7 and 8 discuss how you can use the descriptors to accomplish the following:

- Analyze your own communication.
- Analyze, on your own, specific incidents you have experienced.
- Review an interaction with someone with whom you've had a misunderstanding, assess your perceptions, and plan future actions.
- Pinpoint differences that are making a difference in your daily interactions.
- Analyze team situations to discover hidden differences, areas in which team members may be feeling excluded, and ways they might contribute more fully.
- Prepare yourself for interacting with a group with which you have little history, but for which you have a contact who can use this list to let you know about possible specific behavioral differences you may encounter.

Descriptors Defined

A *descriptor* is a concrete, specific, nonjudgmental word or phrase that can be used to explain the elements of communication style. It is sometimes very difficult to find such words or phrases because many words are inherently open to interpretation, many descriptions are relative, and we often jump to evaluations of the other person's communication style without first trying to note what it is we observed. Individual descriptors are not communication style; rather, they are *elements of an overall communication style*.

These descriptors include the tangible vocal and nonverbal elements that make up communication style as well as points about the flow of conversation, communicative expectations, and the varied uses of compliments, apologies, critiques, and the like. As such, these descriptors represent the key elements one should look for when examining communication style differences and similarities, and can serve as a checklist for what we can see and sense in the actual interaction.

Using the Descriptor Checklist

Just as we mentioned that entering the backstage of the Big Top could be overwhelming, this Descriptor Checklist can be a bit daunting. When reviewing it for the first time, think of a recent conversation in which you believe that a misunderstanding occurred. As you read through the descriptors, consider which specific behaviors and elements may have been a source of the misunderstanding. Our hope is that with practice you will be able to focus on the areas that are most pertinent to your interactions and to help others do the same. At any given time, you may thus end up using maybe 20 percent of the descriptors—or even just one continuum or list.

A descriptor can be analyzed as a continuum, reflecting that a particular behavior may fall along a range of possible behaviors or as a forced choice among specific alternatives. These lists of choices include a space for "other," allowing you to fill in particular behaviors you observed but that are not incorporated into the other choices.

We have grouped the descriptors into three categories, each growing a bit in complexity. The first category is *Discernible Descriptors*—the behaviors that are most readily observable. The second category, *Discoverable Descriptors,* contains descriptors that require some interpretation, questioning, and dialogue with the communicators involved in an interaction. The third category, *Functional Descriptors,* requires you to consider the intended meaning of various phrases or speech acts within the overall interaction.

There are, of course, limitations to this Descriptor Checklist. Our memories are faulty, regardless of how vivid the interactions may feel! Despite our best intentions, we cannot strip ourselves of the interpretations and evaluations we make of others. Our language itself is loaded with bias about what might be considered the most appropriate way to interact. And finally, it is important to acknowledge that the enormous amount of work involved to be solely descriptive would perhaps outweigh the benefit gained in analyzing any one interaction. Despite these cautions and challenges, we believe that using the descriptors moves us forward in our quest for an approach to communication style that includes a more culturally neutral vocabulary, invites dialogue, and honors the richness and depth of human interaction.

The Communication Style Descriptor Checklist is on pages 129–130. Once you have reviewed this checklist, we encourage you to turn to the following explanations of the sixteen elements. For any given descriptor heading, there may be several continua or behavioral lists. Please note that in a few rare places on the Checklist we have simplified the wording from the text in this chapter in order for the Checklist to be a visual that fits onto a copiable handout.

You can use the explanations as a reference, checking for clarification, but not necessarily read these particular pages from the first word to the last. Our belief is that after you understand the checklist, learn about the different descriptors, and practice using them, you will be able to use the Descriptor Checklist to analyze your conversations and train others to do the same.

We include examples to help clarify the meaning of the descriptors. Note that these examples are limited to one behavior in order to simplify the presentation of the material. We do not mean to imply that one behavior signifies a communication style. Rather, we are trying to focus your attention on how easily one behavior may be interpreted so differently and can have a major impact on the message that is perceived. When considering the complexity of communication styles (in that they can include several descriptors and factors simultaneously), the potential for misunderstanding is great.

Category 1: The Discernible Descriptors

The Discernable Descriptors are the most observable of the descriptors; they represent fairly distinct and recognizable behaviors in an interaction. We present five types of descriptors within this category, and we are sure that you and your team members, participants, or students will find communication style behaviors that are

Communication Style Descriptor Checklist

DISCERNIBLE

1. Beginning & Ending a Conversation
1a. Beginning

NV/hesitant ←——————→ Verbal/assertive

1b. Ending

Sudden ←——|——→ Elaborate
Clear closure

2. Presentation of Ideas
2a. Sequencing of function
___ task, ___ relationship, ___ process, ___ other

2b. Sequencing of information
___ general then specific, ___ specific then general, ___ integrated, ___ specific w/o general, ___ general w/o specific, ___ other

2c. Structure of expression
___ outline, ___ storytelling, ___ stream of consciousness, ___ zig zag, ___ other

2d. Degree of preparation

Spontaneous ←——————→ Planned

2e. Links between ideas

Explicit transitions ←——————→ Implied connections

2f. Tools of influence
___ data, ___ experience, ___ proverb/parable, ___ intuition, ___ relationship, ___ emotion, ___ other, ___ none

3. Turn Taking
3a. Timing
___ any time, ___ speaker breath,
___ listener audible breath,
___ speaker finishes, ___ listener moves,
___ at key point,
___ listener assumes speaker finishes,
___ other

3b. Style
___ bowling, ___ basketball, ___ rowing, ___ tennis, ___ other, ___ none

4. Vocal Characteristics
4a. Tone

Formal ←——————→ Casual

4b. Rate

Rapid ←——————→ Slow

4c. Volume

Loud ←——————→ Soft

4d. Vocal sounds
Describe:

5. Nonverbal Characteristics
5a. Eye contact

Hold gaze ←——————→ Look away

5b. Facial expression
Describe:

5c. Gestures
Describe:

5d. Personal distance

Inside personal space ←——|——→ Outside personal space
At personal space

5e. Touch
Describe (kind, frequency, duration):

5f. Silence
Describe (frequency, duration, intended and perceived meaning):

5g. Posture and body language
Describe:

5h. Dress and accessories
Describe:

DISCOVERABLE

6. Expectations of Communication Process
6a. Location of meaning

Explicit ←——————→ Implied

6b. How meaning is created

Individual ←——————→ Mutual

6c. Responsibility for understanding

Listener ←——————→ Speaker

7. Nature of Topics Discussed
7a. Kinds of topics
___ personal, ___ familial, ___ professional, ___ political, ___ spiritual, ___ community, ___ other

7b. Level of self-disclosure

Open ←——————→ Closed

8. Treatment of Emotion
8a. Openness to discuss feelings

Open ←——|——→ Reticent
Subtle

8b. Method of expression

Expresses openly ←——————→ Doesn't express

9. Permeability of New Ideas

Immediate openness ←——————→ Extreme caution

10. Progress of Discussion

Expand/ build ←——————→ Conract/find weaknesses

Note what you have learned about the different ways in which communication style behaviors are used and why:

Source: Communication Highwire: Leveraging the Power of Diverse Communication Styles (Intercultural Press).

Communication Style Descriptor Checklist

FUNCTIONAL

11. Apologies

11a. Frequency

Constant — Intermittent — Never

11b. Quantity

Many words — Few words

11c. Timing
___ beginning, ___ middle, ___ end,
___ throughout, ___ in response to facts,
___ in response to emotions, ___ immediate,
___ after consideration, ___ never

11d. Purpose
___ admission of guilt/regret, ___ empathy,
___ social bonding, ___ courtesy, ___ other

11e. Content

General — Specific

11f. Style
Describe:

12. Requests

12a. Frequency

Constant — Intermittent — Never

12b. Quantity

Many words — Few words

12c. Timing
___ beginning, ___ middle, ___ end,
___ throughout, ___ in response to facts,
___ in response to emotions, ___ immediate,
___ after consideration, ___ never

12d. Purpose
___ accomplish a task, ___ pay a compliment,
___ include someone, ___ assert authority,
___ encourage, ___ other

12e. Content

General — Specific

12f. Style
Describe:

13. Praise

13a. Frequency

Constant — Intermittent — Never

13b. Quantity

Many words — Few words

13c. Timing
___ beginning, ___ middle, ___ end,
___ throughout, ___ in response to facts,
___ in response to emotions, ___ immediate,
___ after consideration, ___ never

13d. Purpose
___ relationship building, ___ request,
___ motivation, ___ confidence building,
___ criticism, ___ other

13e. Content

General — Specific

13f. Style
Describe:

14. Disagreement

14a. Frequency

Constant — Intermittent — Never

14b. Quantity

Many words — Few words

14c. Timing
___ beginning, ___ middle, ___ end,
___ throughout, ___ in response to facts,
___ in response to emotions, ___ immediate,
___ after consideration, ___ never

14d. Purpose
___ improve process, ___ vent emotion,
___ learn, ___ courtesy,
___ disrupt forward movement, ___ other

14e. Content

General — Specific

14f. Style
Describe:

15. Feedback

15a. Frequency

Constant — Intermittent — Never

15b. Quantity

Many words — Few words

15c. Timing
___ beginning, ___ middle, ___ end,
___ throughout, ___ in response to facts,
___ in response to emotions, ___ immediate,
___ after consideration, ___ never

15d. Purpose
___ correct, ___ encourage, ___ guide,
___ insult, ___ gain competitive edge,
___ assert power, ___ facilitate group-building,
___ other

15e. Content
___ specific , ___ general , ___ positive,
___ negative, ___ humorous, ___ other

15f. Style
Describe:

16. Humor and Joking

16a. Frequency

Constant — Intermittent — Never

16b. Quantity

Many words — Few words

16c. Timing
___ beginning, ___ middle, ___ end,
___ throughout, ___ in response to facts,
___ in response to emotions, ___ immediate,
___ after consideration, ___ never

16d. Purpose
___ lighten the mood/relieve tension,
___ empathize, ___ establish rapport,
___ criticize, ___ encourage, ___ other

16e. Content
Describe the topic (kind of info, topic, what it is poking fun at):

16f. Style
Describe:

Note what you have learned about different ways in which speech acts (apologies, requests, praise, disagreement, feedback, humor and joking) are used and why:

Source: Communication Highwire: Leveraging the Power of Diverse Communication Styles (Intercultural Press).

not specifically contained in our list. When you do find an addition necessary, please let us know so that we can continue to build and refine this model.

The Discernable Descriptors include

1. beginning and ending a conversation,
2. the presentation of ideas,
3. turn taking,
4. vocal characteristics, and
5. nonverbal characteristics.

1. Beginning and Ending a Conversation

As simple as it may seem, there are different ways to begin and end conversations— and these seemingly minor differences can have a big impact on the interaction.

1a. Beginning a conversation:

←——————————————————————————————→

Nonverbal/Hesitant   Verbal/Assertive

Other notes:

A difference that has made a big difference in beginning a conversation is whether the speaker simply begins talking as a way to start the conversation or whether one of the communicators requests permission to begin speaking. The communicator can do this verbally by asking a question such as "May I interrupt you?" or nonverbally by standing nearby, touching, knocking, coughing, or using other behaviors. While some argue that this is merely a rule of etiquette, it is our experience that the rules of etiquette vary across experiences and contexts.

> *Joel works in a fast-paced environment and relies on his office as a place to privately regroup and get work done as quickly as possible. When looking at the Descriptor Checklist, he realized that he was judging his coworker Meriem as rude simply because she didn't follow his unstated rule that she should knock before entering his office and speaking—even when his door was wide open.*

1b. Ending a conversation:

Sudden   Clear sense of closure   Elaborate leave-taking

Other notes:

This descriptor encourages you to focus on how the conversation actually ends. *Sudden* refers to a conversation ending mid-sentence ("Okay, we'll have to see. . . .") or with participants simply turning away from each other. To others watching this interaction, it may not be apparent that the conversation is over. However, participants may fully understand that the conversation is over as they realize they have exhausted the topic or have used up the time allotted for the conversation. The middle point of the continuum is marked with a *clear sense of closure* in which there may be a verbal comment (such as an expression that another conversation is needed, an appreciation of the conversation, or a "good-bye") or a simple handshake or kiss. This contrasts with an *elaborate leave-taking* in which the participants note that the conversation is nearing an end and they make several references both verbally (an appreciation for the conversation, discussion of upcoming events, greetings to family members, friends, or colleagues) and nonverbally (head nods, handshakes, hugs, kisses).

> *Tammy grew up in a small town in Wisconsin where saying good-bye at a family gathering could literally take up to an hour. When her Northern European husband first attended these gatherings, he was in the car at the first "good-bye." The two have now negotiated a system in which Tammy tells her husband before the event what the actual "drive-away" time will be, and she begins the elaborate leave-taking one hour before.*

2. The Presentation of Ideas

The set of descriptors for presenting ideas refers to how a speaker conveys a message. It includes elements such as what is discussed first in a conversation—the task, the relationship, or the process; how explicit transitions are; and what tools of influence are used.

2a. Sequencing of functions: (rank order as first, second, etc.)

____ Task

____ Relationship

____ Process

____ Other (specify):

This descriptor lets you sequence the order of which functions happen first, second, and so on in an interaction. *Task* refers to words about work regarding a specific project, event, or duty. *Relationship* refers to acknowledgment of the individuals in the interaction in terms of personal health, state of mind, and general well-being, as well as their co-workers, families, or group memberships. Statements about *process* include questions about how the conversation should proceed ("Should we meet to discuss this?" "Should we invite others to join in this conversation?").

> *Lakeisha was offended when her boss said that her request to share comments about her first week on the job and to invite others to lunch would be addressed at the end of the staff meeting because they would be discussing important items first. For Lakeisha, the order of importance was to let everyone know how much she appreciated their support during her first week—relationship comments. She was thrown off by her boss' request to wait until the end of the meeting, and when it was her turn, she skipped her thanks and focused solely on the lunch invitation, feeling the meeting now had a tone of "all work" and that it would be awkward to make relationship-focused comments.*

2b. Sequencing of information:

____ General context, then specific points

____ Specific points, then general context

____ Integration of general context and specific points

____ Specific points without general context

____ General context without specific points

____ Other (specify):

People can become very impatient when information is delivered in a sequence they do not expect or desire. This descriptor asks you to reflect on the order of the information discussed and to choose whether the general context is established as the first part of the conversation, followed by the specific points, or whether the flow is the reverse. Another option is offered in which the general context and specific points are intermingled throughout the conversation. Also, our experience suggests that in an attempt toward efficient and speedy e-mail communication, there are times when the specific point is made without any reference to the general context. Additionally, the general idea might be presented without any specific details at all.

> *Dianne had requested that all three authors extend a stay at a conference for two days so the three of us would have more time to devote to working on this book, and she offered an explanation of how we might use our time (the first option in this descriptor—the general request for time together is followed by very specific details). Basma sent a lengthy e-mail noting how she liked Dianne's idea of spending time together face-to-face because she was getting tired of working "virtually" via e-mail and phone. She also listed specific pros and cons of extending their stays after the conference (third point—integrating general and specific points). Barbara replied with a quick e-mail stating that she was only able to extend for one day (fourth point; she only gives specific information without any context). Dianne was frustrated with Barbara's response—not because she was saying no, but because there was no explanation (context) given, and thus it appeared the time together was not a priority for Barbara. A phone call was needed to clear up how Barbara's sequencing impacted the message that was heard.*

2c. Structure of expression:

____ Outline form

____ Storytelling

____ Stream of consciousness

____ Zigzag pattern

____ Other (specify):

This descriptor asks you to consider the overall structure of the conversation. Would you describe it as following an outline form in which the points appear ordered by stating a claim and then providing main points and supporting points? Does the conversation appear to be presented more as a story in which the characters and events are described in detail and the goal may include emotionally engaging the listeners? Does the conversation appear to be a stream of consciousness in which the words seem to be spoken as the speaker thinks of them? Or does the conversation follow a zigzag pattern, integrating multiple threads that advance the development of the main claim. Are there periodic advancements toward the main claim supplemented by seemingly tangential remarks throughout the development toward the main claim?

While this descriptor could be related to sequencing of information (for example, it may be common for a *general context then specific points* sequence to be linked with an *outline form* structure), it is our experience that any number of combinations is possible.

> *Bob, a public speaking instructor, had never taught international students before. After Aga gave his speech, Bob literally did not know how to critique the main ideas because he wasn't sure what Aga's main ideas were. Aga's speech seemed disorganized to Bob. When he reviewed the peer feedback, Bob was surprised to find that this apparent lack of order hadn't bothered many students; they were drawn into Aga's storytelling and thus seemed to be able to digest the main idea of what Aga had presented. Bob realized that his expectation of an outline form with a clearly stated purpose for each section of the speech actually became an impediment to his ability to listen to and enjoy Aga's speech.*

2d. Degree of preparation:

Spontaneous   Planned

Other notes:

This descriptor asks you to consider how much preparation was done prior to the actual conversation. *Spontaneous* refers to no preparation before the conversation and *planned* refers to a considerable amount of preparation. If you are the speaker, you will know how much planning took place. If you are describing someone else, you will need to guess based on specific clues in the actual conversation (whether the speaker refers to how much planning was done, whether notes are used, or if reference is made to wanting more time to consider the issues being raised).

> *Suzette and Dean co-led a group of students on a month-long exchange to Australia. Dean was a planner and had detailed notes for every group meeting. Suzette*

was always surprised that Dean seemed "tied to his notes," while Dean was frustrated that Suzette didn't seem to think before she spoke. The difference was clear to the students, and they liked the difference because they found it a good balance. They openly suggested to the leaders that they appreciate each other's strengths more!

2e. Links between ideas:

$$\longleftarrow \hspace{8cm} \longrightarrow$$

Explicit verbal transitions   Implied connections

Other notes:

This descriptor asks you to consider how connections are made between ideas. Some people verbalize the links they see between their ideas as they speak; in this manner they are very explicit in their verbal transitions. Others leave the task of connecting the ideas to the listeners and thus leave the connections implied. Speakers who supply explicit transitions may seem patronizing to people who expect implicit connections, while those who imply the connections may fail to communicate their messages or appear to be disorganized and ill prepared.

Two groups of managers from different facilities agreed that cost-saving measures were a shared and important concern. One group proposed using a cheaper material in their manufacturing process to save money. The second group listened politely, never disagreed, and then proposed a more expensive material for the manufacturing process. The first group became agitated and said, "But you just said you were committed to cost savings!" The second group replied, "We are; that's why we want this higher-quality material." The connection was not clear enough for the first group, as the second group never voiced the explicit connection. Their more explicitly connected meaning would be, "If we are to save money, we need to use the more expensive material, as it will reduce defects and thus save much more money over the longer term."

2f. Tools of influence:

____ Data
____ Experience
____ Proverb/Parable
____ Intuition

_____ Relationship

_____ Emotion

_____ Other (specify):

_____ None

This descriptor addresses the question, "What tools does the communicator use to influence or persuade you?" *Data* refers to the use of information that is tangible and measurable, such as numbers, survey responses, and other items that can be presented as observable reality. *Experience* refers to the use of one's own or the other person's actual encounters with the topic at hand, while *proverb* refers to the use of cultural stories, parables, or life teachings, suggesting that the experiences of others and collective wisdom can be persuasive tools. *Intuition* refers to the use of one's own or the other person's perception of the situation that draws upon a feeling or an energy and may not have an identifiable, tangible explanation. *Relationship* refers to the use of the nature of one's relationship due to status, intimacy, or sense of obligation (for example, a parent using the statement, "Because I am your mother" as a means to influence her child's behavior). *Emotion* refers to the use of feelings to influence—fear or excitement, for example, can effectively stir action.

> *A young advertising executive, newly graduated from a well-respected business school, was recommending a new package design for a major brand of toothpaste. He worked with a senior package designer, Alain, who had thirty years of success behind him. When asked by his supervisors why he had chosen a particular color, the young executive replied, "Because Alain told me this would work." To which his supervisors replied, "But why did he choose that? Did he conduct some marketing studies?" The young executive was trusting Alain's experience. His supervisors, on the other hand, were hoping for a more data-driven explanation.*

3. Turn Taking

Turn taking refers to the way in which the speaker becomes the listener and the listener becomes the speaker, a critical aspect of our daily interactions. How do we take turns in conversations? While this may seem like a great deal of attention to a rather small aspect of our communication, the importance cannot be overstated! There are daily examples of a communicator not feeling respected because of interruptions or disappointed due to lack of interaction. Within these descriptors about turn taking lie the essentials for how and whether people feel validated in their conversations. One of the few human commonalities is that when people want to speak, they want to be heard. The challenge is that our patterns for how we listen, speak, and interrupt each other vary, and thus while we may think we are doing a great job affirming someone, our behaviors may be perceived as invalidating.

3a. Timing of turn taking:

____   At any time while the other is speaking

____   When the speaker pauses to take a breath

____   When the listener takes an audible breath

____   After the speaker finishes speaking and invites others to speak

____   Any time the listener fidgets or moves

____   At each key point

____   After the listener assumes that the speaker is finished

____   Other (specify):

During a technology transfer project, a senior engineer was instructing others in a key process. "Please interrupt me at any time, so that we make sure we are on the same page and understand one another. I'm happy to stop and clarify," he said. "I'll explain five key steps." After each step the engineer paused, hoping for some questions or perhaps a summary from his listeners—something to show that effective communication was occurring. Finally, after he concluded the explanation of the fifth step, one of the trainees raised his hand. "I have a question about the first step," he began. The instructor was shocked. Did this mean that no one had understood anything, and that he'd have to repeat his whole explanation? The instructor expected a back-and-forth turn-taking style, with the listeners providing feedback or questions after each key point. The listeners appeared more comfortable waiting until they had heard the entire explanation, refraining from interrupting the instructor's flow.

3b. Turn-taking style:

____   Bowling

____   Basketball

____   Rowing

_____ Tennis

_____ Other (specify):

While the previous descriptor asks you to focus solely on when and how turns are taken, this descriptor asks you to think about the actual style of that turn taking. We use sports analogies, but music, dance, and many other alternatives can be used to describe turn-taking style. *Bowling* refers to one person speaking at a time, with a clear end (the ball either goes in the gutter or knocks down pins) and a clear transition to the next speaker (the ball is returned underground and appears back where the other players are standing, waiting to take turns). *Basketball* refers to a quick interchange among players, in which the rules are that you can only hold the ball for a short time. *Rowing* is an activity in which there is a leader to guide the group, and individuals stay in the same rhythm, changing cadence only as directed by the leader. *Tennis* refers to a fairly quick exchange between the speaker and listener, but in a more predictable way than with basketball. In basketball, you have the option of holding the ball for a while, while in tennis your goal is to get rid of the ball as quickly as possible. In basketball, there is a concentration on both those who hold the ball and on those who are possible receivers of the ball—a group and an individual focus. Others have also used sports analogies to refer to communication style, including Susan Steinbach in the videotape *Understanding Conversational Styles around the Globe: Bowling, Basketball and Rugby* (1996), and Nancy Masterson Sakamoto in the Japanese and English language comparison article *Conversational Ballgames* (1992).

4. Vocal Characteristics

This set of descriptors refers to critical paralinguistic cues that we give when speaking. We call these types of nonverbal behaviors *vocal characteristics* to be consistent with how these terms are used in the communication literature. From this perspective, the term *verbal* refers to putting thoughts and feelings into words, in effect, using language to communicate, whether it is oral or written, and *vocal* includes everything communicators do with their voice aside from the words themselves. The vocal characteristics involved in this category are tone, rate of speaking, volume, and sounds. Note that while we have attempted to be descriptive here, you will need to make some interpretations as some of these aspects of communication style can only be deciphered in relation to patterns with which you are familiar. For example, we cannot, on paper, convey to you a standard for "loud"—what you are used to determines if something seems loud to you.

4a. Tone:

Formal   Casual

Other notes:

Tone refers to a variety of factors, including the overall cadence of sound in the voice, the rise and fall of the pitch in a voice, and the speaker's intention with changes in the cadence and pitch. For this descriptor, you are asked to give your interpretation of whether the overall tone is one of formality (implying a following of etiquette rules, possibly less familiarity between participants, a sense of clear roles) or more of a casual tone (implying less adherence to conversational rules, relaxed speech in which fillers—e.g., "umm," "know what I mean?"—are used more frequently, an overall sense of friendliness). Tone can greatly affect a communicator's experience of a conversation as positive or negative, and it is very easily misinterpreted.

> *International students attending university in the U.S.A. for the first time are often caught off guard by the casual tone of some of their instructors, misinterpreting the speech as one used between friends. They are surprised when a professor walks into the classroom and says, "How's it going?" These informal phrases and tone, combined with the professor sitting on the desk and drinking coffee during class, challenge the expectation of some of the international students that the professor behave in a formal manner and sometimes confuse them about how to proceed in their own relationship with their professor.*

4b. Rate:

Rapid   Slow

Other notes:

Rate refers to the pace of the communicator's words and is relative to what you consider an appropriate speaking pace. This descriptor asks you to focus on whether the pace is rapid, with very little pausing within or between sentences, or if the pace is slow and more deliberate, with pauses within and between sentences. Rate of speech/communication can mean many different things to different people in different situations. A fast speed could indicate, for example, enthusiasm, irritability, or embarrassment. A slow speed could indicate precision, boredom, confidence, or even a lack of intelligence.

> *A contractor from India was perceived as "sneaky" by his U.S. supplier, in part because he spoke fast (nearly twice the rate of the U.S. businessperson), and the U.S. businessman had difficulty keeping up with what he was saying.*

4c. Volume:

Loud   Soft

Other notes:

For this descriptor, you are asked to interpret the overall volume of the conversation. Does it appear loud, soft, or somewhere in between? This can be an important descriptor, as a loud volume could be misunderstood to represent an "aggressive style" though, in fact, the speaker may simply be using a louder voice than one that you are used to hearing. A softer vocal level may suggest submissiveness to some, respect and elegance to others, or disinterest to still others. Assessing the communicator's volume can help you see if this descriptor affects your interpretation of an interaction.

> *A college instructor let in nearly twenty-five more students than the twenty the registrar had initially indicated for the class. On the first day, students were worried that the teacher would have to be constantly yelling to get everyone's attention.*

Instead, the instructor's soft whisper was nearly magical, leaving students hanging on every word. What perhaps helped this style be so effective was that it was unusual for this academic environment.

4d. Vocal sounds:

Describe what you hear:

This descriptor refers to sounds that are not words but that carry meaning, such as "umm," "ah," and "shh." Vocal sounds are frequently used in communication, and their intended meaning can be easily misinterpreted. Examples include clicking one's tongue, whistling, audibly inhaling, sighing, or laughing.

> *A commercial shipper stopped one evening in a restaurant overseas and was "hissed" at by the proprietor. He said that it made him feel like a vampire or werewolf, while apparently the proprietor was just trying to indicate, since the two didn't share a language, that they were no longer serving.*

5. Nonverbal Characteristics

Nonverbal communication is commonly categorized into several types: oculesics (eye contact), facial expressions, kinesics (body movement such as gestures, posture, and gait), proxemics (use of space), haptics (types and uses of touch), physical appearance, chronemics (use of time), and artifacts (use of objects). Vocalics (vocal sounds), which is also a nonverbal characteristic, was described in the previous section. These characteristics are frequent factors in cross-cultural miscommunication. One woman recalled the first time a senior Chinese colleague grabbed her thigh in a bar. He was merely emphasizing his point, but her sexual antenna went up quickly!

For our purposes here, we venture into the challenging yet important area of developing descriptive, communicative, and neutral terminology for that which eludes description. We encourage you to join us as we attempt to use words for areas we have found to be of critical significance in nonverbal communication.

5a. Eye contact:

$\longleftarrow$ ———————————————————————————— $\longrightarrow$

| Continuously | Frequently | Frequently | Looks away/ |
| holds gaze | holds gaze | looks away | down |

Other notes:

Eye contact includes an assessment of the directness and duration of a communicator's gaze. What is considered acceptable use of eye contact with others varies across cultures, especially when considering communicator roles, gender and power differences, and context. Within any culture, there may be a range of acceptable options for this dimension. Additionally, there are individual differences in how eye contact is used in various settings. *Continuously holds gaze* means that nearly all of the conversation is spent with the speaker attempting to look directly into the listener's eyes. *Frequently holds gaze* refers to conversations when most of the time is spent with the speaker attempting to look directly into the listener's eyes. With *frequently looks away*, the speaker spends more time not looking at the listener than looking at the listener, while *looks away/down* refers to no direct eye contact between the speaker and listener.

> *Dianne remembers her first interest in intercultural communication arose in sixth grade when a Caucasian teacher shouted at her best friend, a Diné, or Navajo, "Look at me when I'm scolding you!" She knew her friend was unable to look directly yet respectfully at the teacher, since she'd been taught that averting eye contact was the respectful way to behave with an authority figure.*

5b. Facial expression:

Describe what you see:

We communicate many emotions and thoughts through our facial expressions. For this element, note anything that stands out to you about the communicators' facial expressions. Consider if movement of the eyes, eyebrows, lips, or cheeks make an impact on you. Can you interpret specific emotions based on these movements or other facial expressions? If so, what about the facial expressions led you to such an interpretation?

> *Silma, an international scholar from Costa Rica, asked her U.S. instructor, "What does it mean when you wink at me?" This question surprised the instructor, because she only then realized how confusing her behavior must have been—she was using winks to indicate camaraderie and support. Silma explained that she thought winks suggested romantic interest. The instructor was glad Silma asked, but was sorry to have put her in the position of having to do so.*

5c. Gestures:

Describe what you see:

For this descriptor, you are asked to assess the communicators' frequency of gesture use, their apparent strength, and what gestures are used. Obviously across cultures many gestures have different meanings and are open to misinterpretation. Gestures most often include finger, hand, and arm movements. Common categories of gestures in the communication literature include *emblems*, which translate directly into words and are specific signifiers of meaning (e.g., the "A-OK" and the "peace" signs in U.S. American culture); *illustrators*, which paint a visual picture for the listener and accent or reinforce the verbal message (for example, a child holding up her hands and saying "I am a big girl!"); and *adaptors*, which often show the communicators' emotional state and help people feel at ease in interactions (for example, smoothing hair or lightly tapping on a desk).

> *We recall an experience on a manufacturing line, when one worker put one arm vertically and the other horizontally to form a "T." To him this meant "time out" or "shut down the line" (it's a hand signal used in American football). The other worker wasn't familiar with the gesture, didn't shut down the equipment, and it resulted in grave injury.*

5d. Personal distance:

<-->

Inside personal space   At personal space   Outside personal space

Other notes:

Proxemics is an important nonverbal category, because most people have fairly specific expectations about how close they like others to be to them, often calling this their "personal space." We may or may not be conscious of these expectations. Many of us have been to cocktail parties or other gatherings at which some people seem to back farther and farther into the wall in a futile attempt to secure more personal space. For this descriptor, consider your own comfort zone and ask, "Is the communicator inside my personal space 'bubble'?" "Is the communicator close but within an expected range of my comfort zone?" "Does the communicator seem distant from me in physical proximity?"

> *When Basma leads student travel courses in Egypt, students often comment on the differences they experience in the use of personal space. In one particular instance, a student standing in a line to enter King Tut's tomb felt like the Egyptians in line behind her were crowding her and trying to push forward. Basma overheard her saying to a fellow student, "Why are they so pushy? We are all going to get in! I don't understand why the Egyptians don't properly follow the concept of a line!"*

5e. Touch:

Describe what you see (include kind of touch, frequency, and duration):

An extension of the consideration of proxemics, this descriptor involves haptics—the actual physical touch between people. Touch may be used for many purposes. Jones and Yarbrough (1985) have identified five different meanings of touch, including *affect* (the expression of positive or negative emotions, such as support, protection, or dislike; for example, a teacher placing a hand on a child's shoulder to encourage him as he struggles through a difficult math problem); *playfulness* (as a means of showing that behaviors should not be taken too seriously, such as tapping someone's arm in jest); *control* (in order to dominate or manipulate a situation, such as the kind of touch someone might use to signal that another person should move over); *ritual* (typical touch behaviors associated with greetings or leave-taking, such as handshakes, bows, or hugs); and *task-related* (the kind of touch that occurs when the doctor examines you or when you get your hair cut). When analyzing an interaction, it can be worthwhile to look at the kind of touch as well as its frequency and duration.

5f. Silence:

Describe what you experience (include frequency, duration, and intended and perceived meaning):

Silence can help communicators feel in sync and at ease with one another—or it can cause extreme discomfort. It is definitely culturally relative, and it varies by personal preference. Silence may be used to indicate many things, including agreement, disagreement, inability to hear, preference for a slower rate of speech, or discomfort with a topic. In our experience it is a frequent and powerful factor in miscommunication.

> *Jackie, a fourth-grade teacher from the East Coast of the U.S.A., was teaching in Guam for a few years. When she confronted one of her students, Jesús, for his misbehavior, she asked him, "What do you have to say for yourself?" Jesús responded with silence. To Jesús, silence indicated respect for his teacher and acknowledgment of his wrongdoing. In Jackie's classroom in the East Coast, such silence would often be interpreted as disrespect.*

5g. Posture and body language:

Describe what you see:

If someone stands straight, tall, and steady with her arms at her side, she may appear confident and comfortable to one person and stiff and nervous to another. A client might take a sip of his tea to indicate his agreement, and you interpret his movements to mean he is not yet ready to commit. This descriptor asks you to focus on how the communicators are holding their bodies. Are they standing or sitting? Do they change position by leaning forward or back? Do they raise or lower their head? Do they slouch or stand tall? Do they prop themselves on a desk while talking to a group or stand at attention? (Note for interculturalists: This descriptor is not about context. Context is one of the factors in Chapter 3, and high- and low-context communication relates to Descriptor 6a, *location of meaning*. In the tea example just cited, a low-context/explicit communicator might not perceive meaning in the tea drinking; he might totally miss it, focusing on the words that are spoken. With this descriptor, you are noting the tea drinking and attempting to understand its intended and perceived meaning.)

> *Knowing that glancing at one's watch can be a signal that a meeting has gone on too long, Mona is anxious. She wants to know how much time is left before the meeting ends to see if she can bring up her complex topic, so she does not want to look at her watch to signal she thinks it should be over. She decides to peek at her watch under the table, hoping no one will notice.*

5h. Dress and accessories:

Describe what you see:

In some cultures, the style of dress and accessories can indicate age, religious affiliation, marital status, sexual orientation, or socio-economic status. However, sometimes how communicators are dressed indicates a meaning that is either intended and not understood, or not intended but perceived.

> *In business training about working in Nigeria, one of the instructors wore traditional dress. He did it for two reasons: to indicate his respect for the traditions of his culture, and because some of the Nigerians these businesspeople would work with would wear such clothing. A couple of the Nigerian employees found his attire very inappropriate. They felt it implied that Nigerians were backward and uneducated. They preferred that the facilitator wear a business suit, as many Nigerian business people would commonly do.*

Category 2: The Discoverable Descriptors

This category contains the elements of communication style that describe how an interaction is experienced by the participants. This category's name, *Discoverable Descriptors*, acknowledges that a person's background, culture, sensitivity, and life experiences influence communicative expectations and behavioral outcomes. Compared to *Discernible Descriptors*, which involve much description and some interpretation, this category involves a mix of some description and more interpretation. For example, as a presenter you may be irritated with an audience whose members don't ask you any questions, but you may not realize that the reason you feel this way because you expect the listeners to be responsible for ensuring understanding. We provide one example for each of the descriptors in this section.

Discoverable Descriptors include
6. expectations of the communication process,
7. the nature of topics discussed,
8. treatment of emotion,
9. permeability to new ideas, and
10. the overall progression of the discussion.

6. Expectations of the Communication Process

6a. Location of meaning:

<--->

Explicit message/words   Implied message/reading between the lines

Other notes:

With this continuum, consider your overall impression: is a majority of the meaning that you derived from the conversation coming from the actual words used? If so, this refers to *explicit message/words*. If most of the meaning involves reading meaning into what is *not* said, this refers to *implied message/reading between the lines*. This concept is directly related to high context (implied message/reading between the lines) and low context (explicit message/words) (Hall 1976).

A young man knew that a young woman was very interested in kayaking. So when he initially wanted to ask her out, he sent a long e-mail detailing a kayaking show he had seen. The young woman read the e-mail and wondered, "How does he have so much time to watch kayaking shows?" She didn't understand that he was showing interest in her and asking her out on a date.

6b. How meaning is created:

$\longleftarrow\hspace{6cm}\longrightarrow$

Individual delivers a message   Mutual co-creation of a message

Other notes:

This descriptor refers to communicator assumptions about how meaning is created and transmitted. In some cultures, the basic assumption is that an individual has an idea or opinion, and that "message," separate from the individual, is encoded and transmitted to another person. In other cultures, the basic assumption is frequently that meaning is created through discussion, empathy, intuition, and life experience. Meaning is a joint creation or perhaps the "hearing" or "sensing" of a fundamental truth.

Two colleagues were working together to prepare a keynote address that they would be delivering together. They both agreed to add content so that the final speech felt comfortable and reflected the feelings of both of them. The challenge was that they had different ways to get to the final speech. Anna drafted the first outline. Kong Mee read it, shared a few differing ideas, and presented a new and very different outline. When the two spoke, Anna spent time understanding Kong Mee's points and acknowledging their validity. She did not feel that Kong Mee had understood her outline, however, and so she explained it. Kong Mee replied, "That's fine. If you prefer to do it your way, I'm easy." The two were speaking past each other. Anna was expecting to co-create meaning by understanding one another and melding the two outlines together. Kong Mee heard Anna's explanation of her outline as an attempt to persuade Kong Mee of its correctness, so she assumed that Anna felt her own outline was the best. She did not understand that Anna was presenting the information not to persuade, but to build an understanding between the two of them that would ultimately lead to co-creating a new outline.

6c. Responsibility for understanding:

←――→

With listener, to ask   With speaker, to be clear

Other notes:

This basic but important dimension asks you to consider whether the responsibility for understanding a conversation lies with the listener or with the speaker. If the responsibility is with the listener, listeners are expected to ask questions for clarification (if roles and context allow); if the responsibility rests with the speaker, then the speaker is expected to thoroughly provide all relevant information.

> *A leader from a large East Asian nongovernmental organization traveled to Australia to meet a new partner organization. He was asked to deliver a speech to the staff. Staff members repeatedly interrupted his presentation to ask questions, and he became very insulted. His expectation was that he was speaking clearly, he was responsible for making sure they would understand, and if they would just let him finish they would understand. Respect for authority also played a factor; as a senior official, he considered their interruptions rude. For their part, the Aussies were expressing interest in what the East Asian had to say. They felt responsible, as listeners, for understanding what he was saying.*

7. Nature of Topics Discussed

7a. What kinds of topics are discussed? (specify)

___   Personal
___   Familial
___   Professional
___   Political
___   Spiritual/belief systems
___   Community
___   Other (specify):

There is a wide range of topics that may be discussed in any given conversation. Topic choice can quickly lead to insult and embarrassment or enjoyment and excitement. In general, we have expectations about what topics we will discuss with whom, and about when, where, and how we will share our ideas with someone on a given topic.

Obviously there are many other categories of topics. The key question is: Does choice of topic make a difference in this conversation?

> *In discussing communication styles with colleagues, someone commented that it is inappropriate to discuss politics across cultures. While this may be clear advice in some areas of the world, it is our experience that this advice is not universal, and expecting it to be so can cause great frustration. Many U.S. Americans who return from work or study abroad remark on how often they were asked about politics by people they met overseas, and how they often didn't feel prepared for these conversations. Some international people living in the U.S.A. likewise express delight when they "finally find an American with whom they can intelligently talk about politics."*

7b. Level of self-disclosure:

←———→

Very open   Very closed

Other notes:

Self-disclosure can be defined as a voluntary act of revealing personal data about oneself to another person including beliefs, values, feelings, and perceptions. Level of self-disclosure refers to the communicator's general approach to sharing personal information during an interaction. In a *very open* approach, the communicator appears to share freely and without inhibition; there is little that is considered private. In a *very closed* approach, the communicator seems careful and cautious about sharing personal information and chooses to keep ideas and thoughts private; there is a broad range of information that is considered private, and few people with whom the communicator usually shares it. Many of us have been in conversations that left us feeling, "Too much information! I didn't need to know that!" Or, at the other extreme, we have been left wondering why someone was so reticent to open up.

> *Angha was enjoying lunch with a few colleagues when she shared a frustration that had occurred the previous evening. At that dinner, Angha's friend Elonor had discussed a family conflict at some length. Elonor had shared details of what family members had done and said, how she had responded, and how angry they had become with each other. Angha told her colleagues that she was extremely uncomfortable because she didn't know Elonor well enough to hear such private information. The stories embarrassed her and she was unable to respond, and she now found herself wanting to avoid Elonor.*

8. Treatment of Emotion

8a. Openness to discuss feelings:

$$\longleftarrow \hspace{10cm} \longrightarrow$$

Open to sharing   Reticent to share/private

Other notes:

This descriptor involves the role of emotions within the interaction. In what way do the communicators share their feelings with one another? *Open to sharing* refers to behaviors that indicate a willingness and ability to tell other(s) how one is feeling and to include discussions about emotional experiences within the interaction. *Reticent to share/private* refers to behaviors that demonstrate either a desire or a need to keep information about feelings to oneself.

> *A very high-ranking Pakistani woman in a major multinational organization confided to her coach that she had had a terrible experience with another facilitator's diversity training exercise in which each participant was asked to step back for each "minority" status he or she had (woman, Muslim, nontechnical education, and so on). As the facilitator listed the minority statuses, the woman stepped farther and farther back. "Yes, this is exactly why I always feel like everything is a battle for me. This is why I'm so exhausted," she was thinking to herself during the exercise. Other participants looked at this high-ranking woman in the back of the room and said, "See? We're inclusive. Even someone with all those minority badges can succeed in our orga-*

nization." She was very upset that they didn't recognize the high emotional, physical, and psychological price she had been required to pay for her success. Yet she didn't indicate any emotion, verbally or nonverbally, during the workshop. She told her coach that she'd never mentioned her experience to anyone outside her immediate family, not even to people she'd worked with for twenty years.

This story illustrates both the previous and the next descriptor.

8b. Method of expression:

←——————————————————————————————→

Expresses openly　　　　　　Subtle　　　　　　Doesn't express

Other notes:

Whereas the previous continuum asks you to consider the degree to which feelings are discussed in a conversation, this descriptor asks you to focus on how obvious the expression of emotion is. There are many different ways of expressing emotional reactions and experiences. One key is to avoid assuming that because emotion is not expressed that it is not there! This descriptor prompts you to identify how you observe emotions being expressed. *Expresses openly* indicates that when feelings are expressed, they are detectable through outward, observable behaviors (sometimes demonstrated through facial expressions, body movements, vocal adjustments, and the like). *Doesn't express* indicates that emotional expressions may be more subtle and perhaps very controlled.

After not seeing each other for more than six years, two Finnish brothers shook hands and smiled. The emotion was intense and an amazing connection was clear— even though there were no hugs or tears.

9. Permeability of New Ideas

←——————————————————————————————→

Immediate openness　　　　　　　　　　　　Extreme caution

Other notes:

When you are excited about a new idea and share it with others, you have expectations not only about how someone should respond but also about how to interpret that response. In a conversation one person may react to an idea with *immediate openness,* stating that the idea sounds good. *Extreme caution* refers to someone who reacts very tentatively, perhaps asking questions to clarify meaning or avoiding any positive feedback. What is challenging across cultures is that both approaches can indicate willingness and commitment, and both approaches can indicate negativity.

> An international student proposed a project to the grant review committee. Hoping to gain some support prior to the meeting, the student contacted one of the reviewers and asked a specific question about the idea and its fundability. The reviewer responded that he needed to do some research and would get back to the student. The word research *appeared to be "extreme caution," and the student e-mailed back that this showed ineptitude on the program management side. The reviewer wrote back, "I'm confused. You asked a question and I said I would research it. What's wrong with that?" What was wrong was that the student had expected more explicit statements of support and more immediate expert advice about the project.*

10. Progression of Discussion

$$\longleftarrow \hspace{6cm} \longrightarrow$$

Expand/build on   Contract/find weaknesses
each other's ideas   in the ideas

Other notes:

This continuum focuses on how communicators intend to further a discussion or conversation. Progression of discussion involves the direction of the conversation—outward and inclusive, or inward and exclusive. To *expand/build* suggests that the communicators affirm and mutually develop the discussion, continuously expanding ideas presented. *Contract/find weaknesses* refers to a progression in which communicators take a critical approach, offering alternative views, debating, and pointing out loopholes. This descriptor is closely linked to the "purpose" descriptors in the Functional categories that follow (Descriptors 11d, 12d, 13d, 14d, 15d, and 16d) but is slightly different in that it refers not to the intended outcome but to the process of the discussion itself.

> *John was a leader of a community organization. He put together a schedule of events and presented it to his team. They began immediately to critique some of John's proposed programs, explaining why they might not work. John became upset. "Hey, we're all volunteers here. I spent a lot of time putting this schedule together. Don't you at least want to give me the opportunity to explain it to you before you tear it apart?" John was very much hoping for empathy and, if not agreement, at least understanding before the debating began. His colleagues, in contrast, were respecting the work John had done by giving it critical attention.*

Category 3: Functional Descriptors

The Discernable Descriptors are designed to encourage us to be as observant as possible of actual words and behaviors. The Discoverable Descriptors are a bit more interpretive in that they encourage both our observation and analysis of the expectations and assumptions underlying words and behaviors. This third category, *Functional Descriptors*, applies the skills of observation and description to more advanced and complicated concepts—*speech acts.*

According to Stephen W. Littlejohn, a "speech act is the basic unit of language used to express meaning, an utterance that expresses an intention. Normally, the speech act is a sentence, but it can be a word or phrase . . . ." (2002, 79). Littlejohn continues, "The meaning of a speech act is its *illocutionary force.* You might, for example, state the proposition 'The cake is good' ironically to mean just the opposite: This cake is the worst I ever ate. Here what appears to be a simple proposition has the illocutionary force of an insult" (79).

Speech act theory is a huge topic area, and we will not attempt to go into detail about it here. We do trust that you will quickly see that the meaning of a speech act, its illocutionary force, is culturally relative. For us to be able to understand another's intended meaning, we need to be able to understand the intended functionality of the speech acts we use: to understand when a statement functions as a request, a compliment, an apology, or a joke. The purpose of this section is to take a step toward integrating speech acts and communication styles into our intercultural work by utilizing the most neutral and descriptive vocabulary possible.

In this category, you need to consider the manner in which the communicators are using speech acts and attempt to understand the meaning the speakers are trying to convey with a given speech act. We highlight some of the speech acts that are most commonly misunderstood across cultures, such as:

11. apologies,
12. requests,
13. praise,
14. disagreement,
15. feedback,
16. humor and joking.

A neutral description of a speech act can be very challenging. We offer you six ways of describing each speech act:

a. its frequency of use in the interaction,
b. the quantity of words involved,
c. the timing of the speech act,
d. the intended purpose of the speech act,
e. the content of the speech act message—its generality or specificity, and
f. the style in which the speech act is delivered and received.

We have left this final aspect, style, is provided to you open-ended, as every speech act can be delivered in a multitude of ways, for example, formal, light-hearted, spontaneous, or hesitant.

It is important to remember that what we intend as descriptions of speech act style—or any neutrally intended descriptors for that matter—may in fact be our interpretations. What seems to you to be formal might appear to another person as rather casual; everything is relative. The goal with the Functional Descriptors is to think about and discuss the intended and perceived meanings of speech acts, so that we can match intention and perception to communicate more accurately. Remember that each of the speech acts may involve many of the discernable behaviors described in Category 1, including the fact that a speech act may function non-verbally. Also, as with previous descriptors, several speech acts may occur simultaneously, intertwining and supplementing one another.

We would like to point out an important distinction between the Functional Descriptors and the goals factor discussed in Chapter 3. Whereas the goals factor allows for a broad view of the overall purposes of the communicators in the conversation, Functional Descriptors allow for an examination of individual and multiple objectives for discrete speech acts within the overall conversation. For example, while approaching a boss to reach the goal of getting a raise, a communicator may want to establish an emotional connection or rapport for the conversation. Does the communicator do this by inquiring about the health of the boss' family members, by apologizing for taking her valuable time, or by sharing a brief update of work she has done on one of her priority projects? Analysis can of course also be done in the reverse, contemplating the reasons behind the frequency of apologies or compliments and the reasons for their use in an interaction.

11. Apologies

The use of apologies can be quite problematic, especially across cultures. We may expect one when none comes. One person may see an apology as admitting guilt, another as social bonding and empathy. One may view apology as weakness or lack of confidence, another as a sign of professionalism and of a good education.

> *One high-profile example of apologies involved a U.S. military plane flying over Chinese airspace without permission from the Chinese government. The Chinese forced the plane to land and held the U.S. crewmembers in China for some time. During that time, an investigation was conducted and it was largely determined that it was a mistake for the plane to have been in that area. The Chinese government requested an apology from the U.S.A. While the U.S. government cooperated with the investigation's findings, they refused to offer a formal apology because from the U.S. cultural perspective, apologizing meant admitting blame and taking responsibility for intentional wrongdoing. From the Chinese perspective, an apology indicated acknowledgment that the incident had happened and provided an opportunity to move forward. National tensions rose and foreign citizens were held, perhaps unnecessarily, for a period of time until this cultural misunderstanding was resolved.*

This apologies descriptor asks you to consider the role apologies play in the interaction you are analyzing.

11a. Frequency: How often does the communicator apologize during the interaction?

←———————————————————————————————————→

Constant   Intermittent   Rare/Never

Other notes:

11b. Quantity of words: How verbose are the apologies used during the interaction?

←———————————————————————————————————→

Many words   Few words

Other notes:

11c. Timing: When do the apologies occur?

____ At the beginning of the conversation
____ In the middle of the conversation
____ At the end of the conversation
____ Throughout the conversation
____ In response to facts
____ In response to emotions
____ As an immediate response
____ Only after consideration and thought
____ Never

11d. Purpose: What does the apology indicate? What is the underlying meaning of the apology?

____ Admission of guilt or regret
____ Empathy

_____ Social bonding

_____ Courtesy

_____ Other (specify):

11e. Content: What kind of information is included in the apology? How general or specific is the information contained in the apology?

$\longleftarrow\hspace{6cm}\longrightarrow$

General   Specific

Other notes:

11f. Describe the style with which the apology is given and received.

12. Requests

Requests are another Functional Descriptor that are very much culturally relative. Someone may repeatedly request something loudly and clearly, yet the other person fails to "hear" it. Or, conversely, a person may perceive that someone is asking for something when that is not the case—the first person was simply trying to connect and acknowledge mutual interests and ideas.

> *A U.S. American introduced a colleague from Cameroon to an employer. One day the Cameroonian said to his U.S. colleague, "I heard from person X that he was paid for a service that the employer requested I deliver for free. I'm really feeling that the employer is taking advantage of me and perhaps discriminating against me due to race." The U.S. colleague heard a complaint, clarified and empathized, and thought the matter closed. It was only later when the Cameroonian asked, "Have you talked to the employer yet?" that the American realized that his colleague had been asking the American to intervene. Because of the cultural differences in how requests are made, the American didn't even realize that he had been asked to do something!*

In discussing requests as a descriptor, it is important to keep in mind that this category includes both the presence and absence of requests and invitations. One person may expect specific requests or invitations to events, social functions, work-related assignments, and the like, while another person mistakenly interprets someone's friendliness as an invitation when none was intended. The following example highlights this challenge.

> *A situation that occurred between Amira and her mother-in-law, Dorothy, illustrates two different interpretations about invitations. Amira had said to Dorothy many times, "You are welcome to come to church with us anytime, Dorothy. We would love to have you join us." Yet over a period of many years, Dorothy never attended church with her son and his wife. One day Dorothy mentioned that she felt excluded from this part of her children's lives. Amira was shocked. "But Dorothy, I've asked you to join us so many times, and you've never come!" Amira told her. "But Amira, you've never actually asked me to come. It was always 'sometime.'" Dorothy needed an explicit invitation to attend church on a particular day in order to feel welcome, while Amira felt that her invitation was welcoming and open-ended. It had never occurred to Amira that, as Dorothy later explained, she would feel like she was imposing on her son's life if she indicated she wanted to join them for church, rather than waiting for what Dorothy considered a more direct and specific invitation.*

This descriptor prompts us to assess the role of requests in the interaction. The key question is this: Does the use of requests make a difference in the interaction you are analyzing?

12a. Frequency: How often does the communicator make requests during the interaction?

←———→

Constant   Intermittent   Rare/Never

Other notes:

12b. Quantity of words: How verbose are the requests made during the interaction?

←———→

Many words   Few words

Other notes:

12c. Timing: When do the requests occur?

____ At the beginning of the conversation

____ In the middle of the conversation

____ At the end of the conversation

____ Throughout the conversation

____ In response to facts

____ In response to emotions

____ As an immediate response

____ Only after consideration and thought

____ Never

12d. Purpose: What does the request indicate? What is the underlying meaning of the request?

____ Accomplish a task

____ Pay a compliment

____ Include someone

____ Assert authority

____ Encourage

____ Other (specify):

Other notes:

12e. Content: What kind of information is included in the request? How general or specific is the information contained in the request?

← —————————————————————————————————— →

General   Specific

Other notes:

12f. Describe the style of how the request is made and received.

13. Praise

Praise can motivate or it can quickly discourage someone. The same message may sound hollow, false, or manipulative to one person and heartfelt to another. There are many ways to deliver praise, including disparagingly.

> *At a recent nonprofit organization event that was extremely well attended and well received, attendees stayed for a long time after the formal program to talk with the speaker informally and amongst themselves. A member of the organization's board praised the executive director by saying, "Too bad we had such a boring program this evening. People couldn't wait to get out the door." It took the executive director a moment to realize that the board member's comment was not an insult, but actually a compliment!*

Praise might also function as its opposite—its purpose may be criticism. "That was graceful" might be said jokingly when someone drops something, for example. Other aspects of praise to consider are where, when, and how praise is communicated—is it saved for a particularly meaningful time? Is it given in public or in private? Does it focus on effort and emotion or on task? This descriptor asks you to reflect on whether praise makes a difference in the interaction.

13a. Frequency: How often does the communicator give praise during the interaction?

←————————————————————————————→

Constant   Intermittent   Rare/Never

Other notes:

13b. Quantity of words: How verbose is the praise during the interaction?

←————————————————————————————→

Many words   Few words

Other notes:

13c. Timing: When does praise occur?

____ At the beginning of the conversation

____ In the middle of the conversation

____ At the end of the conversation

____ Throughout the conversation

____ In response to facts

____ In response to emotions

____ As an immediate response

____ Only after consideration and thought

____ Never

13d. Purpose: What does the praise indicate? What is the underlying meaning of the praise?

____ Relationship building

____ Request

____ Motivation

____ Confidence building

____ Criticism

____ Other (specify):

Other notes:

13e. Content: What kind of information is included in the praise? How general or specific is the information contained in the praise?

⟵————————————————————————————⟶

General   Specific

Other notes:

13f. Describe the style of how the praise is offered and received.

14. Disagreement

The use of disagreement varies tremendously by culture, because it is so closely related to underlying values (harmony or truth) and to the goals of communication (accuracy and specificity or creation of shared feeling and space). As with other speech acts, disagreement can be communicated in a multitude of ways, many of which have already been described in the stories in this book. Silence or failure to respond might loudly communicate disagreement in one situation, while in another interaction disagreement occurs in raised-voice arguments. Some cultures use third-party intermediaries to voice and facilitate disagreement; others trust disagreement only when it is voiced directly and "honestly."

> Jean wanted her colleague Sophie to host a group of foreign students for a weekend during Sophie's ninth month of pregnancy. Sophie repeatedly declined by saying that the timing wasn't right. She disagreed softly yet strongly, she felt, so as not to offend but to be clear. The students came anyway, and Jean expected Sophie to be available to entertain them. Sophie's refusal to host the students and the disagreement about timing was either never heard, not taken seriously, or ignored by Jean. How do we to begin to unravel what actually happened? Was it that Jean expected more explanation of why the timing was bad for Sophie? Did Sophie need to say no more frequently? Or was there something else involved with this disagreement?

This descriptor is meant to encourage us to reflect on whether disagreement (and how it is expressed) affects the process and the outcome of the interaction.

14a. Frequency: How often does the communicator disagree during the interaction?

←——————————————————————————————————————→

Constant   Intermittent   Rare/Never

Other notes:

14b. Quantity of words: How verbose is the disagreement during the interaction?

←————————————————————————————————————→

Many words   Few words

Other notes:

14c. Timing: When do disagreements occur?

____ At the beginning of the conversation
____ In the middle of the conversation
____ At the end of the conversation
____ Throughout the conversation
____ In response to facts
____ In response to emotions
____ As an immediate response
____ Only after consideration and thought
____ Never

14d. Purpose: What is the underlying meaning of the disagreement?

____ Improve process
____ Vent emotion
____ Learn
____ Courtesy
____ Disrupt forward movement
____ Other (specify):

14e. Content: What kind of information is included in the disagreement? How general or specific is the information contained in the disagreement?

←————————————————————————————————————→

General   Specific

Other notes:

14f. Describe the style with which the disagreement is given and received.

15. Feedback

Many of us have preferences for when and how we give and receive feedback. For some people, receiving constant feedback is helpful, whereas other people may find such constant input patronizing. A two-sentence e-mail may be fine for some, whereas several paragraphs may feel insufficient to others. Some people become lost in detail while others crave it. In addition, sometimes we respond to feedback by being motivated, but at other times we may feel overwhelmed. Feedback can assume many styles.

> We recently observed a restaurant manager who walked into one of his dining rooms and realized that a rack of glasses that needed to be moved had not been moved. He said rather sarcastically to the dining room manager, "Mark, we decided not to move these tonight because . . . ?" His subordinate replied, "I've been so busy running your operation and managing the bottom line that I haven't gotten to it yet." This might seem like an exchange of insults or put-downs, and content-wise it is. Yet each of the communicators in this interaction felt satisfied about the exchange, knew that feedback had been given and accepted, and that the glass rack would be moved. The communicators were comfortable with this style of feedback; it resulted in motivation to correct something—it worked for both of them.

This descriptor asks you to think about whether feedback plays a key role in the interaction you are analyzing.

15a. Frequency: How often does the communicator give feedback during the interaction?

←——————————————————————————————→

Constant   Intermittent   Rare/Never

Other notes:

15b. Quantity of words: How verbose is the feedback during the interaction?

←——————————————————————————————————————→

Many words

Few words

Other notes:

15c. Timing: When does feedback occur?

_____ At the beginning of the conversation
_____ In the middle of the conversation
_____ At the end of the conversation
_____ Throughout the conversation
_____ In response to facts
_____ In response to emotions
_____ As an immediate response
_____ Only after consideration and thought
_____ Never

15d. Purpose: What does the feedback indicate? What is the underlying meaning of the feedback?

_____ Correct
_____ Encourage
_____ Guide
_____ Insult
_____ Gain competitive edge
_____ Assert power
_____ Facilitate group-building
_____ Other (specify):

15e. Content: What kind of information is included in the feedback?

____ Specific

____ General

____ Positive

____ Negative

____ Humorous

____ Other (specify):

15f. Describe the style of feedback.

16. Humor and Joking

Humor and joking would seem to be a human universal. Just as we all make requests and give feedback, most cultures and people enjoy humor at appropriate times. But it is this last part that is tricky—what is appropriate humor, when, how often, for what purpose, and what exactly is funny? "Jokes just don't translate" is an aphorism.

There is an urban legend about a joke a former U.S. President made while on a trip to Tokyo. After he made the joke the interpreter said, in Japanese, "The President just made a very funny joke that I am unable to translate. Would you all please laugh so that he doesn't think I am an incompetent interpreter?"

Humor may be subtle or slapstick, verbal or nonverbal, pointed or self-deprecating. Jokes can include plays on words, surprising stories or riddles, the infamous political cartoon, or even a practical joke. And, of course, humor is topical—what is considered "fair game" to joke about varies by culture.

The speech act of humor and joking frequently overlaps with other speech acts discussed in this section. That is because people might apologize or make a request in a humorous way, and humor might be used to deliver feedback or praise. It is important to remember that speech acts are often not distinct and discrete—they intertwine. It may be difficult to determine where one speech act ends and another one begins. What we are concerned about is improving communication—finding a connection point between diverse communication styles. The process of analysis itself can lead to important insights and thus may be more important than being right about a specific speech act.

This descriptor asks you to think about whether humor and joking affect the interaction you are analyzing.

16a. Frequency: How often does the communicator use humor during the interaction?

←————————————————————————————————→

Constant   Intermittent   Rare/Never

Other notes:

16b. Quantity of words: How verbose is the humor during the interaction?

←————————————————————————————————→

Many words   Few words

Other notes:

16c. Timing: When does humor occur?

_____   At the beginning of the conversation
_____   In the middle of the conversation
_____   At the end of the conversation
_____   Throughout the conversation
_____   In response to facts
_____   In response to emotions
_____   As an immediate response
_____   Only after consideration and thought
_____   Never

16*d. Purpose:* What is the underlying meaning of the humor?

____ Lighten the mood or relieve tension

____ Empathize

____ Establish rapport

____ Criticize

____ Encourage

____ Other (specify):

16e. Content: What kind of information is included in the humor? Describe the topic of the humor or joke, what it is poking fun at.

16f. Describe the style of humor.

You have been to the circus backyard and you have discovered some of the meaning behind the magic. These communication style descriptors are powerful tools for helping you to understand the influence of communication styles in your relationships, to manage style differences more effectively, and to access the unique contributions of every member of your team or group. With the Communication Style Descriptor Checklist you can become more adept at identifying the differences that make a difference. We recognize that this task may seem overwhelming, especially at first. The main goal is to work toward a more descriptive analysis of the communication and to resist making premature or inaccurate judgments about the communicator's actions. It is in these specific behavioral descriptions that we can begin to identify the communication style differences that may be affecting our interactions.

The next chapter presents a process for connecting the factors (Chapter 3) and descriptors (Chapter 6), using a Four-Step method that we have used with great success for bridging communication style disconnects. In Chapter 7 we provide you the opportunity to work with the factors and descriptors in more depth.

The following activities will help you to improve your fluency with the communication style descriptors and, thus, your ability to quickly perceive, interpret, and more effectively manage communication style differences.

ACTIVITY *11:* Movie and the Checklist

Watch a movie or favorite television show, and then pick a scene that includes a "miss" in communication. Use the Descriptor Checklist to analyze what actually happened in the interaction. Some of our favorite movies to use for this activity include *Shall We Dance, The Joy Luck Club,* and *Mississippi Masala.* There are also many wonderful international films to enjoy.

ACTIVITY *12:* Journal and the Checklist

Think about a conversation or meeting you have participated in that did not proceed quite as you had expected. Use the Descriptor Checklist to help you decipher what happened.

ACTIVITY *13:* People Watching and the Checklist

Go to a shopping mall, coffee shop, or other public place and observe people, using your Descriptor Checklist! Please, however, be sure to be respectful of others' privacy.

Source: Communication Highwire: Leveraging the Power of Diverse Communication Styles (Intercultural Press). © 2005 Dianne Hofner Saphiere, Barbara Kappler Mikk, and Basma Ibrahim DeVries. All rights reserved.

CHAPTER 7

Leveraging Communication Style Differences

Choreographing the Performance

Chapter 6 gave you a glimpse into life behind the Big Top and introduced the descriptors you can use to understand and appreciate the communication circus more fully. With an understanding of these descriptors and the factors from Chapter 3, we are now ready to choreograph our communication performances. This chapter introduces a method that demonstrates how careful planning and practice can yield performances that flow smoothly, engage the participants, and create the possibility for more effective communication.

We have mentioned previously that description can cause us to quickly lose the core essence of whatever we are talking about. Description can become stale and lifeless, divorced from visceral experience. There is obviously a need for both objective description which can help us to transcend cultural biases, and the richer aspects that reveal themselves when delving into the communication style factors of context, goals, self-concept, values, and communication style repertoire. One way we have found for putting these two components—the factors and descriptors—together is the *Four-Step* method. You can use it to learn about yourself and others and to improve your ability to communicate and collaborate across cultures. We hope that you will experiment with this method, fine-tune and improve it, and add your own adaptations and tools to a hopefully growing literature on communication style.

The Four-Step Method

So what is this Four-Step method? It is an opportunity to "jump onto the band-wagon" going to the circus and engage in a process to learn how to filter out cultural biases and leverage communication style differences. In the Four-Step method we do the following:

1. **Reflect** on our experience to discover our feelings, our intentions, and the reasons we attribute to what others communicated.
2. **Analyze** why we feel the way we do. The goal here is to realize our own expectations, and to see the cause-and-effect links we often unconsciously make between behavior and intentions.
3. **Discuss** with others to understand their intentions and experience. This requires setting aside our own conviction that we are "right" and they are "wrong," at least temporarily.
4. **Decide** how to proceed, including whether we will try to develop a new communication style or skill, how we will collaborate, or perhaps whether we feel it worthwhile to try to collaborate.

Mike and Tanaka—A Date?

Mike frequently traveled to Tokyo on business trips. Tanaka-san always felt upset before even meeting Mike, because he believed that Mike had made management decisions that did not appropriately factor in the needs of the Tokyo organization. Tanaka felt that Mike didn't listen to him, or that he primarily listened to staff in North America or Europe. Tanaka wanted to discuss this with Mike, but he felt hesitant. He wanted to be respectful of his boss, yet he feared his own anger would make him say something he didn't want to say—but he also wanted to let Mike know his true feelings. Because of this complexity of emotion Tanaka would often avert his eye contact, speak softly, and not speak as explicitly or clearly with Mike as he might in more comfortable situations.

So this time when Mike was coming, Tanaka-san thought, "If I can just get Mike alone for dinner or drinks. If we're both relaxed and enjoying ourselves, with no one else around, I'll be able to get up the courage to tell Mike the difficult truth. And he'll be able to hear me because I won't embarrass him in front of anyone else."

So, about 6:30 in the evening on Mike's first day in the Tokyo office, Tanaka-san asks Mike, softly, refraining from direct eye contact, "Would you like to join me for dinner tonight?" Mike is tired from a long day's work in a foreign country and he is very jet-lagged. He knows that once he returns to his hotel, he'll have a lot of e-mail and phone messages that he will still need to deal with, separate from the work he's doing with Tanaka-san. He thinks, "It's so kind of Tanaka-san to offer to give up his night to entertain me. I don't want to impose on his time with his family. I'm sure he has plenty to do, as do I." Mike replies cordially, "Thanks, Tanaka-san, but I think I'd rather get back to the hotel, get some other work done, and make an early night of it."

Tanaka-san says that he understands, and there is an awkward pause. Both men perceive that something has been lost in the communication process. Mike packs up his things, thanks Tanaka for the work that day, and returns to his hotel.

One Step—*Reflecting*

Tanaka-san can start by reflecting on his communication style: How was he communicating? What were his goals and intentions with Mike? Tanaka might note that he finds it difficult to speak up to Mike, but at the same time he very much feels the need to do so. Tanaka-san can also reflect a bit on the judgments he was making about Mike. He might realize he has some very negative feelings about Mike that are no doubt preventing both of them from achieving a more positive working relationship. Tanaka might further discover that he has decided that Mike just does not listen and is not interested in his thinking. Thus, for Tanaka, this first step of reflection utilizes the *goals* and *context* factors described in Chapter 3. In terms of the descriptors, Tanaka might reflect further on the purpose of his request (Descriptor 12d) and realize that Mike may not have understood that he intended to use the dinner out to accomplish a task that was difficult to do in the office.

As for Mike, he needs to realize that the discomfort he felt at the end of the conversation is a sign that he needs to reflect and consider what his *goals* in the conversation were. He will probably decide that he was trying to be polite and respectful of Tanaka-san's family time. Another of Mike's goals is taking care of his own e-mail tasks. In considering the *context,* Mike is feeling the constraint of his own jet lag. If he examines the chronology of their interactions, Mike might come to realize that he has often turned down Tanaka-san's invitations to get together after work hours. Mike might also use the Functional Descriptors from Chapter 6 to discover that Tanaka-san's repeated requests to go out were not extended merely out of politeness and consideration, but out of Tanaka's own interest in creating a space to speak frankly and to accomplish a task.

Two Step—*Analyzing*

At this point, both Mike and Tanaka need to be ready to move beyond reflection and dig deeper into their interactions. Tanaka-san may analyze his own intentions to discover why he uses the communication style that he does with Mike, and then try to figure out why he wanted to speak up to Mike and yet felt unable to do so. He might see that he *values* respecting Mike and controlling his own emotions, and that he also values getting a job done right and having a strong relationship. He might realize that part of the challenge he experiences is due to his negative judgment of Mike and his desire to look good in his boss' eyes. He may realize that the value he places on hierarchy, harmony, and respect are taking priority over his value of being honest and forthright, preventing him from acting in a way he feels would be responsible to the others in the Tokyo organization. During the conversation, these values translated into the fact that Tanaka did not verbally link his dinner invitation with his work concerns (Descriptor 2e); he did not say that he wanted to have dinner with Mike so that they might talk in a relaxed and forthright manner. He averted his eyes when he spoke with Mike (Descriptor 5a) and spoke softly (Descriptor 4c). Tanaka-san may realize that his internal values conflict with each other and that this conflict frequently affects his communication style. He might remind himself that he has the ability to enact more than one communication style (*communication style repertoire*) and might realize that his *self-concept* is often affected by Mike's presence.

Mike's ability to analyze this situation will require some creative thinking about his own behaviors and why these may be bothersome to Tanaka. Mike might realize that he tends to view the *context* of his relationship with Tanaka as that of two adult men equally able to speak up to one another. He *values* egalitarianism and forthrightness. This is in contrast to Tanaka-san's consciousness of his status as being lower in the hierarchy. Thus, Mike fails to notice or allow for Tanaka's hesitancy. In reviewing his communication style, Mike will probably be struck by how he presents his ideas—he may occasionally ask Tanaka how he is doing, but mostly he focuses directly on the tasks they need to discuss (*goals* and Descriptor 2a). He rarely talks about their relationship or their process of communication. Mike tends to see communication as one person sending a message to another, rather than two people together creating meaning (Descriptor 6b). He believes that if Tanaka-san has something to say, he will say it. He looks for meaning in the words that are used, not in implicit messages (Descriptor 6a). Mike might also realize that he tends to end conversations more abruptly than Tanaka (Descriptor 1b). Mike might want to consider a bit more carefully the timing of Tanaka's invitations to go out for drinks and realize that they may indicate that Tanaka has put a good deal of effort and consideration into the request, rather than it being simply a spontaneous comment (Descriptor 12c).

Three Step—*Discussing*

Tanaka-san can explain to Mike his own *goals* or intentions, his *values*, and how they motivate his behavior and communication style (*communication style repertoire*). He may want to ask Mike questions to better understand where Mike is coming from. Tanaka might initiate a discussion with Mike by saying, "You know, Mike, it's difficult for me to speak up and tell you things I feel are difficult or awkward, because I respect you and want to please you. You're my boss. As Japanese, we're taught to maintain harmony and to respect the hierarchy. On the other hand, there are a few things that I feel are impeding our productivity as well as our relationship. I know I can't resolve them myself, so I'd like to take some time with you to figure them out and learn from them." He might ask Mike how he prioritizes his limited time on a business trip, and might ask Mike how he feels about social time with colleagues—whether he sees it as "nice" or "necessary," "polite" or "practical."

From here, of course, Mike must be open and willing to discuss and share his perspective.

During the discussion they might talk about the interaction they just had. Tanaka can explain that he invited Mike so that they could speak in private, and that if they had had enough time, he would have been able to get up the courage to tell Mike what he needed to say. He can explain that it is not that he is afraid of Mike, but that his own biases and style preferences often prevent him from speaking up. Tanaka might also talk about the meaning behind his behavior—his eye contact, voice volume, and links between thoughts (using Descriptors 5a, 4c, and 2e).

Mike, for his part, can explain to Tanaka-san that he realizes that his *goals* are biased in a task-oriented direction, and ask Tanaka to tell him a bit about his expectations of a supervisor. Mike might explain his view of their roles and relationship (*context*) is that the two of them are equally able to speak up, and his *value* is on egalitarianism and honesty. He can ask Tanaka if his views and values are similar. Even better might be if Mike can arrange such a conversation not directly with Tanaka-san, but with a Japanese cultural informant (Descriptor 12f), so that he might learn more about the cultural differences in a triangulated, nonconfrontational way. Then he can double-check the insights he gains from the cultural informant in a discussion with Tanaka-san. Mike might ask Tanaka-san to teach him about Japanese communication style, and share his observation that Tanaka-san averts his eyes and tends to speak in a softer volume than Mike is used to (Descriptors 5a and 4c); he can ask Tanaka-san what those behaviors mean.

Four Step—*Deciding*

If Tanaka takes the initiative and shows his courage through his willingness to discuss his and Mike's communication styles, he can open up the process for both of them to consider alternatives. They can consider scheduling a night out socializing together. Tanaka might be allowed to set meeting agendas once in a while, even though he is the subordinate. Perhaps if Mike makes a point of asking Tanaka how things are going, to ask questions about feelings rather than just facts, and then takes the time and energy to sit and listen, Tanaka might feel motivated to speak his *honne* or personal truth.

If these aspects of their communication are discussed, Mike can make a more informed decision about whether to go out for dinner with Tanaka that night or some other night. The two men can then discuss how they can begin to structure Mike's business trips to allow and encourage Tanaka to speak up, and how Mike might listen to hear what Tanaka-san wants to say.

Mike might consider expanding his *communication style repertoire* by learning to listen for meaning in body language and context as well as words (Descriptor 6a), by allowing more silence (Descriptor 5f) and thus providing Tanaka a chance to supplement his communication, or by asking relationship-oriented questions (Descriptor 2a). Mike might discover that simple things such as slowing the pace of his speech (Descriptor 4b), using less slang and more standard vocabulary (*context factor-language*), and delaying the ending of the conversation (Descriptor 1b) a bit longer will result in improved communication with Tanaka-san. Tanaka-san might find that using more direct eye contact with Mike (Descriptor 5a), repeating his request that Mike join him for dinner (Descriptor 12a), and explaining the purpose (Descriptor 6a) behind his dinner invitation (Descriptor 12d) will help improve their communication.

In this manner, using both the factors and the descriptors to build mutual understanding, the two men have the tools to forge agreement on how they will try to communicate more effectively in the future. And perhaps once they establish a more positive communication pattern, their ability to discuss their communication patterns and decision making processes might come much more freely and naturally, less awkwardly and tentatively. Thus, the Four-Step method can help them to expand their communication style repertoires and to actually use their communication style differences to improve their productivity and relationship.

You may have already realized that this Four-Step method is related to the Observe, Describe, Interpret, Suspend evaluation (ODIS) process identified by Ting-Toomey (1999) and the Describe, Interpret, Evaluate (DIE) process (Bennett, Bennett, and Stillings, 1979; Wendt, 1984) frequently used in intercultural training. We see the relationship as one of cousins, meaning that while they are in the same family of tools, there are notable differences.

The main difference is that we intend our Four-Step method to be used with the factors and descriptors presented in this book. We give you the poles from which you can build your circus tent. Another significant difference is that we purposely incorporate a discussion step in which actual interaction between the parties involved is encouraged in order to build effective relationships and truly leverage communication style differences. In the cases where direct communication between parties is not appropriate, we still encourage dialogue with informed parties who can lend insight not just into what went wrong, but what alternative solutions may be available. The deciding step is an integral element to this model in that the participants involved make a decision about their own actions. Whether in business, communities, families, or academia, this last step of mutually deciding how to share information and make decisions is crucial to effective collaboration and positive relationships.

Use the following story and Activity 14 to see how applying the Factors from Chapter 3 and the Descriptors from Chapter 6 can help you improve your effectiveness—to practice using this Four-Step method. This story is a scene we have acted out in training several times to illustrate the ideas in this book.

At the end of this chapter, you will find the Four-Step Method Worksheet. Your responses to the questions on the Four-Step Method Worksheet can provide you with information that enables you to understand yourself and others, and to consider and reconsider actions you will take to improve your effectiveness. You can use the Four-Step Method Worksheet to help you analyze interactions in which you participate or those that you observe.

The thrill of the Four-Step method would not be complete without giving you a chance to practice a bit of highwire balancing on your own. In Chapter 8 you will have the chance to show that "practice makes perfect" when you integrate the Factors and the Descriptors.

Ling, Sandy, and Chef Bella

Ling and Sandy work for a training firm. Ling is Sandy's supervisor and engages primarily in management and client relations; Sandy mainly facilitates training sessions for clients. Both of them are passionate about their jobs and committed to pleasing their clients. They have extremely busy schedules, and although they work in the same office, they rarely have time to just sit and catch up or talk things through. Today, they are scheduled to meet with a new client—the chef who runs an international cooking academy.

Chef Bella has requested that Sandy deliver an off-the-shelf, standardized training module for her staff. Sandy knows from her needs analysis at the cooking academy that the staff's needs are deeper and broader than the objectives that can be achieved using this off-the-shelf solution. She wants the opportunity to advocate her ideas with the chef before any final decision is made.

As Sandy and Ling are traveling to the cooking academy, Sandy explains the background to Ling. She speaks quickly and animatedly. She relates several stories from the cooking academy that she heard during her needs analysis—stories that demonstrate the need for more in-depth training. Sandy is forthright with Ling, explaining that the chef prefers something quick and easy, but that she's afraid this approach won't really accomplish what the chef wants to accomplish.

Ling listens to Sandy quietly. She nods her head frequently and maintains a pleasant expression. She asks a few questions about the chef's requests, budget parameters, and concerns. Ling does not directly respond to Sandy's comments, and it seems to irritate Sandy that Ling is not sharing her sense of urgency.

Sandy then asks Ling directly to support her in advocating to the chef a training design that is more in-depth and customized to the cooking academy's needs. Ling listens carefully, and tells Sandy that she very much

Source: Communication Highwire: Leveraging the Power of Diverse Communication Styles (Intercultural Press).

appreciates Sandy's competence, experience, passion, and commitment to excellence. She says she knows that Sandy shares her conviction to meet the chef's expectations. Ling speaks softly and much more slowly than Sandy, pausing frequently.

The two women walk into the school and are conducted to the chef's office. Chef Bella greets them in a loud, hospitable voice, with a large smile and animated expression on her face, and ushers them into her office on one side of a noisy kitchen. Ling buttons her jacket as they enter the chef's office and maintains a rigid posture and restrained body language. She tells Chef Bella how much her firm appreciates the cooking academy's business, and how committed they are to delivering the best services to the academy. Chef Bella speaks quickly and expresses excitement about the off-the-shelf training that Sandy is going to conduct for the academy. She says she is confident it will be "just the thing" to help the staff and students understand one another better and function more effectively as a team. She praises Sandy's abilities effusively, based on her contact with Sandy so far and on comments she has heard about Sandy's trainings from other professionals in the hospitality industry, and she gets out a calendar to discuss possible dates for the training.

Sandy interrupts (Chef Bella speaks very quickly and without pausing, so she sees interruptions as the only option if she wants to speak) to tell the chef that her needs assessment has shown a few things that the off-the-shelf training will not address. She suggests that perhaps they all consider a more customized training design before making a final decision. Chef Bella responds to Sandy's suggestion with a jovial laugh, and restates that she has complete confidence in the off-the-shelf training program and in Sandy's abilities. She explains that the thing to do is get it on the calendar so that it actually happens!

By now Sandy seems quite fed up that Chef Bella "believes in her abilities" and yet won't listen to her! She turns to her supervisor, Ling, in hopes that Ling will support her line of reasoning. The chef also looks at Ling, who pauses, then slowly and softly says, "So, Chef Bella, it sounds as if you are quite excited about this method, and would just like to confirm a date for the training?"

Sandy's jaw drops open. She feels incredibly disappointed with Ling, and shocked that Ling wouldn't act more responsibly with the client by attempting to convince Chef Bella of a better approach. Ling, Chef Bella, and Sandy agree on a training date, and the meeting finishes.

On the way back to their offices, Sandy says to Ling, "I can't believe you didn't support me in there, after I'd asked you straight out for your help!" She has obvious emotion in her voice. Ling looks at Sandy and says, "I'm sorry, Sandy. I didn't mean to upset you. You mean a lot to this firm. You are our senior trainer. I want to keep you happy. But the chef had already made up her mind. She knew what she wanted to do. What would be the sense in arguing with the client?"

ACTIVITY *14:* Using the Four-Step Method to Appraise the Ling, Sandy, and Chef Bella Story

The following handout summarizes the Four-Step method, while the Worksheet presents questions to guide you through it. Be sure also to make a copy of the chart, "Questions to Consider When Analyzing the Factors," from the end of Chapter 3, and answer those factor questions also. You may want to take notes or discuss your answers with someone else. You can also use the Four-Step Method Worksheet to analyze your own interactions, those you observe, or the examples in the next chapter.

THE FOUR-STEP METHOD

This is an opportunity for you to "jump on the bandwagon" and engage in a process for reflecting on a specific interaction, for filtering out cultural biases, and to learn from and use communication style differences with the Four-Step method:

1. **Reflect** on your experience to discover how you are feeling, your intentions, and the reasons you attribute to what others have done.

2. **Analyze** why you feel the way you do. The goal here is to realize your own expectations, and to see the cause-and-effect links often unconsciously made between behavior and intentions.

3. **Discuss** with others to understand their intentions and experience. This requires setting aside your own conviction that you are "right" and they are "wrong," at least temporarily.

4. **Decide** how to proceed, including whether you will try to develop a new communication style or skill, how you will collaborate, or perhaps whether you feel it worthwhile to try to collaborate.

Source: Communication Highwire: Leveraging the Power of Diverse Communication Styles (Intercultural Press).

THE FOUR-STEP METHOD WORKSHEET *(continued)*

Take a few moments to ask yourself the following questions. You may want to take notes or discuss your answers with someone else.

1. **Reflect** on your experience of the interaction:
   - How do you feel about each of the people in the interaction?

   - How might you describe each of them?

   - Do you empathize with one of them more than the others?

   - Do you have theories about why each of them behaved the way they did?

   - Do you feel anyone was "right" or anyone else was "wrong?"

   - Do you have recommendations on how the interaction might have been handled better?

THE FOUR-STEP METHOD WORKSHEET *(continued)*

2. **Analyze** the communication styles used in the interaction:
   - Why do you feel the way you do? What values, beliefs, or expectations do you have that cause you to feel the way you do about the people participating in the conversation? What does your reaction to this interaction tell you about yourself?

   - Try to put yourself in the shoes of each of the people in the conversation. What values, beliefs, or expectations did each of them appear to have?

   - Use the chart "Questions to Consider When Analyzing the Factors" to further analyze the interaction.

   - Use the Descriptor Checklist to analyze the behaviors of the people in the interaction and how that behavior influenced the interaction and outcome. Look back at your answers to the questions above. What links do you make between behavior and deeper culture, between actions and intentions?

Source: Communication Highwire: Leveraging the Power of Diverse Communication Styles (Intercultural Press).
© 2005 Dianne Hofner Saphiere, Barbara Kappler Mikk, and Basma Ibrahim DeVries. All rights reserved.

THE FOUR-STEP METHOD WORKSHEET *(continued)*

3. **Discuss** (in small groups) the communication styles used in the interaction.

    - Take a moment to formulate a few questions you might ask of the people in the interaction. Attempt to describe the behavior you saw and the words you heard, and then try to figure out how the people intended their behavior. What motivated their behavior? Do you think your perceptions were correct? Was there more that you were missing?

    - Think about how you could ask your questions or obtain the characters' perspective most productively. How might you word your questions? In what order would you ask them? Might you say something up-front to contextualize your questions and intentions? How might you filter out your own judgments so that you could truly hear the other person's perspective?

    - You might try out some of these questions with a partner or small group to see their effects in real life.

THE FOUR-STEP METHOD WORKSHEET *(continued)*

4. **Decide** how to proceed, or brainstorm options for how those in the inter-action might proceed.
   - What could the people in the interaction do to more accurately interpret one another's communication style in the way it was intended?

   - What are some strategies that people in the interaction might have used to improve the accuracy and good feeling of their communication and collaboration?

   - In what ways might the people in the interaction have attempted to ex-pand their communication style repertoires? What new behaviors might they have tried?

   - What strengths did each of the people in the interaction possess? What potential value did they add to the interaction—talents or insights they want to take care not to lose?

   - How might the people in the interaction have more effectively used one another's strengths and unique contributions?

Next Steps

We have introduced you to three very different yet powerful tools for working with communication style: the factors presented in Chapter 3, the Descriptor Checklist in Chapter 6, and the Four-Step method in Chapter 7. You have had an opportunity to practice using each of these tools via activities, worksheets, journals, and dialogue.

Chapter 8 provides you with the opportunity to practice all three tools together, and Chapter 9 offers several more activities on the topic of communication style. This concluding section lets you and your colleagues master the tools contained in this book, and helps you refine your abilities to make full use of the assets that each of you bring to your organization or community.

Using the Factors and Descriptors

Practice Makes Perfect

You have been through an incredible circus journey! Chapter 7 gave you a process to tie it all together, the Four-Step method. In this chapter we provide you two more opportunities to practice applying the Factors and Descriptors to build your understanding, confidence, and fluency with them. The chapter has two in-depth examples accompanied by some questions. You may want to read through the "Factors and Descriptors Worksheet" first so that you know what to look for as you read each story. Then, as you read the stories you can write your answers to the questions on separate sheets of paper.

After you have spent some time working on each of these examples and questions, you may want to refer to our thoughts in the "Author Insight" section at the end of this chapter. These are not necessarily the "correct" answers, but they will help you understand our thinking. The goal, again, is exploration, dialogue, and reflection. No peeking!

ACTIVITY *15*: *Jintsuu*

Make copies of the "Questions to Consider When Analyzing the Factors" from Chapter 3, the Star Chart from Chapter 4, and the Descriptor Checklist from Chapter 6, along with the "Factors and Descriptors Worksheet" on that next page, to analyze the *Jintsuu* story.

Source: Communication Highwire: Leveraging the Power of Diverse Communication Styles (Intercultural Press).

FACTORS AND DESCRIPTORS WORKSHEET

Questions for reflection and analysis:

1. Explain the key factors in this scenario and how they affected the interaction. You may want to use the chart "Questions to Consider When Analyzing the Factors" and a copy of the Star Chart from Chapter 4 to aid you in your analysis.
2. Use the Descriptor Checklist to help you describe those differences that really seemed to make a difference in the interaction.
3. Use the Four-Step Method to gain insight into how the participants in the story could learn from this interaction and enhance their communication in the future.

Jintsuu

Six colleagues were enjoying after-work drinks in a bar in Tokyo: four Japanese men (including Hirose-san and Akiba-san), a Venezuelan man (Roberto), and a U.S. American woman (Judy). The colleagues had been working together for four years. The Japanese spoke English fairly well, the non-Japanese spoke Japanese quite fluently, and they all knew each other and enjoyed one another's company. The night's outing had no agenda other than enjoyment and relationship building. The group was seated around a low table, with a padded booth seat on one side and bar stools on the other. The following is an English translation of their conversation.

Judy: Speaking in Japanese, in a singsong voice, while playing with her drink, with her eye contact moving between the drink and the various members of the group, and with a smile on her face.

> *She was thinking:* I hope they are not going to think I am totally inane. This is a pretty stupid joke. My answer is a play on words, *nihonjin*, which means "Japanese person," or in a tricky way, can also mean "two bottles of gin." Hopefully it will get a laugh. And then everyone will start telling some riddles of their own. I love learning new ones.

"I have a riddle for you all. How do you order two gins in Japanese?"

> *She was feeling:* I am having a good time, and these guys are a lot of fun.

A short, two- to three-second pause.

Hirose-san: With a huge smile on his face and looking directly and in a sustained manner at the others, speaking the first syllable clearly, then holding up two fingers and loudly enunciating the final syllables.

> *He was thinking:* This is a good answer. I'm pretty clever. I know it's not what Judy had in mind.

"Jintsuu." (This literally means "labor/birthing pains," but is intended as a play on the English words *gin* and *two*.)

> *He was feeling:* I feel good about myself and how clever I am with Japanese word riddles. This is a fun group.

Everyone except Roberto: Spontaneous loud laughter.

Everyone except Roberto was thinking: Wow! Hirose-san was quick with that one! That's a great answer!

Everyone except Roberto was feeling: This is fun.

Roberto: Eventually joining in the laughter.

He was thinking: I get that *jintsuu* is "gin-two," but what else does the word mean?

He was feeling: Good, a chance to learn a new vocabulary word. I sure don't feel like I'm ever going to master this language.

Akiba-san: Speaking to Hirose-san while smiling mischievously.

"That's a great answer! Much better than what Judy was thinking! Jintsuu . . . . You are quick."

He was thinking: That's a very creative answer. It shows how even silly riddles can get interesting with the right people.

He was feeling: This is a good group.

Roberto: Speaking quickly, looking directly at Hirose-san, with almost no pause after Akiba-san's comments.

"What is jintsuu?"

He was thinking: I don't know that word; I have never heard it before. It sure must make for a funny joke.

He was feeling: I want to laugh, too. I want to know what it means.

Source: Communication Highwire: Leveraging the Power of Diverse Communication Styles (Intercultural Press).

Hirose-san: Inhaling air audibly through his teeth, turning his head sideways and making a grimace with his face.

"Yes, hmmm . . . jintsuu . . . ."

He was thinking: Oh no. This is going to get embarrassing. Maybe I wasn't so clever. How in the world am I going to explain *jintsuu*?

He was feeling: I am embarrassed and confused. I am not sure what to say. I hope I can find a way to explain.

Everyone except Roberto: Sitting quietly. A couple of people smiling; a few wrinkling their brows.

They were thinking: Explain *jintsuu* to Roberto? This is such a typical difficulty when communicating across language differences.

They were feeling: We don't want Roberto to feel left out. Defining *jintsuu* is going to be difficult. We don't know if anyone could do it.

Akiba-san: After a quiet pause of four or five seconds, Akiba-san leans back against the padded back of the booth, lifting his right hand and arm and laying it across the back of the seat, his grimace shifts into a slight smile.

"My wife's name is Hiroko. We met at university; we were both on the tennis team."

He was thinking: I've got an idea now. I'll be able to explain Hirose-san's joke to Roberto.

He was feeling: Excitement. Anticipation.

Everyone, including Roberto: Another round of laughter.

They were thinking: This is going to be a long, detailed story! Akiba-san's communication is not the clearest; will he be able to do this?

They were feeling: This is going to be funny and interesting.

Source: Communication Highwire: Leveraging the Power of Diverse Communication Styles (Intercultural Press).
© 2005 Dianne Hofner Saphiere, Barbara Kappler Mikk, and Basma Ibrahim DeVries. All rights reserved.

<u>Roberto:</u> Watching
Akiba-san quite intently.

> **He was thinking:** So, *jintsuu* must mean
> "courtship" or "dating." Or, perhaps it means
> "university-love . . . ."

> **He was feeling:** Curiosity.
> Eagerness.

<u>Judy:</u> Looking at her watch
to see what time the story was
beginning.

> **She was thinking:**
> Oh my, this is going to be a
> long, detailed story, and I'll bet there
> will be no clear definition at the
> end!

> **She was feeling:**
> This is going to be fun.

<u>The Japanese:</u> Bemused smiles
on their faces, watching Akiba-san
and sipping their drinks;
intermittently chuckling.

> **They were thinking:** Akiba's never
> going to be able to explain this.

> **They were feeling:** He's always so con-
> fident of his storytelling; it ought to
> be interesting.

<u>Akiba-san:</u> Speaking intently,
explaining in detail to Roberto
for twenty-three minutes.

> **He was thinking:**
> Roberto seems to be following
> me; he'll understand. Everyone
> seems to be enjoying my story.

*"Our first date was at a coffee
shop . . . . I proposed marriage to
her in. . . . We were married at . . . .
We rented an apartment at . . . ."*

> **He was feeling:** I'm
> enjoying these old memories.

Source: Communication Highwire: Leveraging the Power of Diverse Communication Styles (Intercultural Press).
© 2005 Dianne Hofner Saphiere, Barbara Kappler Mikk, and Basma Ibrahim DeVries. All rights reserved.

Roberto: Listening quietly, looking at Akiba-san, his drink, and the others at the table. Fidgeting with his drink.

He was thinking: Now I'm really confused. I have no idea what *jintsuu* means. Why is Akiba-san telling me his life story?

He was feeling: I am getting really tired of this; can't he just get to the point?

Everyone else: Watching the interaction with slight smiles, briefly asking a few questions for clarification, making a few supportive comments as Akiba-san is talking.

They were thinking: Akiba sure loves to tell stories. He's really trying to explain this to Roberto. There's no way he's going to be able to.

They were feeling: He is so funny. It's wonderful how much he loves his wife. We empathize with his difficulty, but we're not sure how to help, either.

Akiba-san: Leaning forward in his seat, speaking a little bit louder on these last sentences, gesturing with his hands indicating a baby coming out.

"Hiroko got pregnant . . . and on December 13 our first son, Tatsuaki, was born."

He was thinking: I did a pretty good job of explaining that. Roberto no doubt now understands what *jintsuu* means.

He was feeling: That was fun and helpful.

Roberto: Puzzled expression on his face.

"Well, that's all interesting, but what is **jintsuu?**

> **He was thinking:**
> What the heck is *jintsuu*? I still have no idea. Why can't he just tell me what it means? I keep asking and that's the best way to learn vocabulary.

> **He was feeling:**
> Exasperation.

Everyone else:
Peals of laughter.

> **They were thinking:** If we let Akiba-san answer Roberto's question, he's going to start all over again! We have to interrupt and give a direct definition. At least Roberto should ask a question about the birth—where Akiba-san left off—to get us closer to the answer and spare us another long story.

> **They were feeling:** Oh no, we can't sit here for another twenty-three minute story! We've got to put an end to this; it was fun while it lasted.

> **Akiba-san was thinking:** This fun joke is turning into misery. I do wish Roberto would understand already!

> **Akiba-san was feeling:** I may have to say more—that makes me feel stressed.

Judy: Looking directly
at Roberto, and switching to English.

*"Jintsuu means 'labor pains'—
like when giving birth to a child."*

She was thinking: Poor Roberto. We've got to just let him know what it means and get on with it. We don't want to miss the last train home—it's an expensive taxi ride.

She was feeling: I've had enough of this trip down memory lane.

Japanese colleagues' and Roberto's internal thoughts: Oh, that's how you say *jintsuu* in English!

Everyone else: Laughing,
fidgeting.

Japanese colleagues' internal feelings: Relief that they didn't have to search for how to explain the word.

Use the Factors and Descriptors Worksheet to analyze and interpret the *Jintsuu* story.

Source: Communication Highwire: Leveraging the Power of Diverse Communication Styles (Intercultural Press).

ACTIVITY *16:* That's Undemocratic!

Make copies of the "Questions to Consider When Analyzing the Factors" from Chapter 3, the Star Chart from Chapter 4, and the Descriptor Checklist from Chapter 6, along with the "Factors and Descriptors Worksheet" to analyze the "That's Undemocratic!" story.

Source: Communication Highwire: Leveraging the Power of Diverse Communication Styles (Intercultural Press). © 2005 Dianne Hofner Saphiere, Barbara Kappler Mikk, and Basma Ibrahim DeVries. All rights reserved.

That's Undemocratic!

This example took place during a cross-cultural awareness and skill development training session designed for one hundred faculty from Eurasia who had been competitively selected to come for one year of professional development at a U.S. university. One day during this ten-day training, at the end of a session, participants were to be given the opportunity to sign up for evening events. The morning lecture session, held in a large auditorium, had ended late, leaving little time for the event sign-up to take place right before lunch. Since the goal of the events was to get the nearly 100 participants into smaller groups, providing them with the opportunity to network with each other and to enjoy an outing in the U.S.A., each event had limited space. The participants were told they would have a choice of events, but that they might not get their first choice. Rather than have participants sign up on a first-come first-served basis, the facilitators decided to give out random numbers from 1 to 100 and have participants sign up in the order of the number received. When the sign-up began, facilitators called out numbers one to ten to begin the process. Instead of ten people with numbers one to ten standing up, approximately fifteen participants with varying numbers rushed to the sign-up sheets, and approximately ten others came forward to speak to the facilitators. Several others shouted out questions to the facilitators and to each other. Amidst all of this, a participant, Elena, approached Mary, the program director, and the following exchange took place. During this exchange, three other participants were waiting to talk to Mary.

<u>Elena:</u> Looking the program director in the eye when speaking and maintaining steady eye contact, with a tight facial expression, as if clenching her teeth, and speaking louder than in previous conversations.

"This is not fair! This is not a democracy! I do not get my choice!"

Elena was thinking: Because this is so unfair, I must say something. Because Mary is the program director, I should tell her what I think. It's okay to be critical because the staff is always asking for feedback. It's important that she know this experience did not meet my expectations. This should have happened a different way.

Elena was feeling: I am frustrated. If the U.S. really promotes equal opportunity and democracy, these people should run their programs in a better way. This program director should change her ways.

<u>Mary, Program Director:</u> Stepping forward to be closer to the participant, not smiling, and looking directly at the participant.

"Tell me why this is not democratic."

Mary was thinking: I am going to give a directive, rather than ask a question or apologize for the sign-up process. I anticipated this reaction from some participants and this is an important learning moment.

Mary was feeling: Wow; she's angry! I forgot how it feels to be yelled at like this. Ugh! I am frustrated that the process did not work—even though I knew it was a risk. To be told this is unfair is really insulting.

<u>Elena:</u> Responding in the same tone as with the first statement, with the exception that the final words are spoken slightly louder and with more conviction.

"If I have a choice, then I get to go where I want. And I cannot. That's undemocratic!"

Elena was thinking: It's clear what is wrong.

Elena was feeling: I am getting more frustrated. It's obvious what is wrong. But I also feel glad that she is talking to me about this. "That's undemocratic" came out easily because it's something I say and hear a lot at home when I want to express the irony of a situation.

<u>Mary:</u> Maintaining eye contact but not raising her voice to match Elena's, and smiling slightly when saying "Oh!"

"Oh! I have a different view of choice. To me, it does not mean getting what you want; it is having some choice in options. There were a variety of options presented to you."

Mary was thinking: I am trying to acknowledge that this is the heart of the difference.

Mary was feeling: Interesting! I am understanding something exciting here!

Source: Communication Highwire: Leveraging the Power of Diverse Communication Styles (Intercultural Press).

Elena: Gathering up her materials to leave for lunch. Less sustained eye contact, and with the same volume and pitch as her last statements.

"It is undemocratic. This should not happen in the U.S."

Elena was thinking: The program director is not making sense. Either I am right or she is. And I don't think I'm wrong! It's time to go to lunch. Why didn't she see that I'm pointing out the irony of this happening in her country—I'm not personally insulting her? And all this for a silly night out. I'm here to do important work—not to go out and have some fun.

Elena was feeling: I can't believe it! Why does she try to make this into cross-cultural differences? It is about what's the best way to do things.

Mary: Moving her head down to try to get eye contact with Elena and changing her voice slightly to sound firmer.

"I would like you to consider your strong reactions and why this is so upsetting to you."

Mary was thinking: I am not going to apologize and I am not backing down. I see something here that she doesn't. I need to challenge her to see it.

Mary was feeling: Did I cross a line here by pushing this? She's not interested in what I am saying. The conversation is over. I'm overwhelmed at her expression of emotion and relieved this might end soon.

The exchange ended when the participant left the room. Another participant standing nearby during the exchange commented, "If we didn't have choice, you should just have signed us up for events yourself."

Author Insights *Jintsuu*

Note: In debriefing this example, we received direct input from all of the participants, and therefore the comments here reflect their actual thoughts and feelings.

Question 1: Factors from Chapter 3

CONTEXT

1. Physical context: A bar, at night, group in a circle, in Tokyo, Japan. The physical environment was important as it led to a shared assumption that the goal of the evening was to have fun and get to know one another better. Thus, the power dynamics and the hierarchy of these colleagues were not extremely important in this physical setting on this night.

2. Roles: They were colleagues who worked with one another. The expectations regarding the colleagues' roles in this bar setting were very different from their respective roles in the office. In this setting, the expectations of one another were to be friendly and have a good time.

3. Historical context: The shared histories and their perceptions of the cultural groups interacting did not directly impact this scenario.

4. Chronology: The people in the story all had ongoing business relationships with one another. They worked for the same company and had known each other for at least four years. They had not previously discussed this specific topic.

5. Language: Language was at the center of this example. The participants had no language in which they shared complete fluency. There were four native Japanese speakers who also spoke English, with varying levels of fluency; Roberto was a native Spanish speaker who was fairly but not completely fluent in Japanese (since he didn't know the word *jintsuu*); Judy was a native English speaker who spoke Japanese and Spanish. Akiba's English was not very good. As such, language completely dominated the flow of the conversation as Roberto continued to ask for an explanation of *jintsuu*. In turn, language affected the experience of the evening in that it potentially interfered with the goal of the evening (see notes in the "Goals" section).

6. Relationship: As mentioned in the explanation of physical context, the physical setting had a significant impact on the relationship here. This group of friends/colleagues were out to enjoy the evening. They had known each other for four years. The specific status relationship was that Roberto was the overall boss, with Hirose, a department manager, being the most senior beneath him. Akiba, an independent contributor, also reported to Roberto. The two remaining Japanese were a section chief (who reported to Akiba) and a lower-level employee (who reported to the section chief). Judy was an external human resources/training contract employee, unrelated to the formal hierarchy.

7. Constraints: One important constraint was making the last train home. While certain participants may have *felt* constrained in what behavioral options they had available to them, these types of constraints reflected the values involved in the interaction (see notes on values later in this section).

GOALS

The dynamic was that of a typical Japanese after-hours drinking session with work colleagues. The main goal shared by all was to enjoy the evening. A way to reach this goal was to have some fun with jokes and language riddles and thus share humor. For Roberto, the goal became to understand the joke in the same way that others understood it. In this way, Roberto's goal differed from the others in that he wanted to ensure he was a part of the group and understanding this joke became one small way—in his own mind—to test his membership.

Judy sensed that Roberto's goal of understanding the joke was potentially interfering with the goal of having fun. Thus, Judy wanted the stories to stop so they could all be enjoying the conversation; she sensed the others' discomfort and wanted to release Akiba from what she had rightfully understood was becoming a misery for him. In addition, she also wanted the conversation to return to some sense of balance—Akiba had talked for a long time while everyone else had listened.

SELF-CONCEPT

While the new "answer" to the joke was greeted with glee, the Japanese men were slightly embarrassed and hesitant to talk about the "personal" and "female" nature of *jintsuu* (labor pains). This awkwardness probably resulted in a more circular style than normal. Also, because Akiba-san was enjoying telling his own story, the "definition" became longer and longer.

Roberto saw himself as skilled at language acquisition (he spoke English and Spanish completely fluently, he spoke several other languages, including Japanese, fairly well), and he was an eager lifelong learner. Thus, he grabbed the opportunity to learn a new vocabulary word. While this situation may have left some people doubting his language skills, Roberto was still feeling good about himself because he was asking questions and considered himself to be inquisitive.

Judy saw herself in this interaction primarily as a facilitator of group process. She was attempting to keep things lively, help the conversation flow smoothly, and help all of the people at the table participate comfortably. Judy's view of herself differed from her prescribed role in the situation in that she was not viewed by others, nor was it assigned to her, to be the facilitator.

VALUES

This case clearly illustrates conflicting personal values.

- *Politeness.* In this situation, all involved valued the Japanese norm that it is not polite to interrupt a story. At the same time, permitting a friend to suffer is rude, and Akiba was struggling. Others wanted to help but they were caught in these two conflicting desires.
- *Face.* The notion of "face" was involved in that they did not want to make English mistakes (while trying to save Akiba) or look stupid and become embarrassed.
- *Appropriate topics of conversation.* The subject of birth was uncomfortable for a group of Japanese male work colleagues, though none of them had a command of the necessary vocabulary even if they had wanted to quickly interpret *jintsuu* into English. While they were fairly fluent in work-related English, they were not as fluent in this sort of English.
- *Insider/Outsider.* Despite the strong relationships among these colleagues, the value placed on being an insider may have come into play for the Japanese. Even though the group was at a bar and in an after-hours drinking setting,

there were two foreigners, one of whom was a woman, so the Japanese may have felt it was still a "formal," not completely *uchi* (insider) situation. They still had a fair amount of *enryo* (hesitation or discomfort) about discussing *jintsuu*, which was very personal in nature.

- *Relationships.* Predominant in this situation for all participants was the importance of relationship, to get to know one another better personally and to form a good group feeling or atmosphere. They also had a task orientation—to define the term *jintsuu* for Roberto. The Japanese had a stronger value on enjoying the process as it unfolded, as compared to Roberto in particular.

COMMUNICATION STYLE REPERTOIRE

Communication style repertoires were the key issue in this scenario. Akiba-san was using a background-first, circular storytelling style; indeed, many Japanese like to give the context of a story before getting to the main point. Frequently, the speaker may not even state the main point, believing that it is obvious, since he has so carefully taken the listener to the exact location in which to find the answer. To many Japanese, the explicit verbal statement is not necessary and can seem to disrespect the listener, as if talking to a child. Roberto in this case was looking for an explicit definition; he wanted to understand the riddle's punch line and to learn a new vocabulary word.

Since Roberto wanted an explicit answer and was probably growing agitated and increasingly confused, he would have been wise to ask a different question at the point when Akiba-san had stopped, rather than repeating his initial question. Roberto could have asked, for example, "So *jintsuu* means 'having a son'?" Then, Akiba-san may have answered explicitly or, if he had answered in a circular style, the two would have been much closer to shared understanding.

Judy's repertoire was very broad in this situation. She was able to see that Roberto was becoming distressed about his inability to understand, and that Akiba-san was becoming distressed by his inability to explain. These negative emotions were conflicting with the goal of the evening, which was for everyone to enjoy being together. Judy understood the emotions and was able to determine when it was appropriate to use an explicit explanation.

Question 2: Descriptors from Chapter 6—Differences That Made a Difference

The following comments reflect descriptors that seemed to have the most impact on the interaction.

- Hirose-san was using storytelling (Descriptor 2c) to express his meaning, and everyone shared the expectation that Hirose would speak until he finished his story (Descriptors 3a and 3b). The location of meaning for Hirose-san was implied (Descriptor 6a), while Roberto expected a more explicit definition with clear links between the story and the definition of *jintsuu* (Descriptor 2e).
- Judy's smile (Descriptor 5b) and singsong voice (Descriptor 4a): These behaviors indicated playfulness. These behaviors communicated her intention.
- Hirose-san's huge smile (Descriptor 5b) and enunciation (Descriptors 4a and 4b): Indicated pride in a good answer. Communicated his intention.
- Everyone's laughter: Indicated approval of Hirose-san's answer/enjoyment. Communicated their intention.
- Roberto's laughter: Meant that he didn't understand but was trying to fit in with the group mood. Didn't communicate his meaning—others thought he understood the joke.
- Akiba-san's mischievous smile (Descriptor 5b): Signaled his enjoyment at giving Judy a hard time, good-naturedly. Communicated his intention.
- Roberto's direct eye contact (Descriptor 5a) and quick speech (Descriptor 4b): Indicated that he didn't want to interfere with the group mood but wanted to understand. Communicated his intention.
- Akiba's "air inhale" (Descriptor 4d): Indicated embarrassment and difficulty/confusion. Communicated his intention. There was a gap in expected degree of preparation (Descriptor 2d) here, in that Akiba-san found it difficult to respond "off the cuff" or without preparation, while Roberto didn't expect it to be so difficult. There was also difficulty around nature of topics discussed (Descriptor 7a), since labor pains aren't exactly normal "male" terrain.
- Akiba's leaning back (Descriptor 5g) and grimacing (Descriptor 5b): Indicated he was about to commence a long and difficult story. His level of

self-disclosure (Descriptor 7b) also indicated his desire to help Roberto understand. Communicated his intention.

- Roberto's question: Indicated a direct and linear style (Descriptor 2c), and that he expected an explicit answer to his question (Descriptor 6a). This was the difference that made a difference in this story—Akiba-san was unable to respond in a manner that communicated meaning to Roberto, so he just did his best, winding around the main point with his story.

- Judy's looking at her watch (Descriptors 3a, 5c, and 6a): Signaled she knew there was a major gap in communication going on, and that she was thinking about intervening. Communicated her intention.

- Akiba's intentness (from Descriptors 5a, 5b, and 5g): Indicated he was trying his best to communicate meaning to Roberto. Communicated his intention.

- Akiba's gestures (Descriptor 5c), louder volume (Descriptor 4c), and forward lean (Descriptors 5d and 5g) at the end of his story: Indicated that he had arrived at his main point, even though he did not state that main point verbally (Descriptor 6a). This was the other side of the difference that made a difference. Showed he was giving an implied answer to Roberto's question. Communicated his intention to everyone except Roberto, who was not sure how to clarify.

- Roberto's puzzled expression (Descriptor 5b): Indicated that now that he had taken all this time and ruined the enjoyable mood of the evening, he really wanted to understand the meaning of the term *jintsuu*. He wanted it direct, explicit, and now (Descriptor 6a)! Communicated his intention to everyone, but the Japanese felt unable to answer in the manner required.

Question 3: Four-Step Method from Chapter 7

In this scenario, it was probably Roberto who would have benefited the most from applying the Four-Step method. Why? Roberto didn't understand that his desire to gain vocabulary was conflicting with the overall goal for the evening, nor did he understand that there was a way to meet his own goal as well as that of the group. If Roberto *reflected* upon his discomfort in not reaching his goals more quickly or directly, he might have found more patience and flexibility, and might have been able to relax and enjoy the process. Second, if Roberto were to *analyze* and *discuss* the situation with Judy or his Japanese colleagues, he could develop an understanding of the communication style strategy of asking questions in such a manner that the entire story would not need to be retold. Finally, if Roberto could *decide* how he could adapt his repertoire to include this question-asking skill, he would be able to meet his needs, as well as the group's goal of enjoying the evening without placing undue stress on his colleagues.

Author Insights, *That's Undemocratic!*

Note: In debriefing this example, we received direct input from Mary, the program director, and therefore we know what her thoughts and feelings were. Our insights about Elena come from several Ukrainians and experts in the area and thus reflect assumptions about the participant.

Question 1: Factors from Chapter 3

CONTEXT

1. Physical context: A large auditorium (seats 185) on a university campus in the United States.
2. Roles: Mary, the program director, designed the program format, was responsible for the training process, and was the decision maker about the intercultural content and process. She was not faculty, but rather was a professional staff member of the university. Participants were competitively selected, so it was a great honor to be a participant. She was a university faculty member in Ukraine. In academia, deans and department heads have the highest status, followed by faculty. Since the program director was not faculty, Elena may not have viewed Mary as having much status, or she may have had some confusion about Mary's status because a comparable position may not exist in her institution.
3. Historical context: The cultural history has two components. First, there is much discussion throughout Eurasia about whether it is okay to like U.S. Americans, but it is generally not viewed as favorable to *be* like one. As a result, it is very acceptable to criticize and to resist U.S. approaches. Second,

there is often frustration among the faculty that their dramatic reforms in education are not acknowledged when they come to the U.S.A., nor are the accomplishments they achieved within the Soviet system. Therefore, Elena may well have been engaging in the interaction from a position of distrust and resentment. The comment "That's undemocratic" reflected some of this history.

4. Chronology: This was day four of a ten-day orientation program for the visiting faculty. At the end of the ten-day program, the faculty would travel to their U.S. universities for the academic year. Elena and Mary did not know each other well, yet by this point in the program their roles were clear.

5. Language: The majority of the program, as well as the cross-cultural awareness pieces and the directions for this specific activity, were conducted in English. The sign-up instructions may not have been clear to Elena due to linguistic and cultural barriers.

6. Relationship: Mary and Elena had met for the program each day, but because of the size of the group, had only personally exchanged a few words, a few questions, and responses.

8. Constraints: This session to get the participants signed up began a bit late and was therefore rushed. Also, lunch immediately followed the sign-up process, so people were hungry.

GOALS

Elena's main goal in talking to the program director was to point out the problem. While an ideal outcome would have been for Mary to change the sign-up system, this outcome was not truly expected. For Mary the main goal was to have Elena recognize that there were undoubtedly cultural differences involved. As the conversation unfolded, Mary wanted Elena to see that the heart of the problem was a different perception about "choice." Mary's ultimate goals were:

1. to have Elena and the other participants process what it felt like to experience the difference and to understand (not necessarily accept) why a U.S. American might develop this type of sign-up system;

2. to have the participants sign up for the evening events (as a result of this

sign-up outcome, the process was repeated the following day, followed by a debriefing of the overall sign-up process); and

3. to give participants a chance to experience a "choice-making" process that they would likely encounter at U.S. universities.

SELF-CONCEPT

Elena thought, "If I don't argue and express myself, who am I?" She expected the program director to take more responsibility for having a better process. Elena was still experiencing jet lag. Also, she knew she was in the U.S.A. for a fairly short time and therefore felt impatient to experience a great deal in a short amount of time. She was not expecting to have fun during the orientation; she would have preferred to go to a work-related event during the evening.

While preferring in general to avoid conflict, Mary needed to challenge herself to hold her ground. She viewed her job as helping the faculty understand and process their reactions to U.S. culture, not trying to make them happy. This program's goal was to help the faculty understand the U.S. system, so while many accommodations were made during the program, having the faculty experience dealing with choice seemed to be a critical element for their preparation. In addition, there was the practical matter that the faculty had to get signed up for these evening events in a timely manner. There were limited spaces for each of the events. It was frustrating and a bit demeaning that the process did not work the first time and had to be repeated the next day.

Also, Mary had many years of experience working with people from countries of the former Soviet Union, and this interaction represented just one among many. Thus, she anticipated some problems and had learned that to back down and apologize for the action was not going to help her credibility and, more important, would not help the participant six months later when she might be struggling with U.S. American culture.

VALUES

Some of the key values potentially involved for Elena were as follows:

- *Maintain her identity.* Elena felt that it was important not to accept U.S. American values as her own; she wanted to ensure that she didn't become too Americanized during her year in the U.S.A.

- *High-power distance.* She expected to be treated according to her status. Elena was a distinguished faculty member and considered it an honor to have been selected for the program. In addition, she did not quite know how to view the program director, who was not a faculty member, but she did not view her as an equal.
- *Work before play.* Elena regarded entertainment as secondary to the role of work. She expected to work hard during this week at the program and wasn't really interested in participating in these events "just for the experience" or "just for fun." "No wonder," she thought, "that U.S. Americans are often not taken seriously—they treat everything as if it were a game."
- *Literal interpretations.* Elena remembered that Mary had said on the first day of the program that she was interested in reactions to the program and that she would welcome suggestions at any time, so Elena felt that now she had some feedback to share.
- *Interpretation of the concept of democracy.* Elena regarded the discussion of democracy as a contentious topic in Ukraine. While Ukrainians differ greatly on their opinion of what a true democracy should mean and be, Elena felt that democracy should mean a complete freedom of choice.

Some of the key values involved for Mary were as follows:

- *Obedience.* Mary believed that when a process is explained, it should be followed, and while disagreements are fine, ultimately the participants should follow the process she described.
- *Flexibility.* She wanted the participants to get to know other faculty at these events and to enjoy life in the U.S.A. outside of the classroom. Mary felt that it was important for the participants to be flexible and go and simply enjoy the events.
- *Harmony.* Mary considered the best way to express disagreements was with questions and concerns, not with demands or with pointing out flaws so quickly.
- *Friendliness does not mean laissez-faire.* Mary had never intended to portray the program as democratic. Decisions were made in advance, and while she took

the faculty's opinions into account, she had not intended on changing this process by vote or by hearing the faculty's views. While Mary was open and friendly, that did not mean she would jump to change things merely because the participants wanted her to change them.

COMMUNICATION STYLE REPERTOIRE

Elena was tapping into a skill repertoire that told her to take on a confrontational style to demonstrate the emotions she felt about this incident. When growing up in Ukraine, she learned that it is not insulting to be confrontational and, in fact, this can help avoid conflict. Within this framework, it was important not to back down from this disagreement. Thus she used this style while defending her arguments, with irony and sarcasm, about U.S. American democracy. When the conversation appeared to be over, when there was nothing more to say, leaving the room was the best option. She sensed that the program director was frustrated with her honesty, but she didn't know that Mary perceived her as angry. Elena was friendly during the next days and even gave a big hug to Mary at the airport, feeling no clash between the disagreement over the sign-up and her friendly nature toward the director.

Mary was balancing meta-level processing (trying to get to the heart of the difference), self-monitoring (thinking about how her behaviors were interpreted), and style switching (moving out of her comfort zone and engaging in the conflict).

Mary had several years of experience working with what seemed to her as a very direct and confrontational style. That was why she stepped in—to actually engage in the argument rather than step back and cool down. Elena, recognizing that Mary was engaging in the argument, continued her role and did not back down.

However, later in the program, Mary was surprised when she realized she had underestimated how much her own style had influenced her perception of the participant. Much to Mary's surprise, Elena did not seem to hold any grudge against her and, in contrast to Mary's expectations, Elena was quite warm and friendly. Thus, while Mary was able to switch behaviors and "act" in the other style, she did not fully understand the ramifications of the style, and she was not personally comfortable with it. In short, she had overestimated Elena's anger and missed the possibility that the key statement "That's undemocratic" reflected Elena's view of irony in the situation, and had continued to judge Elena from a very relational-style orientation. When the two parted at the airport, Elena hugged Mary and was very teary-eyed. While this reaction was not uncommon among the participants, Mary was not expecting it from Elena.

In this example, the communication style repertoire of the program director was perhaps the most critical factor in that it led to her developing a better understanding of the interpretation of the word *choice* and the values placed on this word. This revelation was helpful when Mary facilitated a debriefing on the participants' reactions to the sign-up activity: she used this information to ask questions about the participants' perspectives on choice, to share her viewpoint, to invite other U.S. Americans to share their interpretations, and to plant a seed about how emotional reactions can be a sign of encountering cultural differences.

Question 2: Descriptors from Chapter 6—Differences that Made a Difference

The following comments reflect descriptors that seemed to make the most impact on the interaction.

- Elena's direct and sustained eye contact (Descriptor 5a), tight facial expression (Descriptor 5b), and loudness (Descriptor 4c): These behaviors indicated a desire to express an opinion. There was probably a gap in expectations about beginning a conversation (Descriptor 1a).
- Elena saying "This is not fair": Indicated the passion and importance of her feelings (Descriptors 14a and 14b) and conversation movement (Descriptor 10). Communicated her intention.
- Mary's repositioning herself to move closer to Elena to speak face-to-face (Descriptors 5a and 5d): Indicated a desire to continue the conversation. Communicated her intention.
- Elena's enhanced volume (Descriptor 4c) and conviction (Descriptor 4a): Indicated strong belief in being right and communicated her intention. Mary interpreted the treatment of the emotion to be on the surface (Descriptor 8b). As Mary's preferred way to treat emotion would be reserved reactions (Descriptor 8a), this was a place of much discomfort for the director, and her

continuing to ask questions was possibly due to her history (context factor) with participants from this region of the world.

- Mary's slight smile (Descriptor 5b) and "calm" voice (Descriptor 4a): Indicated Mary's professionalism and control of the situation. Probably did not communicate her intention—Elena probably thought Mary was being superficially friendly and thus insincere.

- Elena's gathering her materials to leave (Descriptor 5g) and diverted eye contact (Descriptor 5a): Indicated that Elena had said what she wanted to say and was ready to finish the conversation with clear sense of closure (Descriptor 1b). Communicated her meaning.

- Mary's attempt to get eye contact (Descriptor 5a) and firmer voice (Descriptor 4a): Indicated she wanted to continue the dialogue. With Elena already having ended the conversation, this meaning was probably not communicated at this time. The revisiting of the topic and Mary's asking of questions on subsequent days may have been more effective in continuing the dialogue than any specific behaviors during this exchange.

Question 3: Four-Step Method from Chapter 7

In this example, the Four-Step method was critical for the program director in three significant ways. First, Mary *reflected* on and *analyzed* her past experiences before this program began, and thus she was somewhat prepared for this particular interaction. She further analyzed the interaction with fellow staff members, including representatives from Elena's home country. Mary then *discussed* aspects of the interaction with the entire group, gaining additional understanding of the participants' perspectives on choice. During that debriefing, while she *decided* for the group what the sign-up process would be, she gave more information about why the sign-up procedure was designed the way it was.

The second way was that Mary directly invited the participants to engage in the Four-Step method: She asked them to consider their reactions as an opportunity to *reflect* and *analyze* and then to *discuss* their experiences with staff. Ultimately, they each needed to *decide* how to come to terms with communication style differences they encountered during their stay in the U.S.A.

Of course, in many ways the Four-Step method never quite ends. The final way in which it was applied was that the program director, when asked to submit this example for this book, shared this story with many people from Eurasia. Having the example written down provided a profound opportunity to further *reflect* on not simply what occurred but also on others' reactions to this example. One respondent was critical in helping Mary to further *analyze* the comment "That's undemocratic" and come to understand the role of irony in the interaction. This analysis involved *discussing* the history and the use of irony and required Mary to be open to new interpretations. All of this information and understanding influenced the sign-up process used later in this program, and moreover left Mary to *decide* how to proceed in the future about her own communication style.

We hope that the two stories in this chapter, your analysis, and our own thoughts have reconfirmed for you the power of communication style. If we take the time and effort and use the tools presented in this book, from a simple miscommunication we can learn a lot about ourselves, the other person (or people), and the communication process and enhance our future collaborative competence.

CHAPTER 9

More Activities

Taking the Show on the Road!

This book has provided you a variety of models, methods, and tools for harvesting the potential that communication style provides. We invite you and those with whom you live and work to continue developing your communication style competence by using the additional 10 activities described in this chapter. With motivation and skills, you will be able to distinguish the elephant from the mosquito (or the mountain from the molehill) from multiple points of view. Using these activities and those you have already completed, you will be able to give a mesmerizing communication highwire performance.

ACTIVITY *17:* When Styles Are Out of Sync

Objectives: Participants will learn what communication style differences are, and they will recognize when differences become a "hot button" for themselves and for a group. Participants will be able to explore these questions: When have communication styles been out of sync? How do I recognize when communication style differences are making a difference?

Assumptions/Theory Inherent in the Activity: Communication style factors and the Descriptor Checklist as presented in Chapters 3 and 6.

Time Frame: 30 minutes to 2 hours, depending on the depth of facilitation.

Parameters: This activity works well after a presentation about communication style differences, including an introduction to the factors in Chapter 3 and the Descriptor Checklist in Chapter 6.

Materials, Supplies, and Handouts: The handouts "When Styles Are Out of Sync" (at the end of this activity)

Trainer Preparation: If you have had previous experience with the group, consider carefully what types of communication style differences they may have encountered. Consider how to incorporate your insights into the group's reporting of communication style differences.

How to Facilitate:
1. Begin by asking participants to reflect on the question, "When have you encountered communication styles being out of sync in this group?" Then ask them to record their thoughts.
2. Have participants pair up and share their experiences.
3. Collect responses from the group and record these on a whiteboard or flipchart paper.
4. Ask the group to review this list of responses and ask what strikes them about the list. What commonalities are there about the experiences? What differences?

Source: Communication Highwire: Leveraging the Power of Diverse Communication Styles (Intercultural Press).

5. Ask the participants to go back to their initial notes and consider, "How did you know that communication style differences were making a difference?"

6. At this point, revisit the factors and the Descriptor Checklist and have a free-flowing conversation about how these could have come into play in the experiences. For example, you may note that most of the experiences involve a value difference. Ask the group to consider why this may be the case. Or perhaps there are specific behavioral differences that seem to have the biggest impact, such as how conversations are started or what constitutes evidence. This may lead into a conversation about what the (perhaps unstated) group norms and rules are.

Tips: Be prepared to probe with questions to help facilitate the group's learning—this activity is an exploration with no right or wrong answers.

Adaptations: These questions can be used as assessment material with clients.

WHEN STYLES ARE OUT OF SYNC

When trying to determine if communication style is the factor causing difficulty in an interaction, it is helpful to explore the various ways that communication style conflicts may come into play. We have divided these into three categories: one-on-one interactions, groups, and the relationship between process and individual expectations. These three levels build on and dovetail with one another; they are not distinct and separate things. The following tips may indicate that misunderstanding could be due to communication style differences.

- Styles are out of sync in one-on-one interactions:
    1. One party will not let go of an issue or topic, perhaps repeating it several times in varying ways. This could be a method to indicate the topic's importance, a sign that the speaker does not feel heard or appropriately acknowledged, and/or that the speaker expects you to ask questions about the topic to understand the point in more depth.
    2. A communicator seems to suddenly shift style, consciously or unconsciously. This can happen even in a quick interaction in a store: a friendly clerk suddenly becomes "official" or "professional" or a vivacious talker suddenly falls silent and thoughtful.
    3. Someone appears confused or has a "blank" face. The person may be wondering what point you are trying to make, what your real message is, or is shocked at what she thinks she is hearing.
    4. Conversations with a particular person frequently leave you exhausted. Perhaps you hesitate to complain because you know it will require so much energy to communicate what you want.
    5. Tension permeates the communication climate and strains the communication process. Each party seems superficially cheerful and cautious or perhaps angry and agitated.
    6. Communicators seem to avoid face-to-face interaction, avoid certain conversational topics that elicit difficult communication styles, appear

WHEN STYLES ARE OUT OF SYNC *(continued)*

to limit nonverbal cues while focusing on verbal aspects, or seem to emotionally or psychologically "check out" of a conversation.

7. One party uses exaggerated compensatory behaviors, whether consciously or subconsciously, as a response to the communication style of another person. Perhaps the person speaks more loudly or gestures more profusely.

8. Two individuals are in agreement, but they don't recognize it. Others need to point their agreement out to them.

- Styles are out of sync in a group:

1. Someone who seemed committed to an issue stops attending group meetings, or someone who was doing a lot of work starts doing visibly less.

2. A member of a group expresses that she must "stop being herself" and learn to communicate like everyone else.

3. A group member speaks and other group members roll their eyes or show other behaviors of discontent.

4. When asked to work on a project together, people resist or are hesitant, even if they agree on the main goal.

- There is a mismatch between the process and the expectations of the participants:

1. A process is described and yet what is explained does not happen. For example, a meeting is proclaimed to be a place where "people can speak their minds," but very little disagreement occurs openly at the meeting. Then, when the meeting ends, there are many side conversations disagreeing with decisions made during the meeting.

2. A group member complains about the group's decision making; for example, it is too quick or does not take into account important information.

Source: Communication Highwire: Leveraging the Power of Diverse Communication Styles (Intercultural Press).

ACTIVITY *18:* Cultural Shifts/Communication Shifts

Objectives: Participants will be able to see the changes over time of what are considered appropriate communication behaviors in specific cultures. They will realize the situational and ever-changing nature of communication style.

Assumptions/Theory Inherent in the Activity: Expected and appropriate communication styles change over time within a culture. To understand this point, it is helpful to think about possible generational differences in how we think about communication styles, or the challenges created when an organization attempts to or is forced to change during a merger. There are underlying cultural values that shape communication styles within any given time period. It may be insightful to explore these shifts over time within a specific context, for example, in the workplace or within a particular professional field.

Time Frame: 15 to 30 minutes for generational focus; 30 minutes to 1½ hours for organizational focus.

Parameters: This is a useful activity for groups in which multiple generations are represented. It is also useful if the particular organization or group experiences any tensions because of differences resulting at least in part from changes over time (such as a merger of departments or companies) and across generations.

Materials, Supplies, and Handouts: None are necessary. Depending on your adaptation of this activity, it might be useful to have paper, markers, and tape available for participants to write observations and to make labels.

Trainer Preparation: Carefully think about the implications of using this activity because you are asking participants to delve into their real communication situations and not hypothetical differences. Do your background research on making connections between participant observations and possible historical events and shifts over time.

How to Facilitate:

1. Divide participants into groups, possibly based on generational characteristics or on work teams.

2. Give general and specific questions to the groups based on the context you have chosen. For example:

Generational Questions	Organizational Questions
Have participants brainstorm communication styles they have experienced with people from a particular generation. Have them discuss possible shifts over time in what they have observed about communication styles. For example, you could ask:	Have participants brainstorm communication styles they have experienced across different departments or as a result of a major organizational change (downsizing, a merger, new product brought to market). Have them discuss possible shifts over time in what they have observed about communication styles. For example, you could ask:

a. *What messages did you receive as a child about communication style?* Participants will discuss different expectations of the appropriate ways for children to communicate in different cultures and families. For example, some may say that their parents were much stricter with them than they are with their children, that children used to be more respectful of their elders and rarely volunteered their opinions.

b. *What messages do you give your children?* Participants will talk about the communication styles used by parents in different cultures and family settings. For example, one parent may be solicitous of a child, teaching the child interdependence and consideration, while another parent encourages the child to think and act independently.

a. *What messages did you receive when you first began working at this organization?* Depending on their start date and department, participants may discuss such varying messages as "I was told I'd have to fend for myself" or that "You are a valued employee and we are committed to taking care of you."

b. *What messages do you give your staff? What messages are shared with other departments?* Participants will talk about what is valued within the organization and within specific departments, and how these values are communicated.

Source: *Communication Highwire: Leveraging the Power of Diverse Communication Styles* (Intercultural Press).

Generational Questions	**Organizational Questions**

c. *What messages do you now receive as an adult?* Participants will discuss the expectations of others about their communication style currently. For example, participants may say they are expected to speak up to help solve a problem, or that they are expected to confer with other adults in order to proceed as a team in a cooperative manner.

d. *How do you account for the communication style differences between adults and children?* Participants will discuss whether they have different communication style expectations for children and adults, and if so why, and whether communication style differences of adults and children have changed over their lifetime.

c. *What messages do you feel are hidden from or not obvious to other departments or new employees?* Participants will discuss messages that are implicit to members of the "in" group, to members of the organization or specific departments. How did they learn/obtain those messages?

d. *How do you account for the communication style differences across your organization?* Participants will discuss whether they have different communication style expectations for people in different functions in the organization, at different hierarchical levels, and with differing lengths of employment.

Note: You could frame the discussion questions based on the particular group's situation and generational and/or historical effects (experiences during a time of war or famine can create different predominant styles of communication, for example).

3. Debrief the activity based on how you used it. Be sure to fully address underlying reasons for shifts in communication styles over time, the development of new communication styles, and our increasing exposures to different communication styles as the world becomes "smaller," more interlinked, and more mobile. Make sure to validate the feelings of frustration that change can bring for some, as well as a feeling of optimism that can result from new opportunities.

Tips: Think about your training goals for the specific group of participants and carefully weigh the potential benefits and disadvantages of dividing the group in certain ways. This can be a powerful tool, but it is also potentially divisive.

Adaptations: There are various ways of using this activity: participants could do role plays, groups could represent different generations, groups could debate the positive and negative outcomes of the styles they have identified, and so on.

ACTIVITY *19:* The Great Gender Debate

Objectives: Participants will gain skill in seeing how socialized gender roles affect expected communication styles and will explore possible ways that gender tendencies may transcend cultural differences. This activity also helps participants realize the power of the assumptions they often make about gender in their messages and the dangers of over-generalizing gender differences.

Assumptions/Theory Inherent in the Activity: Many theorists in communication and linguistic fields have discussed the socialization of gender roles and the effects on communication. Many have criticized researchers for placing too much emphasis on gender differences and for perpetuating myths about the extent of communication and other differences based on gender. This activity shows how gendered messages have influenced our thinking and behaviors, and how we may be surprised at similarities across the gender divide.

Time Frame: 30 minutes to 1 hour.

Parameters: This activity could work with various-sized groups, and it should be used with groups that include at least males and females or a more diverse mix of gender indentifications. This activity is not recommended for groups in which there are only a few participants from one gender group and many more participants from the other.

Materials, Supplies, and Handouts: Paper and pens for notetaking; possibly a flipchart, depending on how you decide to run the debate and debrief the activity. If you want, you could provide research information on gender communication tendencies and references for further exploration of this topic.

Trainer Preparation: Be sure to read background information on gender communication research and the critiques of this research. Be prepared to share your own views on your perceptions of gender roles and the effects on communication interactions. Have a plan for when and how you will end the activity, and be sure that plan is clearly communicated to the participants. For example, you may decide that the debate will last a certain amount of time and then break that time into structured increments, or you can implement a certain number

Source: Communication Highwire: Leveraging the Power of Diverse Communication Styles (Intercultural Press).

of "rounds," allowing for the presentation of ideas and then a response from the other side. You may also inform participants that the debate will end when you determine major points have been sufficiently discussed or if the interaction begins to get out of hand.

How to Facilitate:

1. Divide the group into small groups (three to six people each, depending on group size) according to their self-selected gender affiliations. You may also want to ask for two or three volunteer observers to walk around during the activity to make notes about communication styles they observe. After the debate, when processing the activity, you may ask the observers for comments.

2. Ask each group to generate a list of communication styles generally used by people of another gender. Ask them to discuss in groups why each communication style is challenging, helpful, confusing, amusing, or frustrating. In doing so, they will likely discuss or use their own preferred communication styles.

3. Instruct each group to come up with a debate plan, in which they present arguments for the usefulness of their own style of communication and argue against another gender's preferred approach. Have them discuss how and why they would defend their own communication style, and why, specifically, they find the other gender's communication style problematic.

4. When groups have had ample preparation time, conduct a large group debate: have the small groups present their ideas and respond to the ideas of others. There are various ways you could set up and conduct the debate.

5. When the debate is finished (there will likely not be clear resolution, as different approaches to communication will still exist and, hopefully, be seen as equally valid, and there will undoubtedly be similarities noted as well), debrief the experience.

6. During the debriefing, focus attention not so much on what is positive or negative about the style differences, but on what the participants' perception is of where the style differences come from: lived experiences,

Source: *Communication Highwire: Leveraging the Power of Diverse Communication Styles* (Intercultural Press).

messages from family, school, media, and other influences. You may also discuss choices participants have made to adopt a particular gender style, strategies they have used in communicating across some of the identified differences, and insights they have gained in noting some of the similarities.

Tips: The topic of gender-based communication style preferences is potentially very volatile, so use this activity with caution and for the right purposes. Be prepared to respond to the tension or disagreements that might arise. Be sure to emphasize that the purpose is not to attack other communication approaches, but to explore some of the ways underlying cultural values and messages have influenced our gender roles. Be sure to stress the idea that the gender research, while sometimes based on true physiological differences between males and females, is debatable and represents only general tendencies, not absolute distinctions that are true of everyone. Be open to discussion of how biology and life experiences have influenced roles and differing enactments of "male-ness" and "female-ness."

Adaptations: Ask participants to debate the merits of other genders' preferred communication styles—a sort of switching places.

Source: Communication Highwire: Leveraging the Power of Diverse Communication Styles (Intercultural Press).

ACTIVITY *20:* How Would I Say That?

Objectives: Participants will explore communication style differences in situation- and goal-specific settings.

Assumptions/Theory Inherent in the Activity: Different communication styles emerge in different contexts and when we are communicating for different purposes. This activity demonstrates that styles are not types, nor are they static. Differences come out quite clearly when we have specific objectives we are trying to accomplish, such as making an apology, giving a compliment, or using humor. These actions are referred to as speech acts. For additional information, see Chapter 6 and the appendix (page 259).

Time Frame: 15 minutes to 1 hour, depending on the number of situations explored and the extent to which each is discussed.

Parameters: This activity is highly adaptable to various training contexts and audience sizes. Participants may work in pairs, small groups, or as a large group observing selected participants interacting. This activity works best with a multicultural mix of participants.

Materials, Supplies, and Handouts: Prepare index cards or note cards. Copy the "How Would I Say That?" handout (at the end of this activity), cut up the copy to separate the speech acts, and then tape or glue one speech act to each note card.

Trainer Preparation: Make cards with specific speech acts. Divide participants before the training to form diverse cultural groups for this activity. Prepare a list of ways different cultures might enact the same speech acts (see examples throughout this book).

How to Facilitate:

1. Give a brief (three-to-five minute) overview of speech acts (see page 235).
2. Divide participants into small groups. Give each group one card with a particular speech act—for example, giving a compliment to a coworker (see handout).

3. Ask each group to discuss how each individual would enact the speech act they have been given. Instruct participants to pay attention to the diversity of ways they might meet the same communicative goal.

4. Ask participants to discuss cultural influences on their approaches to the different speech acts.

5. Debrief the activity with the large group, discussing the participants' observations and what they found the most interesting and/or surprising.

Adaptations: It is possible to do this activity in front of a large group, asking for volunteer respondents.

HOW WOULD I SAY THAT? SAMPLE SPEECH ACTS

1. Give a compliment about the clothes someone is wearing.
2. Give a compliment about a well-written memo, e-mail, or paper.
3. Request time off from work or class to attend a family funeral.
4. Request more challenging projects at work or school.
5. Use humor to lighten the mood after a stressful meeting.
6. Explain that you will not meet a deadline.
7. Request new office furniture or a transfer to a new dormitory.
8. Thank someone for his or her help with a project.
9. Praise a colleague for a well-run conference or event.
10. Critique a supervisor or teacher for being late to a meeting.
11. Critique a subordinate or friend for being late to work.
12. Tell a family member you are not going to a family dinner.
13. Tell a family member you are not going to a cousin's wedding.
14. Apologize for taking a week to respond to an e-mail.
15. Apologize to your friend for forgetting that you had made a dinner plan with him or her and now you have another commitment.

Source: *Communication Highwire: Leveraging the Power of Diverse Communication Styles* (Intercultural Press).
© 2005 Dianne Hofner Saphiere, Barbara Kappler Mikk, and Basma Ibrahim DeVries. All rights reserved.

ACTIVITY *21*: Create Ground Rules for a Team

Objectives: Participants will discuss and agree on how they would like to function as a team or group, particularly how they would like to manage communication styles. This activity works especially well with ongoing teams or groups (e.g., students, community board, work group/team, etc.).

Assumptions/Theory Inherent in the Activity: Advantages and disadvantages of diversity on a team; the need to create a third culture or intercultural space in which to operate.

Time Frame: 45 minutes to 2 hours, depending on the depth of the discussion. The decisions made during this activity will need to be revisited frequently.

Parameters: An intact work team or other long-term group.

Materials, Supplies, and Handouts: Copies of the form "Individual Styles—Components of Team Effectiveness" (at the end of this activity) for each participant; a flipchart or whiteboard for taking notes and recording decisions. You will need access to a photocopy machine to make copies of each individual's completed form.

How to Facilitate:

1. Explain to the team or group how important it is for a multicultural or cross-functional team to have clear ground rules in order to work together effectively and to bring out the best of what each team member has to offer. Use the analogy of a sports game: if we all play by different rules, we will each believe the other is cheating. It is important to agree on the guidelines we will use for communicating with one another: how we will share information, make decisions, and resolve conflict (our communications style). You may also want to explain that while it is common for groups to simply brainstorm a list of ground rules, this approach typically results in a list that does not pay attention to cultural differences, and as a result it typically reflects the dominant culture and is loaded with assumptions about how to enact the rules (for example, "be respectful" may mean raising one's

hand when you want to speak or it may mean that it is okay to speak while someone else is speaking). Instead of using an open brainstorming approach, this activity provides an opportunity for everyone involved in the group to provide input about the ground rules based on an analysis of their individual and group communication styles.

2. Ask each team member to complete the handout "Individual Styles."

3. Make enough copies of each group member's completed form to give to all of the participants. Then pass the forms out to all of the group or team members so that each person has a copy of everyone else's answers.

4. Lead a discussion with two purposes: (1) to understand one another's preferred communication, decision-making, and conflict-resolution styles, and (2) to agree on norms or guidelines for communication, decision making, and conflict resolution in this team or group.

5. During team or group meetings, post a copy of these ground rules for everyone to see. Be sure to have the group revisit the norms regularly and to modify, update, delete, or add to them as needed. You can ensure that this is done if you normally facilitate this group, or you can have group members themselves agree to take responsibility to make this happen.

Tips: Be sure to remind the group that all styles have value, and encourage team members to make sure they are doing all they can to utilize the contributions, in the preferred styles, of each member. Encourage them to look at how information is elicited, shared, and presented (verbal, written, visual); what language is used when; how decisions and transitions between topics are indicated; and the purpose of formal versus informal meetings.

Adaptations: Depending on the group's needs, you may want to substitute the situations described in the form's left column. For example, "Describe your preferred style when working under a tight deadline" or "Describe your preferred style when communicating virtually."

Source: Communication Highwire: Leveraging the Power of Diverse Communication Styles (Intercultural Press).
© 2005 Dianne Hofner Saphiere, Barbara Kappler Mikk, and Basma Ibrahim DeVries. All rights reserved.

INDIVIDUAL STYLES—COMPONENTS OF TEAM EFFECTIVENESS

The strength of a team is that its members can more thoroughly analyze the relevant factors involved in a decision from diverse viewpoints. Team members also bring a variety of styles of communicating, decision making, and resolving conflict, which when blended together well, improve a team's overall effectiveness.

Describe your preferred style:	On a team, when do you feel most productive, like you're contributing your best?	When do you feel most ineffective, misunderstood, frustrated, or powerless?	In what type of situation is your preferred style most useful?	How can your style be negatively perceived/ when is it a disadvantage?
When communicating with cross-functional peers (making a point, understanding others).				
When participating in an important decision-making process.				
When faced with direct disagreement or conflict among team members.				

Source: Communication Highwire: Leveraging the Power of Diverse Communication Styles (Intercultural Press).
© 2005 Dianne Hofner Saphiere, Barbara Kappler Mikk, and Basma Ibrahim DeVries. All rights reserved.

ACTIVITY 22: Hand Clapping

Objectives: Participants will experience the need to figure out new rules when none are provided (similar to having to create ground rules for a group of people with different communication styles) via a very energizing activity. This hand clapping activity is adapted from one originally used by Bernie DeKoven (*www.deepfun.com*) for a different purpose at a NASAGA (North American Simulation and Gaming Association) Conference.

Assumptions/Theory Inherent in the Activity: Change management, management of uncertainty, cultural bridging, third culture creation, differences between intended and perceived meaning.

Time Frame: 10 to 30 minutes, depending on how you debrief the activity.

Parameters: Works particularly well with a large group of people (more than thirty) in a large, empty space. Requires sufficient space for groups of three or four people to stand comfortably.

Materials, Supplies, and Handouts: A bell or chime can come in handy for stopping the activity, as it tends to get very noisy. You also want a room with doors and privacy, in a place where some noise will not be a problem. No handouts are required, but you could create some about the topic of managing change or dealing with the unknown.

Trainer Preparation: Become comfortable with the clapping sequence and your ability to teach it. Be clear about your purposes for using the activity, how you want to debrief it, and what you want participants to gain from it.

How to Facilitate:

1. Tell participants that you would like to lead them in an energizing activity that will provide some learning about working with different communication styles in a group.

2. Demonstrate with a partner a children's hand clapping game. You can use any simple clapping game that is normally done in pairs and with which you and the group is familiar.

3. Ask the participants to pair off and begin practicing the clapping. You may want to demonstrate again, and you will definitely want to encourage people to have fun with the activity.

4. After most of the pairs seem to have the basic motions, encourage the participants to try to go faster. You might ask them to clap louder or softer.

5. When most participants seem to be able to do the clapping, stop the participants. Provide positive feedback. Ask them to think a moment about how this experience felt.

6. Tell participants you would like to increase the challenge. Ask them to assemble in groups of three and continue the clapping activity, this time as a group of three. If they protest that they don't know how, explain that you have every confidence that they can figure it out. Participants may find a way to do the same clapping routine in a threesome, or they may alter the clapping routine in order to accommodate the threesome configuration.

7. Again, once most groups are clapping as a threesome, encourage them to clap louder, softer, faster, and slower.

8. After most of the threesomes are clapping, stop them again. Provide positive feedback. Ask them to reflect on how they feel and how this experience was. Ask them to think about how it felt to change from pair clapping to a threesome, how they dealt with uncertainty.

9. Finally, ask the participants to assemble into groups of four and do the clapping as a group. Again, reassure them that they can figure it out. Urge them to go faster or louder. Stop the participants after they have clapped fairly successfully.

10. For the debriefing, ask the participants about their experiences at each stage: in pairs, threes, and fours. They will no doubt talk about how difficult it was, how they had different styles of clapping as well as communicating and deciding; that each team did things a bit differently. Make sure to point out how groups ended up with different ways to approach the task (some may have done pairs, then switched pairs; some may have developed a new rhythm; some may have figured out a way to keep the same

clapping pattern with all three or four by forming a circle and using one hand with one partner and the other with another partner. Ask participants to reflect on how they decided how to clap: Who took initiative and how? What type of communication style was used? Did all feel that they were able to contribute and participate? If so, what enabled this collaboration and inclusion? If not, what impeded collaboration and inclusion across different communication styles.

11. Summarize the activity by agreeing on some key points for leveraging communication styles—steps to take to ensure that different styles are recognized, welcomed, understood, and utilized.

Tips: As with any training activity, you must believe in the activity, feel comfortable with it, and trust in its process in order to have a positive experience with it. It is important for you to encourage the participants to have fun and enjoy themselves, to experiment, and affirm that they will learn from the experience. It is also key to use participants' comments during the debriefing as jumping-off points to do short (thirty second) "teachings" on bridging communication styles and leveraging differences.

Adaptations: Participants could do the activity without speaking to focus on nonverbal communication.

ACTIVITY *23:* E-mail

Objectives: To provide participants the opportunity to practice bridging group members' different styles of written communication (via e-mail) to enhance productivity in the workplace.

Assumptions/Theory Inherent in the Activity: Style switching for task accomplishment.

Time Frame: 1 hour to 90 minutes.

Parameters: This activity works well with any group of participants who frequently use e-mail. Tables and chairs for teams of three to five participants; an even number of groups.

Materials, Supplies, and Handouts: Paper and pencil, or flipchart and markers; a written scenario for each group with communication style descriptions (handouts at the end of this section); "E-Mail Activity Scenarios," "Guidelines for Feedback," "Tips for International/Intercultural E-mail."

How to Facilitate:

1. Explain the purpose and overall flow of the activity.
2. Assign each small group a scenario to work with and give them twenty minutes or so to draft one e-mail to the colleague described in the scenario. They should consider the communication style factors and descriptors, and write an e-mail using a communication style they feel will be effective in the given scenario.
3. Once the e-mails are written, have each group send their e-mail via "server" (you, the facilitator) to their colleague (another small group). Pair the small groups so that they exchange e-mails with each other.
4. Each group reads the assigned scenario and their colleagues' e-mail that they have just received, then writes their feedback according to the guidelines that follow this activity. This takes about ten to twenty minutes.
5. The two teams meet and share their feedback verbally with one another, attempting to learn from the other team's observations.

6. Participants discuss whether they used any communication style behaviors (Chapter 6 descriptors) that they might not normally use, or if they used behaviors differently from how they are accustomed to using them. Ask participants to discuss how they might broaden their communication style repertoires to be able to communicate more effectively with a wider variety of people. Ask participants to summarize their learning from the activity, and how they'll use this learning in everyday work.

7. Conclude with a few key learning points participants obtained from the exercise, for example, a list of tips for writing international/intercultural e-mails (sample follows this activity).

Tips: Keep track of time, as participants can very easily spend more time than you might want crafting their e-mails and their feedback. Participants may voice resistance to trying new communication style behaviors; be prepared to deal with this response.

Adaptations: Use culture-specific scenarios for a group learning about a specific culture. Use real scenarios for an intact team's continuous improvement.

E-MAIL ACTIVITY SCENARIOS

1. You have a Chinese colleague, Aling, whom you have known for several years. You are currently working on a project with Aling and have been putting time and energy into the project while also balancing your other work. You have a deadline to meet on Aling's project, but it now looks as though you will not be able to meet the deadline because of some technical challenges as well as your staff's summer vacation schedule. You know that Aling will be very upset, and that she has little respect for the fact that so many of your staff take vacations at the same time. You want to reassure Aling that you are doing your best and will continue to try to meet the deadline. Please e-mail Aling to let her know. In her communication style Aling tends to value and express concern for others, social niceties, such as apologies for difficulties, a strong work ethic, and predictability and commitment.

2. You are planning a trip to Cameroon to make presentations on a new program you are introducing. Arnaud, your contact there, has worked very hard to plan your week's schedule, and has managed to make appointments for you with several high-profile people. Your boss, however, has just told you to delay your trip for one week. Please e-mail Arnaud to let him know. In his communication style, Arnaud tends to share background information and to tell stories. He expresses a concern for group welfare while trusting age, education, and experience. He values his word and his commitments. Arnaud also seems quite comfortable expressing both his positive and negative emotions.

3. Karl, one of your German international student volunteers, wrote to you that he could not come to help at an orientation as planned, but you never read that e-mail. You get back to your desk and are ready to write a very short e-mail demanding to know where he was when you realize he did send an e-mail to you. You feel that Karl's e-mail was very brief and you really do not know why he missed the orientation. You had a very hard time without him. How do you respond?

Source: Communication Highwire: Leveraging the Power of Diverse Communication Styles (Intercultural Press).

E-MAIL ACTIVITY SCENARIOS *(continued)*

4. You have a Venezuelan colleague, Jaime, with whom you need to coordinate your work efforts. Jaime has given you several different dates for when he will be finished with his portion of the work so that you can begin, and you want to confirm the correct information. Please e-mail Jaime to straighten this out. In his communication style Jaime tends to talk about pleasurable experiences inside and outside work. You know him to be a very proud man who sees himself as incredibly trustworthy and sincere.

5. You have been working on a joint development project with a Dutch colleague, Henk. He promised to create and get to you some drawings that you need. Henk gave himself a deadline that passed three weeks ago, and this delay is negatively influencing your work. You need to know when you can actually expect the drawings, and how you might help him to get them done more quickly. Please e-mail Henk so you can get this matter resolved. In his communication style, Henk tends to be concise and forthright. He does not use a lot of "social lubricants" and appears to appreciate honesty and explicit communication. You know that Henk hates to be told what to do, and that he approaches teamwork and decision making from a consensual orientation.

6. Your U.S. college student, Megan, sends you a long e-mail detailing why her assignment is late. In her e-mail, she discloses a lot of personal information regarding her family situation, her problems at work, her feelings about her other instructors and their lack of understanding about her situation, and confidential information about her roommate, who you also have as a student in one of your classes. Her high level of disclosure, especially about people you know, and her explicit and open manner of communicating makes you uncomfortable. Because it is Thursday evening, and you do not have classes on Friday and will not be seeing Megan until the following week, you feel that it is important to respond via e-mail, yet you are unsure of what to say and how to say it. How would you respond to Megan's message?

Source: Communication Highwire: Leveraging the Power of Diverse Communication Styles (Intercultural Press).

1. Write what you feel is positive about the communication style your colleague or student used in his or her e-mail and why (the positive effect that it would have).
2. Write what you would change, if anything, about your colleague's or student's communication style in this e-mail and why (the negative effect you predict), and how you would suggest writing it instead.

Source: Communication Highwire: Leveraging the Power of Diverse Communication Styles (Intercultural Press).
© 2005 Dianne Hofner Saphiere, Barbara Kappler Mikk, and Basma Ibrahim DeVries. All rights reserved.

TIPS FOR INTERNATIONAL AND INTERCULTURAL E-MAIL

- Use greetings and social expressions in the receiver's native language.
- Consider adjusting your style to the receiver's in order to motivate the receiver toward getting the job done and collaborating effectively.
- Use "standard" dictionary language and avoid idiomatic expressions. Use short sentences and vocabulary with clear meaning.
- Format your e-mail for easy review by a nonnative speaker, with headings or section titles and numbered points.

Source: Communication Highwire: Leveraging the Power of Diverse Communication Styles (Intercultural Press).

ACTIVITY *24:* Toothpicks

Objectives: Participants will explore the ways in which nonverbal differences affect our communication styles and the meanings that we communicate or perceive.

Assumptions/Theory Inherent in the Activity: Nonverbal differences, impact of small differences on how we interact, importance of the Communication Style Descriptor Checklist in understanding communication style.

Time Frame: 30 to 45 minutes.

Materials, Supplies, and Handouts: Toothpicks (enough for ten for each participant); overhead projector or flipchart; cards made by copying the handout at the end of this activity and cutting out one card for each participant. Mark the cards in some way (stickers, highlighting, gluing behavioral instructions to colored paper, etc.) so that each type of behavioral instruction is marked differently, enabling participants to easily distinguish people who have different behavioral instructions from themselves. You may want to make multiple copies of the handout sheet (which includes six different behavioral instructions), and you may also make up your own behavior cards.

Trainer Preparation: Consider the level at which participants may have an emotional reaction and be prepared to facilitate this reaction. For example, novices to intercultural issues may be overwhelmed at how much one minor difference can affect the situation. More experienced participants can be very surprised that despite good intentions, they still behave inappropriately and they cannot decipher exactly why. Be prepared to help participants understand the strategies they use to avoid getting toothpicks.

How to Facilitate:
1. Explain the objectives of the activity.
2. Put these rules on an overhead or flipchart:
    - Follow the rules on your card.
    - Find someone with a different colored or marked card.
    - Do not share what is on your card.
    - Try to figure out your differences with nonverbal communication.

3. Give one card to each participant.

4. Encourage them to interact, discussing a common topic (for example, "What is one of your favorite movies and why?").

5. Make sure when the nonverbal rules are violated that each participant gives a toothpick to the person breaking his/her nonverbal rule (this usually happens very easily!). For example, if your nonverbal rule is that you find direct eye contact offensive and another participant is looking you directly in the eye, give that participant a toothpick.

6. After the group has interacted for five to ten minutes, invite the participants to end the role play and begin the debriefing. During the debriefing, ask the following questions:

   • What did it feel like to participate? To give toothpicks? To receive them?

   • How easy or hard was it to discover what someone else's nonverbal rules were?

   • What does this suggest about how easy or difficult it can be to interact when you do not know the rules?

   • What were the nonverbal differences encountered? What are other ways nonverbal behaviors can differ?

   • In what ways did the nonverbal differences affect your own communication? Your interaction with others?

7. Make sure to include this last question, as it connects nonverbal behaviors to communication style.

Tips: This brief activity can have quite a bit of power if participants feel they are interculturally savvy but they keep getting toothpicks! If this is the case, this activity lends itself well to a discussion that knowing about differences is very important, and that knowing when a particular difference makes a difference is an additional skill.

Adaptations: Could use other supplies, such as points that would be added up and with the lowest scorer receiving a prize.

You find direct eye contact offensive. When you speak, you try not to look people directly in the eye; instead, you avert your eye contact from listeners. If someone looks at you in the eye, give that person a toothpick.

You like to know that people listen when you speak, and you expect that people show they are listening by nodding their heads. You nod your head when others speak. When you are speaking, if listeners are not nodding their heads, give them a toothpick.

You find people standing closer than about eighteen inches or one-half meter away from you offensive. Stand at quite a distance from people and give them a toothpick if they stand too close to you.

During conversations, you find tapping one's feet or fingers or fidgeting offensive. Try not to do this when you speak to people, and give them a toothpick if they do this when you are speaking with them.

You like it when people get their ideas out quickly in conversations, and you are easily distracted by vocalized fillers such as "um," "ah," and "er." If people do not speak quickly enough or if they use vocalized fillers, give them a toothpick.

When speaking, you pause frequently, and you do not like to be interrupted until you have finished speaking. You do not interrupt others when they speak. If people interrupt you and do not give you enough time to pause, give them a toothpick.

ACTIVITY *25:* The Music in Our Heads

Objectives: Participants realize how the messages we tell ourselves or hear in our minds affects our communication style.

Assumptions/Theory Inherent in the Activity: Power of perception, impact of communication styles on behavioral choices, connection between Factors and Descriptors (between motivation and behavior).

Time Frame: 10 to 30 minutes, depending on how you debrief the activity.

Parameters: Works great with a small or large group of people in a large space. Requires sufficient space for movement and for pairs of participants to interact comfortably.

Materials, Supplies, and Handouts: CDs of different instrumental music styles (we suggest upbeat classical music, slow waltzes, circus music, parade music, rock music, music from different cultures, etc.); ask participants to bring their individual CD players to listen to the music. (If individual players/earphones are not available, you can use two different stereos and adapt the activity.)

Trainer Preparation: Be prepared for all kinds of responses regarding the effects of the music. Think carefully about your goals in using this activity and plan accordingly in terms of what kinds of roles, situations, and music would be most useful in accomplishing those goals.

How to Facilitate:

1. Instruct participants to pair up, and then give each participant a CD player with a different style music CD than his or her partner.

2. Advise participants that they should designate one partner as Person A and one partner as Person B.

3. Instruct participants to begin listening to their music, getting a feel for the music, and moving around individually as the music "moves" them.

4. After a few minutes of allowing participants to get into the feel of their music, ask them to find their partner. Once paired, give them a specific instruction about their roles, for example, tell them that Person A is the supervisor and Person B is the employee, and that they are meeting to dis-

cuss Person B's perception that he or she desires an extended holiday/vacation. Participants are told to begin a conversation on this topic with their partner using a style that their music suggests. (Please note that you can use different kinds of situations for this activity, depending on your participants and your intentions in using this activity. You can instruct them that Person A and Person B are adult siblings and they are discussing a family issue; that Person A and Person B are co-workers on a project under deadline, and Person A is up for promotion this quarter and Person B is considering leaving the company for another job opportunity at the end of this quarter; or that Person A and Person B are roommates who have different ideas about how weekly "chores" should be divided and completed.)

5. After discussing this topic according to their styles, instruct partners to switch roles (the employee is now the supervisor) but not styles, and to have a second conversation trying to achieve the same goal, but this time with roles reversed.

6. Continue this activity for several rounds. Use different situations (see suggestions in step 4 or create your own) and perhaps have participants switch CDs to give them a chance to try out different styles.

7. Debrief the activity by asking participants how they interpreted the different music styles, how they felt, what it was like interacting with others, how they were affected by the constant "music in their heads," how the assigned roles affected their enactments of styles, and so on.

Tips: This activity can be quite powerful because of the effects of music on participants' moods and approaches to communicative situations. Often, participants engage in a discussion about how much they are affected by music, and share with the group the strong influences music has in their lives and how it prompts them to shift moods, engage in certain behaviors, think in certain ways, visualize different life experiences, and so on. Utilize the power of music's influence in this activity. It may also work well to use this activity to introduce different kinds of ethnic music and to discuss the effects of participants' level of familiarity with the music on their experience in this activity.

Adaptations: As noted above, if personal disc players are not available, or if you do not have enough for each participant, you could use two CD players playing two different kinds of music instead. In this case, put the disc players on opposite sides of the room and set the volume so that everyone can hear both, but can hear one song more distinctly. In larger groups, you could ask for several volunteer pairs who would play the roles in the assigned situation while the others act as observers of the interaction. It is also possible to experiment with this technique by having two volunteers act out a situation with their assigned music styles, while three or four others move around them using music styles that are potentially supportive, disruptive, encouraging, and so on.

ACTIVITY *26:* The Circus Goes On!

Objectives: Participants will be able to understand the strengths of a variety of communication styles via a circus performance metaphor. Participants are encouraged to expand their own communication style repertoires.

Assumptions/Theory Inherent in the Activity: Understanding the strengths of various communication styles is critical to helping participants embrace a range of styles and develop a broad repertoire.

Time Frame: 30 minutes to 1 hour, depending on the depth of facilitation.

Parameters: This activity challenges the facilitator to balance a sense of playfulness, creativity, and depth of exploration.

Materials, Supplies, and Handouts: Copies of the handout "Potential Performers" (at the end of this activity); whiteboard and/or flipchart paper.

Trainer Preparation: Be prepared to help participants stretch their view of their own capabilities. Based on your previous work with the group, provide specific examples of when group members exhibited various roles from the "Potential Performers" handout.

How to Facilitate:

1. Ask participants to review the "Potential Performers" handout and consider the roles they most frequently play in communication. Clarify that the goal in presenting these categories is not at all to imply that there are communication style types. (If you have read the previous chapters, we certainly hope this message is loud and clear!) Instead, this list represents a set of competencies essential in daily intercultural interactions, and thus the ideal world would be one in which we could all enact all of these roles and help others to understand the power in each of these roles.

2. Ask participants to consider the time and place when they might productively use each of these roles. Then ask participants to share their responses in small groups or with a partner.

3. Ask participants to commit to observing their communication style behaviors over the course of one week, documenting when they use various roles.

Adaptation: If the circus metaphor does not ring true to you, then gently set the metaphor aside and focus on the behaviors and patterns of each of the approaches listed in the handout.

Source: Communication Highwire: Leveraging the Power of Diverse Communication Styles (Intercultural Press).

POTENTIAL PERFORMERS

The Tightrope Walker

Key skills and behaviors: Balancing, recognizing crucial decision points, ignoring distractions (or focusing despite distractions), acting courageously, acknowledging potential consequences of small missteps; does not attempt new tricks without practice.

The Clown

Key skills and behaviors: Making people laugh, engaging in a lighthearted approach, not taking oneself too seriously, creating diversions, masking one's own reactions in order to keep the conversation going, knowing when to focus on the negative, taking time for serious concerns, shining a spotlight on important information without putting on "airs."

The Unicyclist

Key skills and behaviors: Balancing, always moving, persevering, continually practicing, changing directions quickly, moving quickly, able to fluidly adjust to change, ending with abrupt dismount; excellent solo performer and able to focus on practical aspects of the interaction.

The Trapeze Artist

Key skills and behaviors: Working together/coordinating efforts, trusting others, continuously learning new skills, revealing honest reactions as colleagues see all, acknowledging potential consequences of small missteps, making leaps of faith, working with or without support, co-creating their interactions, always accountable to others.

POTENTIAL PERFORMERS *(continued)*

The Stagehands/Backstage People/Roustabouts

Key skills and behaviors: Making the show run, coordinating many people and events, solving problems and troubleshooting, managing crises; facilitative, supportive, does not need to be in the limelight.

The Ringmaster

Key skills and behaviors: Running the show (at least in outward appearance), exercising power and control, providing a voice for others, helping people focus attention (on important goings-on), maintaining a common focus and sense of purpose, maintaining a unified energy/atmosphere.

The Magician

Key skills and behaviors: Mastering distraction, creating "curiosities" and illusions, knowing lots of key information; incorporates assistants, able to build mystery and excitement, entices focus and concentration, maintains a distance yet is engaging.

The Lion Tamer

Key skills and behaviors: Controlling own fear, interacting with different work roles, coordinating movements of colleagues, knowing potential for danger exists; has a team of assistants, able to command respect, courageous, strong.

The Mime

Key skills and behaviors: Communicating nonverbally, storytelling, capturing attention of key constituents; able to harness the imagination of others, creative, physically involved/whole body communication, able to create and share a vision.

Source: Communication Highwire: Leveraging the Power of Diverse Communication Styles (Intercultural Press).

POTENTIAL PERFORMERS *(continued)*

The Juggler

Key skills and behaviors: Keeping multiple tasks going at one time, including multiple perspectives, performing by oneself or with others, dealing proficiently with complexity, blocking out distractions, maintaining energy and excitement.

The Hawker

Key skills and behaviors: Persuading people, capitalizing on the "excitement" felt by stakeholders, capitalizing on potential customers' relationships with one another, involving people; able to command attention, persuasive.

The Spectator

Key skills and behaviors: Willing to buy into a vision; looking for excitement, newness, or thrill; supporting others' abilities; gives positive feedback and encouragement, demands quality.

Tracing the Heritage of Communication Styles

As we mentioned in the Introduction, when we began this book we were surprised to find that very little had been written about communication style. In our extensive review of the literature, we found work relating to the topic in sociolinguistics and linguistics, interpersonal communication, anthropology and ethnography of communication, and intercultural communication. However, we were not able to find a source that traced and summarized these varied roots of communication style in one volume. The way the different academic disciplines and practitioners define *communication style* reminded us of the blind men defining the elephant: it all depended on the frame of reference!

Our goal for this book was to present new tools for understanding and leveraging communication styles. While conducting research for this book, we gathered a great deal of material that was not immediately applicable to the practical nature of this book, but that is nevertheless an important contribution to the field. In this appendix, we highlight some of the key thinking about communication style to show you the richness of the literature and to encourage you to explore the roots that are of interest to you in greater depth. As educators, team leaders, and trainers, we all need to understand the key theoretical models and research that have contributed to the phenomenon of communication style so that we can prepare others to understand and maximize differences in communication styles.

The following table summarizes the key contributions to communication style theory from the various academic disciplines. After the table, we offer brief synopses of the main communication style concepts that we see growing out of each discipline. As you examine the table and read this appendix, keep in mind that many of these historical roots overlap and that, in some cases, they developed simultaneously. Even within each discipline, many of the categories dovetail with one another so that it is difficult to distinguish clearly where one concept ends and another begins. It is our goal with the chart to provide a simple overview, not to box in concepts or scholarly works as exclusively one thing but not another. Finally, we will explain six main themes that we can draw from this review of the communication style literature. Additionally, we include an extensive bibliography with a variety of sources on communication style. We hope this information inspires your thinking about communication styles, motivates you to learn and apply your knowledge of communication styles to enhance your work and relationships, and encourages further inquiry into the topic of communication style. We plan to publish the results of our literature review in a more comprehensive form at a later date, most likely in an intercultural journal. Please look for it.

Sociolinguistics and Linguistics

Linguists have contributed a great deal to the study of communication style, and particularly to the descriptive and analytical approach we suggest in this book. On a basic level, linguists such as Kaplan (1988) have assisted us in considering how our daily interactions are affected by our thinking patterns, and about how these cognitive structures are related to our language backgrounds. Additionally, linguists have spent much time and effort training themselves to describe observable behavior and to use this as a starting point for understanding a language community. From linguists, we have learned to focus on different aspects of the interaction, such as the affective and semantic tones used by communicators, and the role of turn taking in conversational development. This attempt to capture what is personally, culturally, and contextually relative into a neutral, descriptive terminology is essential for the approach to communication style presented in this book, and has greatly influenced the development of our descriptors in Chapter 6.

Several linguists, including Gumperz, Lakoff, Tannen, and Kochman, help us explore the intersection of language and social phenomena by looking more closely at these observable behaviors in individual interactions. Through their research, we understand that communicative and conversational style differences can be

Summary Table of the Disciplinary Contributions to Communication Style

Sociolinguistics and Linguistics	Interpersonal Communication	Anthropology and Ethnography of Communication	Intercultural Communication
Communication style varies by language family (Kaplan)	The Coordinated Management of Meaning Theory (Pearce and Cronen)	Emic and etic (Pike)	The values connection (Barnlund, Casse, Gudykunst, Ting-Toomey)
Elaborated and restricted codes (Bernstein)	Communication Accommodation Theory (Giles and others)	High and low context (Hall)	Linking the individual and the individual's culture (Barnlund, Gudykunst, and Kim)
Importance of the observable (Gumpertz, Lakoff, Tannen, and Kochman)	Expectancy Violations Theory (Burgoon and Hale)	Origins of nonverbal behavior studies (Birdwhistell, Ekman and Friesen, Hall)	Typologies (Gudykunst and Ting-Toomey, Bennett and Paige)
Communicative style (Lakoff); Conversational style (Tannen)	Communicator Style (Norton)	Ethnography of communication and culture-specific patterns (Hymes, Philipsen, and others)	Communication style as a window to deeper culture (Barnlund, Bennett, Ting-Toomey, and others)
Speech Act Theory (Austin; Searle)		Role of silence (Basso)	Culture-specific patterns (Condon, Carbaugh, and others)
			Emphasis on developing intercultural competence that can include developing communication style skills (Bennett, Hammer, and Martin)

insights into cultural patterns and beliefs. Finally, the linguistics discipline has introduced the notion of *speech acts*—patterned, routine utterances that speakers use regularly to perform a variety of functions, such as apologies, complaints, requests, refusals, and compliments. Researchers such as Cohen have examined speech acts as a fundamental avenue to understanding differences across cultures in order to be a more effective language learner.

Interpersonal Communication

Interpersonal communication researchers have proposed many different theories and approaches to understanding interaction, and in particular, miscommunications. The Coordinated Management of Meaning Theory (CMM) developed by Pearce and Cronen is a good example of the interrelatedness of theoretical ideas across disciplines; it integrates ideas from speech act theory and systems theory, among others. CMM helps explain how people are thought to interpret and act in any communicative situation on the basis of rules and within a series of embedded contexts. The contexts they discuss are related to several of the factors covered in Chapter 3.

Other interpersonal researchers explore ways that communicators adapt their communication to others, as in the Communication Accommodation Theory (CAT) of Giles and others (which has been an important vehicle for examining the extent to which communicators diverge and converge in their communication patterns, in terms of language choice and verbal and nonverbal behaviors), and the Expectancy Violations Theory developed by Burgoon and Hale (which focuses on expectations communicators have for nonverbal behaviors in a given interaction situation). Some of these interpersonal communication theories are particularly relevant to the examination of interactions among communicators from different ethnic, cultural, regional, and/or linguistic backgrounds, as they address the process of making communicative adaptations and the behavioral implications of communicators' choices. Some of this work informed the questions in Chapter 3 that we encourage you to use to guide your analysis of the factors in your own communication interactions.

Finally, Norton and Miller are credited with first identifying communicator style types when they proposed that people were predisposed to behave in certain ways while interacting with others. Norton (1978) conceptualized "communicator style" as "the way one verbally and paraverbally interacts to signal how literal meaning should be taken, interpreted, filtered, or understood" (99). As we mentioned at the beginning of this book, one of our main motivators for doing this work was to help trainers and educators move beyond one-word style "types" and into more descriptive terminology to explain the complexities of communication style.

Anthropology and Ethnography of Communication

Pike, considered to be both an anthropologist and a linguist, applied the linguistic concepts of *phonemic* (sound units in a given language) and *phonetic* (physical sounds and their descriptions) to culture, and created the notion of *emic* (what is valid for one specific culture) and *etic* (an analysis from outside the cultural perspective) (Pike 1954). This development of validity for an emic perspective is the foundation for cultural-specific work in nearly any discipline, and the etic perspective has contributed to communication styles by establishing a precedent for the application of universal theories (such as high and low context discussed later), and the importance of value comparisons, which is one of the main factors in the model detailed in Chapter 3.

A prime example of how deep cultural understanding may be applied to specific communication behaviors is demonstrated by Hall's work on high- (emphasizing implicit messages and reliance on contextual cues for meaning) and low- (focusing on explicit verbal messages and specific communication messages) context communication. Many intercultural scholars (e.g., Gudykunst, Kim, and Ting-Toomey) have been greatly influenced by Hall's conceptual frame of high and low context. A specific example of this influence is Gudykunst and Kim's (2003) linking of indirect and direct communication styles to Hall's concept of high and low context. We are also influenced by these broad concepts, and yet have misgivings about an oversimplified relationship portrayed between high context and indirect communication and between low context and direct communication. We have incorporated the concept of high and low context into our descriptor list as explicit and implicit understanding. We link motivations and behaviors in our factor model and descriptors, but do not assume a one-to-one correlation between explicit and implicit communication and any particular behaviors or cultures.

Anthropologists such as Birdwhistell (often referred to as the founder of kinesic studies) made important connections between nonverbal behaviors, ideas from linguistics, and reflections of cultural differences. Ekman and Friesen's focus on facial expressions led to an important concept that one behavior, even an eye blink, can lead to different interpretations based on one's background. We include descriptors for analyzing these kinds of behaviors in Chapter 6.

The anthropological roots also include the contributions of what has been named *the ethnography of communication*, the process of describing the patterns of speech in a particular community. Hymes (1974) detailed a mnemonic framework—SPEAKING (setting and scene, participants, event, act sequence, key, instrumentalities, norms, and genres)—that has guided much of the work in this area. The connection to communication styles is that scholars have utilized ethnographic methods and Hymes' mnemonic framework to analyze countless communities' patterns of specific cultural communication, such as Philipsen (1975), Carbaugh (1990), Katriel (1986), and Fitch (1998). They explain a particular culture's communication with a depth and richness that is offered not through a search for universals or answers to specific hypotheses, but rather via an exploration of how to understand these patterns from the perspectives of those inside the culture. Also of note is Basso's ethnographic work on Western Apache language and culture and his attention to silence. The factors we present in Chapter 3, as well as the descriptors in Chapter 6, aim at understanding intended meaning from the perspective of the communicator, so that meaning can be shared and understanding can occur.

Intercultural Communication

Interculturalists have shed a great deal of light on the critical importance of communication style in understanding intercultural encounters. On a general level, interculturalists view communication style as a window into other cultures as well as our own. From an intercultural communication perspective, several researchers have explained communication style in relation to cultural values and different cultural orientation systems. Bennett (1998) notes that, "Habitual patterns of thought are manifested in communication behavior. Since our habits of thought are largely determined by culture, in cross-cultural situations we should see contrasts in these styles of communication" (20). The contributions by interculturalists here echo the contributions of Gumperz, Lakoff, Tannen, and Kochman in that an individual's behaviors can be understood, in part, by examining cultural patterns and beliefs. In other words, the link between the individual and the individual's culture can be seen (sometimes literally) through one's communication style. The approach we present in this book builds on these notions of communication style as a window to deeper values and worldviews.

Noting the effects of values on shaping communicative events, Gudykunst and Ting-Toomey (1988) identify key themes and foci that help when trying to understand a culture and the role of communication in context. Casse (1980) viewed values as so integral to the concept of communication style that his typology is entirely based on how individuals respond to value dimensions. In this book, we acknowledge the power of our underlying value systems and in how they manifest themselves in our preferred communication styles (see Chapter 3 for our discussion of the values factor).

Other notable researchers, such as Barnlund (1975), encouraged scholars and practitioners to look holistically at this concept and defined communication style as

> . . . the topics people prefer to discuss, their favorite forms of interaction—ritual, repartee, argument, self-disclosure—and the depth of involvement they demand of each other. It includes the extent to which communicants rely upon the same channels—vocal, verbal, physical—for conveying information, and the extent to which they are tuned to the same level of meaning, that is, to the factual or emotional content of messages (14–15).

Samovar and Porter (2001) took a slightly different approach to defining communication styles by directly linking style to "characteristics that compose a communication personality" (281). In describing how to improve one's intercultural communication, these authors argued that recognizing one's communication style—"the manner in which you present yourself to others" (281) —is essential.

Additional typologies abound in the actual practice of conducting intercultural communication courses and workshops. Academic sources for these typologies are frequently Gudykunst and Ting-Toomey (1988), Ting-Toomey (1999), and Bennett and Paige (1993 and 1996). We have experienced the practical value of typologies in processing intercultural encounters. The key contributions we have observed from the typologies developed by interculturalists are that they give educators and participants the language to talk about communication style differences; they are usable and efficient approaches to examining communication style differences; and perhaps most important, the identified styles ring true to people's experiences. A challenge of using a typology alone is that it does not typically reflect the richness of our communicative interactions, including the multiple interpretations of the particular words used to describe the styles (consider, for example, Tanaka's and Mike's differing interpretations of "direct" communication discussed throughout the book).

One of the major contributions of the intercultural field to understanding communication style comes in the form of culture-specific resources. Examples here include Condon's (1984) classic book, *With Respect to the Japanese*, in which he builds on the link between Japanese "group" mentality values and communication style; Vossestein's (2001) book, *Dealing with the Dutch*; and Shahar and Kurz's (1995) *Border Crossings*, which includes information about Israeli communication style. Another innovative tool for understanding culture-specific values and communication style differences is the *Cultural Detective* (Nipporica Associates, see description in Other Tools, page 279) for analyzing over thirty different cultures.

The roots of intercultural communication are grounded in practice (Leeds-Hurowitz 2002; Pusch 2004). As a result, much emphasis has always been placed on how to apply theory and research to everyday interactions. To us, this practice includes one's skill and repertoire of utilizing different communication styles. Concepts such as intercultural communication competence (Martin 1993), intercultural perspective-taking (Chen and Starosta 1996; Steglitz 1993; Kappler 1998), intercultural conflict styles (Hammer 2003) and the Developmental Model of Intercultural Sensitivity (Bennett 1993), greatly influenced our approach to communication styles in that we integrate the ability to use a variety of communication behaviors into our factor model.

Key Themes in the History of Communication Styles

From our analysis of the literature, which we report only in summary form here, we have discovered six key themes that inform this book. These themes, interwoven with one another, are as follows:

1. Communication typologies are useful, yet limiting.
2. Communication styles have underlying rules.
3. Neutrally describing communication styles is critical to understanding their complexity.
4. There is a complex link between communication style and several key factors, including values.
5. Communication style patterns are embedded in culture.
6. Leveraging communication style requires a flexible, dialectical approach.

Communication typologies are useful, yet limiting. Researchers from various disciplines find it useful and efficient to identify and discuss lists of specific communication styles, and to propose categorical ways we can understand communication style differences. Indeed, in training and educational settings, the types of communication styles developed across the disciplines seem to resonate with participants' experiences, and they are able to apply these types to their lives with relative ease. It is also clear that such approaches to communication style can be rather limiting. We have noted earlier the great benefits of these contributions, as well as some of the challenges we see in typological schemes. The approach we have described in this book is an attempt to account for the complex nature of intercultural interactions while leveraging the assets of typologies.

Communication styles have underlying rules. Several theories from different academic roots focus on the rules underlying both interaction events and the styles used by the communicators. Based on Gudykunst's notion of uncertainty avoidance, which is what often motivates people to communicate in a given situation, the basic human desire to understand the "rules" seems fundamental to effective communication in many cases. In intercultural situations, this need becomes particularly salient, as many people experience discomfort because of what is not known. Figuring out the rule systems and appropriate communication behaviors is the first step in communicating effectively across cultural differences (national, ethnic, racial, religious, gender, and so on). Situations in which there is a disconnect between communication styles highlight the power of these rules and the need for greater understanding. The Four-Step method of reflection and discussion presented in this book is designed to facilitate discovery and understanding of the rules underlying communication style.

Neutrally describing communication styles is critical to understanding their complexity. One of the most challenging aspects of writing this book on communication styles centered on a concern to utilize neutral descriptions in how we talk about communication style. As understanding of cultural differences related to values, norms, communicative behaviors, and patterns evolved, new terms were necessary to fully address the richness and complexity of these cultural variations. One indicator of the increasing need to neutrally describe communication style is how much overlap we found across various disciplines regarding some of the root concepts associated with communication styles. We have used the concept of the observable (emphasizing a more neutral approach) as a foundation for our Descriptor Checklist, which is designed to facilitate a focus on and open discovery about the differences that make a difference. We look forward to your feedback and ideas as we continually strive toward the evolutionary development of a culturally neutral, descriptive terminology for communication style.

There is a complex link between communication style and several key factors, including values. One of our goals in this book has been to view communication style from a larger cultural perspective, as influenced by many different cultural and linguistic factors, to assist readers in gaining further insights into the impact and effects of communication style. Tracing the roots of communication styles has shown that scholars from many disciplines have explored the complex link between how we communicate and a diversity of cultural influences. The five core factors we present in Chapter 3 and the interaction discussions of those factors in Chapter 4 offer you the chance to examine the intricate and creative ways people balance such fundamental influences as values, self-concept, and goals in enacting various communication styles.

Communication style patterns are embedded in culture. The valuable contributions made by culture-specific researchers across disciplines shows us that communication styles are frequently situation based or context specific, and that all the layers of culture exert a strong influence over the kinds of communication styles that might be observed within those particular cultures or contexts. Much of the work in this area focuses on explaining communicative behavior in sufficient detail to enable us to perceive, correctly interpret, and practice a new style. In this book we have made a very conscious effort to enable the reader to decipher and leverage personal as well as cultural influences on communication style. Just as individual differences underlying communication styles are significant, there are enormous variations in cultural interpretations of communication styles as well.

Leveraging communication style requires a flexible, dialectical approach. Interculturalists Martin and Nakayama (2000) recommend a dialectical approach to the study of intercultural communication, an approach that weaves the contributions of all three traditional approaches (social science, interpretive, and critical) into an approach that is processual (recognizing that cultures and people change, that patterns evolve, and that any study is merely a snapshot in time), relational (for a contextual, holistic view), and that allows for the contradictory (for example, reality is both internal and external; behavior is predictable and creative and changeable). We have very much endeavored in this book to follow a dialectical approach to the analysis and management of communication style, introducing you to several different and hopefully complementary ways of identifying, analyzing, and working with communication styles. It is in this spirit of openness and flexibility that we believe greater satisfaction and productivity in relationships, both professionally and personally, may continuously expand.

Conclusion

Examining the connections among language, culture, and communication style provides insights into the complexity of human communication and the seemingly unending possible approaches to and interpretations of communication style. Past scholars and researchers laid a significant framework for developing an awareness of and appreciation for this complexity. Communication style grew out of the roots of many theoretical backgrounds and continues to flourish from its multidisciplinary influences.

We believe that we are at a crossroads in terms of understanding those around us. As we continue to live, work, and play in a world made increasingly and accessibly diverse by technology and travel, we are motivated to achieve deeper levels of understanding and to avoid the potentially dangerous constraints resulting from strict categorizations or limited appreciations of others. It is our most sincere hope that the theories and approaches summarized in this appendix, and the methods we propose in this book, will serve as steps in the direction of helping us all to recognize, value, and leverage the diversity of our global, multicultural society.

References

Althen, Gary. 2002. *American Ways: A Guide for Foreigners in the United States.* 2d ed. Yarmouth, ME: Intercultural Press.

Austin, John L. 1962. *How to Do Things with Words.* Cambridge: Harvard University Press.

Bales, Robert F. 1970. *Personality and Interpersonal Behavior.* New York: Holt, Rhinehart, & Winston.

Barnlund, Dean C. 1998. "Communication in a Global Village." In *Basic Concepts of Intercultural Communication: Selected Readings,* edited by Milton Bennett, 35–52. Yarmouth, ME: Intercultural Press.

_____. 1975. *Public and Private Self in Japan and the United States: Communication Styles of Two Cultures.* Tokyo: Simile Press.

Basso, Keith H. 1990. *Western Apache Language and Culture.* Tucson: University of Arizona Press.

_____. 1970. "To Give Up on Words: Silence in the Western Apache Culture." *Southwestern Journal of Anthropology* 26, no. 3: 213–30.

Bennett, Janet M., Milton Bennett, and Kathryn Stillings. 1979. DIE (Describe, Interpret, and Evaluate) Model Handout. Unpublished.

Bennett, Janet M., and R. Michael Paige. 1996, 1993. *Communication Styles Handout.* Portland, OR: Intercultural Communication Institute.

Bennett, Milton. J., ed. 1998. *Basic Concepts of Intercultural Communication: Selected Readings.* Yarmouth, ME: Intercultural Press.

Bennett, Milton J. 1993. "Towards Ethnorelativism: A Developmental Model of Intercultural Sensitivity." In *Education for the Intercultural Experience,* edited by R. Michael Paige. 2d ed., pages 21–71. Yarmouth, ME: Intercultural Press.

Bernstein, Basil. 1971. *Class, Codes, and Control: Theoretical Studies toward a Sociology of Language.* London: Routledge & Kegan Paul.

Birdwhistell, Ray L. 1970. *Kinesics and Context.* Philadelphia: University of Pennsylvania Press.

Bourhis, Richard Y., Howard Giles, and William E. Lambert. 1975. "Social Consequences of Accommodating One's Style of Speech: A Cross-National Investigation." *International Journal of the Sociology of Language* 6: 55–72.

Brown, Penelope, and Steven Levinson. 1987. *Politeness.* Cambridge: Cambridge University Press.

Burgoon, Judee K., and Jerold L. Hale. 1988. "Nonverbal Expectancy Violations: Model Elaboration and Application." *Communication Monographs* 55: 58–79.

Cameron, Carrie. 1993. *How Is Politeness Expressed across Cultures?* Unpublished paper.

Carbaugh, Donal, ed. 1990. *Cultural Communication and Intercultural Contact.* Hillsdale, NJ: Lawrence Erlbaum.

Casse, Peter. 1980. *Training for the Cross Cultural Mind.* Washington, DC: SIETAR.

Chen, Guo-Ming, and William J. Starosta. 1988. *Foundations of Intercultural Communication.* Boston: Allyn & Bacon.

Cohen, Andrew D. "An Introduction to Situationally Appropriate Utterances: Speech Acts." Summary of a lecture presented at the Japanese Association of College English Teachers' Summer Seminar on "Pragmatics in Second Language Acquisition: A Focus on Speech Acts," 19–22 August, 2003, Kusatsu, Gunma, Japan.

Cohen, Andrew D., and Noriko Ishihara. (Forthcoming in 2005). A Web-Based Approach to Strategic Learning of Speech Acts. CARLA Research Report. Minneapolis, MN: Center for Advanced Research on Language Acquisition. [www.carla.umn.edu/about/profiles/Cohen]

Condon, John C. 1984. *With Respect to the Japanese.* Yarmouth, ME: Intercultural Press.

Condon, John C., and Fathi Yousef. 1975. *Introduction to Intercultural Communication.* New York: Bobs Merrill.

DeKoven, Bernie. 2003. *The Well-Played Game.* Lincoln, NE: Writers Club Press. *www.deepfun.com.*

Ekman, Paul, and Wallace Friesen. 1975. *Unmasking the Face.* Englewood Cliffs, NJ: Prentice-Hall.

Fitch, Kristine L. 1998. "A Ritual for Attempting Leave-Taking in Colombia." In *Readings in Cultural Contexts,* edited by Judith N. Martin, Thomas K. Nakayama, and Lisa A. Flores, 179–86. Mountain View, CA: Mayfield.

Fowler, Sandra M., and Sheila Ramsey. 1999. "Epilogue: Intercultural Training: The Future." In *Intercultural Sourcebook: Cross-Cultural Training Methods, Vol. 2,* edited by Sandra M. Fowler and Monica G. Mumford. Yarmouth, ME: Intercultural Press.

Gallois, Cynthia, Howard Giles, E. Jones, A.C. Cargile, and H. Ota. 1995. "Accommodating Intercultural Encounters: Elaborations and Extensions. In *Intercultural Communication Theory,* edited by Richard Wiseman, 115–47. Thousand Oaks, CA: Sage.

Giles, Howard, and Nikolas Coupland. 1991. *Language: Contexts and Consequences.* Milton Keynes, UK: Open University Press.

Giles, Howard, and Kimberly A. Noels. "Communication Accommodation in Intercultural Encounters." In *Readings in Intercultural Communication: Experiences and Contexts,* 2d ed., edited by Judith N. Martin, Thomas K. Nakayama, and Lisa A. Flores, 117–26. Boston: McGraw Hill, 2002.

Gonzalez, Alberto, Marsha Houston, and Victoria Chen, eds. 2004. *Our Voices: Essays in Culture, Ethnicity, and Communication.* 4th ed. Los Angeles, CA: Roxbury.

Gorden, Raymond L. 1995. *Living in Latin America: A Case Study in Cross-Cultural Communication.* Lincolnwood: National Textbook Company.

Griffin, Em. 2003. *Communication: A First Look at Communication Theory.* 5th ed. Boston: McGraw-Hill.

Gudykunst, William B., and Stella Ting-Toomey. 1988. *Cultural and Interpersonal Communication.* Newbury Park, CA: Sage.

Gudykunst, William B., and Young Yun Kim. 2003. *Communicating with Strangers: An Approach to Intercultural Communication.* New York: McGraw Hill.

Gumperz, John J., ed. *Language and Social Identity.* Cambridge: Cambridge University Press, 1982.

Hackman, Michael Z., Kathleen Ellis, Craig E. Johnson, and Constance Staley. 1999. "Self-Construal Orientation: Validation of an Instrument and a Study of the Relationship to Leadership Communication Style." *Communication Quarterly* 47: 183–95.

Hall, Edward T. 1976. *Beyond Culture.* Garden City, NY: Doubleday.

———. 1966. *The Hidden Dimension.* New York: Random House.

Hall, Edward T., and Mildred Reed Hall. 1990. *Understanding Cultural Differences.* Yarmouth, ME: Intercultural Press.

Hammer, Mitchell. 2003. *Intercultural Conflict Style Inventory, Interpretive Guide, Facilitator's Manual.* www.hammerconsulting.org/ics_inventory.html

Hart, Roderick P., R. E. Carlson, and William F. Eadie. 1980. "Attitudes toward Communication and the Assessment of Rhetorical Sensitivity." *Communication Monographs* 47: 1–22.

Herrmann, Ned. 1996. *Whole Brain Business Book.* New York: McGraw-Hill.

Hofner Saphiere, Dianne, ed. 2004. *Cultural Detective.* www.culturaldetective.com

Hofner Saphiere, Dianne, and Nipporica Associates. 2000. *Redundancía: A Foreign Language Simulation.* Leawood, KS: Nipporica Associates. www.nipporica.com/prod.htm

———. 1998. *Ecotonos: A Multicultural Problem-Solving Simulation.* Yarmouth, ME: Intercultural Press.

Hofner Saphiere, Dianne, and Yuko Kipnis. 2002. *Shinrai: Building Trusting Relationships with Japanese Colleagues.* Leawood, KS: Nipporica Associates. www.nipporica.com/prod.htm

Hofstede, Geert. 1980. *Culture's Consequences.* Beverly Hills, CA: Sage.

Hoijer, Harry. 1994. "The Sapir-Whorf Hypothesis." In *Intercultural Communication: A Reader,* 7th ed., edited by Larry Samovar and Richard E. Porter, 194–200. Belmont, CA: Wadsworth.

Huchendorf, Karen, and Fran Brew. 2004. *Cultural Detective: Australia.* Leawood, KS: Nipporica Associates. www.culturaldetective.com

Hymes, Dell. 1974. *Foundations of Sociolinguistics: An Ethnographic Approach.* Philadelphia: University of Pennsylvania Press.

Johnstone, Barbara. 1989. "Linguistic Strategies for Persuasive Discourse." In *Language, Communication, and Culture: Current Directions*, edited by Stella Ting-Toomey and Felipe Korzenny. Newbury Park, CA: Sage.

Kaplan, Robert. 1996. "Cultural Thought Patterns in Inter-Cultural Education." *Language Learning* 16: 1–20.

_____. 1988. "Cultural Thought Patterns in Intercultural Education." In *Toward Multiculturalism: A Reader in Multicultural Education*, edited by Jaime Wurzel. Yarmouth, ME: Intercultural Press.

Kappler, Barbara. 1998. "Refining Intercultural Perspective Taking." Unpublished doctoral dissertation. University of Minnesota, Minneapolis.

Kappler Mikk, Barbara, and Rhonda Davy. 1999. Training materials (from Chapter 1). Unpublished handouts from nonprofit training on communication style and working with nonnative English speakers.

Katriel, Tamar. 1986. *Talking Straight: "Dugri" Speech in Israeli Sabra Culture.* Cambridge: Cambridge University Press.

Kochman, Thomas. 1981. *Black and White Styles in Conflict.* Chicago: University of Chicago Press.

Kramarae, Cheris. 1981. *Women and Men Speaking.* Rowley, MA: Newbury House.

Lakoff, Robin. 1975. *Language and Women's Place.* New York: Harper & Row.

Leeds-Hurowitz, Wendy. 1998. "Notes on the History of Intercultural Communication: The Foreign Service Institute and the Mandate for Intercultural Training." In *Readings in Cultural Contexts*, edited by Judith N. Martin, Thomas K. Nakayama, and Lisa A. Flores. Mountain View, CA: Mayfield.

Lewis, Richard D. 1999. *Cross-Cultural Communication: A Visual Approach.* UK: Transcreen.

Littlejohn, Stephen W. 2002. *Theories of Human Communication.* 7th ed. Belmont, CA: Wadsworth.

Loeffler, Robert. J. 2003. "Candy and the Circus Go Hand-In-Hand." *Bandwagon* 47, no.1: 4–15.

Lustig, Myron, and Jolene Koester. 2003. *Intercultural Competence: Interpersonal Communication across Cultures.* 4th ed. New York: HarperCollins.

Martin, Judith N. 1993. "Intercultural Communication Competence: A Review." In *Intercultural Communication Competence: International and Intercultural Communication Annual*, edited by Richard L. Wiseman and Jolene Koester, 16–32. Newbury Park, CA: Sage.

Martin, Judith N., and Thomas K. Nakayama. 2000. *Intercultural Communication in Contexts.* 2d ed. Mountain View, CA: Mayfield.

Martin, Judith N., Thomas K. Nakayama, and Lisa A. Flores. 1998. *Readings in Cultural Contexts.* Mountain View, CA: Mayfield.

Masterson, Sakamoto, Nancy 1992. "Conversational Ballgames." In *Encountering Cultures,* edited by Richard Holeton. Englewood Cliffs, NJ: Prentice-Hall.

Miller, L. D. 1977. "Dyadic Perception of Communicator Style: Replication and Confirmation." *Communication Research* 4, no.1: 87–112.

Miller, Sherod, and Phyllis A. Miller. 1997. *Core Communication: Skills and Processes.* Littleton, CO: Interpersonal Communication Programs.

Montgomery, Barbara, and Robert W. Norton. 1981. "Sex Differences and Similarities in Communicator Style." *Communication Monographs* 48: 121–32.

Ngomsi, Emmanuel. 2002. "Working Effectively with Nigerian Colleagues." In *Beyond Boundaries: Developing Intercultural Competence for Business Effectiveness.* Leawood, KS: Nipporica Associates. Proprietary training material. *www. nipporica.com.*

Norton, Robert W. 1983. *Communicator Style: Theory, Application, and Measures.* Beverly Hills, CA: Sage.

_____. 1978. "Foundation of a Communicator Style Construct." *Human Communication Research* 4, no. 2: 99–112.

Norton, Robert W., and L. D. Miller. 1975 "Dyadic Perception of Communicator Style." *Communication Research* 2, no.1: 50–66.

Paige, R. Michael, Andrew D. Cohen, Barbara Kappler, Julie C. Chi, and James P. Lassegard. 2003. *Maximizing Study Abroad: A Students' Guide to Strategies for Language and Culture Learning and Use.* Minneapolis: Center for Advanced Research on Language Acquisition, University of Minnesota.

Pearce, W. Barnett, and Vernon Cronen. 1980. *Communication, Action, and Meaning.* New York: Praeger.

Philipsen, Gerry. 1998. "Places for Speaking in Teamsterville." In *Readings in Cultural Contexts,* edited by Judith N. Martin, Thomas K. Nakayama, and Lisa A. Flores, 217–226. Mountain View, CA: Mayfield.

_____. 1975 . "Speaking 'Like a Man' in Teamsterville: Culture Patterns of Role Enactment in an Urban Neighborhood." *Quarterly Journal of Speech* 61: 13–22.

Pike, Kenneth L. 1954. *Language in Relation to a Unified Theory of the Structure of Human Behavior.* Glendale, CA: Summer Institute of Linguistics.

Pusch, Margaret. 2004. "History of Intercultural Communication." In *Handbook of Intercultural Training,* edited by Dan Landis, Janet M. Bennett, and Milton J. Bennett. 3rd ed., 437–52. Thousand Oaks, CA: Sage.

Renwick, George. 2004. "Afterward: Reflections on the Future of Training." In *Handbook of Intercultural Training,* edited by Dan Landis, Janet M. Bennett, and Milton J. Bennett. 3rd ed., 437–52. Thousand Oaks, CA: Sage.

Samovar, Larry A., and Richard E. Porter. 2001. *Communication between Cultures.* 4th ed. Stamford, CT: Wadsworth/Thomson Learning.

Samovar, Larry A., and Richard E. Porter, eds. 2003. *Intercultural Communication: A Reader.* 10th ed. Stamford, CT: Wadsworth/Thomson Learning.

Searle, John R. 1969. *Speech Acts.* London: Cambridge University Press.

Shahar, Lucy, and David Kurz. 1995. *Border Crossings: American Interactions with Israelis.* Yarmouth, ME: Intercultural Press.

Sitaram, K. S., and Roy T. Cogdell. 1976. *Foundations of Intercultural Communication.* Columbus, OH: Bell & Howell.

Staley, Constance C., and Jerry L. Cohen. 1988. "Communicator Style and Social Style: Similarities and Differences between the Sexes." *Communication Quarterly* 36: 192–202.

Steglitz, Inge. 1993. "Intercultural Perspective-Taking: The Impact of Study Abroad." Unpublished doctoral dissertation, University of Minnesota.

Steinbach, Susan. 1999. *Body Language: An International View. www.TheSeabrightGroup.com.* Video.

_____. 1996. *Understanding Conversational Styles around the Globe: Bowling, Basketball and Rugby. www.TheSeabrightGroup.com.* Video.

Steinfatt, Thomas M. 1989. "Linguistic Relativity: Toward a Broader View." In *Language, Communication, and Culture: Current Directions. International and Intercultural Communication Annual,* edited by Stella Ting-Toomey and Felipe Korzenny. Vol. 13, 35–75. Newbury Park, CA: Sage.

Stewart, Edward C., and Milton J. Bennett. 1991. *American Cultural Patterns.* Rev. ed. Yarmouth, ME: Intercultural Press.

Summerfield, Ellen. 1993. *Crossing Cultures through Film.* Yarmouth, ME: Intercultural Press.

Tannen, Deborah. 1996. *Gender & Discourse.* New York: Oxford University Press.

Thiagarajan Sivasailam. 1996. "Chatter." in *Simulation Games by Thiagi.* Bloomington, IN: Workshops by Thiagi. *www.thiagi.com.*

Ting-Toomey, Stella. 1999. *Communicating across Cultures.* New York: Guilford Press.

Vossestein, Jacob. 2001. *Dealing with the Dutch.* Amsterdam: KIT Publishers.

Wendt, Jon. 1984. "DIE: A Way to Improve Communication." *Communication Education* 33: 398–401.

Wood, Julia T. 1997. *Gendered Lives: Communication, Gender, and Culture.* 2nd ed. Belmont, CA: Wadsworth.

Wurzel, Jaime. 2002. *The Cross-Cultural Conference Room,* Intercultural Resource Corporation, *www.irc-international.com.* Video.

Summary of Key References by Topic

The above is a rather extensive bibliography, and we know from experience that it can be helpful to have a bit more direction than a standard bibliography permits. Therefore, we have taken the liberty here of summarizing some of the major works on communication style by topic area. We do not relist the complete reference; for the complete citation, please see the References. We hope that this list, while certainly not exhaustive, provides you with some starting points to your own pursuit and approach to communication style.

Sociolinguistic and Linguistic Heritage
(Language Family, Codes, Communicative Style, Conversational Style, Speech Acts)
> See Austin; Bernstein; Brown and Levinson; Cameron; Cohen; Kaplan; Lakoff; Searle; and Tannen.

Interpersonal Communication Heritage
(Coordinated Management of Meaning, Communication Accommodation, Expectancy Violations, Communicator Style)
> See Bourhis; Giles and Lambert; Burgoon and Hale; Gallois, Giles, Jones, Cargile, and Ota; Giles and Coupland; Giles and Noels; Miller; Montgomery and Norton; Norton; and Pearce and Cronen.

Anthropology and Ethnography of Communication Heritage
(Emic and Etic, High and Low Context, Nonverbal Behavior, Ethnography of Communication, Role of Silence)
> See Basso; Birdwhistell; Carbaugh; Hall; Hymes; Philipsen; and Pike.

Intercultural Communication Heritage
(Values and Orientations, Context, Definitions of Communication Style Typologies, Culture-Specific, Practical, Dialectical Approach)
> See Barnlund; Bennett; Bennett and Paige; Carbaugh; Casse; Condon and Yousef; Gudykunst and Kim; Gudykunst and Ting-Toomey; Hofner Saphiere; Hofstede; Katriel; Kochman; Martin and Nakayama; Pusch; Samovar and Porter; and Ting-Toomey.

Typologies
(Theorists who have developed typologies to discuss communication style)
> See Bennett and Paige; Gudykunst and Kim; Kaplan; Norton; and Ting-Toomey.

Other Tools

In this section, we share some additional educational tools that can be used to explore communication styles. We welcome you to share your favorite tools with us as we continue building on one another's expertise in communication styles. Again, complete citations are included in the Reference Section.

Body Language: An International View. Steinbach. Video. Short clips of people from different countries demonstrating nonverbal communication, with interesting short quizzes interspersed.

Chatter. Thiagi. Simulation Game. An easy-to-use interaction game in which all participants are given a specific communication behavior instruction and then chat informally in small groups while enacting their assigned behaviors. The game shows participants how simple behaviors, considered by some to be polite and by others to be impolite, can have a big impact on communication and on the success of interactions. Thiagi has many tools available on his website, www.thiagi.com.

The Cross-Cultural Conference Room. Wurzel. Interactive CD-ROM, video, and DVD. This interactive tool chronicles the naturally different meeting styles of three national groups of business people: Argentineans, Japanese, and U.S. Americans. Includes a final Japan–U.S. meeting. This is an excellent tool that allows viewers to see communication style differences in simulated meeting settings.

Cultural Detective. Hofner Saphiere et al. Culture-specific training materials. A series of situation-based, culture-specific training materials that emphasize the interactive nature of intercultural communication and the link between observable behavior and underlying values, beliefs, and "common sense."

Ecotonos: A Multicultural Problem-Solving Simulation. Hofner Saphiere and Nipporica Associates. Simulation game. Participants form three different cultures with different sets of rules work on a task (building a bridge or community, making a decision in a case study). Participants then emigrate, forming multicultural groups, and continue working on their tasks. This simulation game allows participants to practice maintaining their identities while collaborating effectively across cultures. Rule cards include several communication style differences (listening style, explanation style, customs regarding space and touch, gestures and eye contact, approach to problem solving) as well as instructions for creating your own rules and tasks.

Includes two valuable tools for bridging communication style differences: The *Four Phase Model* and the *Diverge/Converge Model*.

The Joy Luck Club. Wang. Video (referenced in Chapter 6).

Mississippi Masala. Nair. Video (referenced in Chapter 6).

Redundancía: A Foreign Language Simulation. Hofner Saphiere et al. Simulation activity. A ten-minute simulation plus debriefing that allows participants to experience how our communication style is affected when we speak a language less than fluently. Participants learn how communication style affects our ability to communicate competence, expertise, confidence, enthusiasm, and personality. This activity also allows participants to practice different styles of listening to nonfluent speakers.

Shall We Dance. Suo and Chelsom. Video (referenced in Chapter 6). Originally a Japanese movie remade into a U.S. American movie starring Richard Gere and Jennifer Lopez, that presents a terrific contrast in styles.

Shinrai: Building Trusting Relationships with Japanese Colleagues. Hofner Saphiere and Kipnis. A 53-minute audio CD and 24-page instructional manual describing how to communicate trustworthiness to Japanese colleagues, including verbal and nonverbal behavior and key phrases.

Shower. Video. Zhang. A Mandarin Chinese movie with English subtitles available at *www.cthv.com* and through major online booksellers. The opening few minutes are a wonderful juxtaposition of a science-fiction sort of bathing experience: automated, step-by-step, linear, low context; and, at the same time, a traditional communal bathing experience: relationship-focused, many things at one time, holistic, high context. Could be a wonderful introduction to a discussion of how every style has advantages and disadvantages, and situations in which each is appropriate.

Whole Brain Business Book. Herrmann. This is a typologies piece: organizer, visualizer, personalizer, and analyzer. Focuses on thinking styles/thought processing. Also includes communication style behavioral characteristics and an assessment tool similar to Casse's.

Activities and Stories

List of Activities

We have included many activities in this book in hopes that you will participate in them yourself, as well as with your colleagues or in a more formal learning environment. To help you locate activities more easily, we list them here with their page numbers.

List of Stories

The stories in this book illustrate specific points and also accompany activities. Stories are such powerful and flexible learning tools that you may find many independent uses for them. Here is a list of the more developed stories in this book, with their page numbers. Please note that Chapter 6 contains a wealth of shorter vignettes that you also may want to use.

Index

A

advantages/disadvantages to every style, 11–12

analysis of interactions, initial vs. deeper insight, 110, 118

analyzing (step 2, Four-Step method), 174, 176–77, 212, 219, 220

anthropological roots, 263–64

apologies, 8–9, 66, 157–59

assertive style, 9, 55

B

behavioral differences as cause of disconnects, 123–25

benefits of communication style competence:
authenticity, 21, 22–25
critical mass, 22, 30–33
intentionality, 22, 26–30

C

CAT (Communication Accommodation Theory), 262

choices, conscious vs. habitual, 26–30, 265

CMM (Coordinated Management of Meaning) theory, 262

communication:
components of, 13
definition of, 12
differentiated from communication style, 13–14

communication style:
description/definition of, xi–xii, 5–12
multiple influences on. *See* synchrony/chaos

communication style repertoire factor, 72–78, 80–81
and descriptors/Four-Step method, 176, 177, 179, 210, 217–18
and Star Chart, 85, 88, 89, 107, 108, 116

See also under leveraging differences, deeper-insight practice

communicators, 13, 52, 264

communities/organizations, creating productivity in, 30–33

compliments/praise, 104, 107, 162–63

context factor, components of, 13, 52–53
chronology: number/nature of interactions, 54, 56, 58, 79
constraints: time available/medium used, 55, 57, 59, 78
historical background shared, 54, 58
language used, 13, 54, 55–56, 57, 58, 78
physical setting, 53–54, 58, 78
relationship, nature of, 54–55, 58–59, 79
roles, perception of, 54, 58, 79
and Star Chart, 87, 89, 104, 105, 108, 115, 116
as used with descriptors/Four-Step method, 176, 177, 178, 179, 207, 208, 213, 214

cultural bias, 173, 174

cultural relativity, xi, 8–9, 12–13

D

deciding (step 4, Four-Step method), 174, 178–79, 180, 213, 219, 220

DeKoven, Bernie, 239

descriptors:

categories of. *See* Discernible Descriptors; Discoverable Descriptors; Functional Descriptors

checklist, 127–28, 129–30

definition of, 126–27

overview of, 125–26

use of, 126, 175–79, 211–12, 218–19

DIE (Describe, Interpret, Evaluate) process, 179

direct/indirect as culturally relative labels, xi, 124, 263